BEST OF
Lone Star ★ Legacy
COOKBOOKS

Published by
Cookbook Resources
in cooperation with
Austin Junior Forum

Best of Lone Star Legacy Cookbooks is published by Cookbook Resources in cooperation with the Austin Junior Forum, Austin, Texas for the preservation of great American Family Recipes. Cookbook Resources salutes Austin Junior Forum for the publishing excellence of *"Lone Star Legacy"*, *"Lone Star Legacy II"* and *"Changing Thymes"*. These cookbooks preserve the American way of life and are superior examples of America's most authentic book form, the Community Cookbook.

1st Printing   July 2001
2nd Printing   October 2003

Copyright © 2001
Cookbook Resources, LLC, Highland Village, Texas

ISBN 1-931294-04-6

Manufactured in China
Designed and Published by

cookbook
resources
Cookbook Resources, LLC
541 Doubletree Drive
Highland Village, Texas 75077
972-317-0245
Toll-Free Orders: 866/229-2665
www.cookbookresources.com

Introduction

est of Lone Star Legacy Cookbooks has been published to preserve the great American Family Recipes found in our country's most authentic cookbooks, the Community Cookbook. Austin Junior Forum published **Lone Star Legacy**, the first of a series of three Community Cookbooks, in 1981 for the purpose of raising money to restore an historic Austin mansion to be used for civic purposes.

After several years of work and countless volunteer hours, the members of Austin Junior Forum created a cookbook that has sold more than 200,000 copies and continues to sell in its original form today. In 1985 members again gathered their best recipes for their second cookbook, **Lone Star Legacy II**. Meeting with continued success and acceptance of an exceptional volume of family-tested recipes, the Forum published their third cookbook, **Changing Thymes**, which brought a modern version of family meals and friendly entertaining. Today, more than 350,000 cookbooks have been sold by Austin Junior Forum and they stand as a monumental publishing success.

With no knowledge of cookbook publishing, no money for the printing and binding, the women of Austin Junior Forum had a vision of an ongoing fundraising project and the determination to make their vision a reality. Today, the Caswell House stands as a mighty tribute to these brave women, past and present, who dare to make things happen and who are determined to do good things for others.

Through their cookbooks, the women of Austin Junior Forum have helped preserve American Family Recipes. They have invited us into the homes and kitchens of families in Austin, Texas and have made us feel welcomed and we are grateful. **Best of Lone Star Legacy Cookbooks** is a lasting memorial to the women of Austin Junior Forum and to the American way of life. It preserves the best of authentic American regional traditions, family values and a way of life through its recipes.

May each of you who read this cookbook feel the same warmth and comfort of **Lone Star Legacy, Lone Star Legacy II** and **Changing Thymes** preserved here in these pages.

Sheryn R. Jones

Publisher

$\mathcal{T}able\ of\ \mathcal{C}ontents$

Here's a perfect start with quick and easy and really different dips, spreads and appetizers. And the drinks are on the house.

These salads and salad dressings work with any main dish and favorites like Grandma's Hot German Potato Salad and Layered Salad keep everybody happy.

Warm-up on a cold winter's night or sink into a favorite easy chair to enjoy the best soups and sandwiches you'll ever find.

There's nothing like the smell of these hot breads to make you feel warm and fuzzy. And jazz up your weekend or holiday brunches with super breakfast treats especially for you.

MIND YOUR CACTUS 161

Here are vegetables, rice and pasta the whole family loves. This great selection gives you all the choices you need for everyday and every occasion.

COME AND GET IT 199

Come and get the best of all those chicken, beef, pork and seafood dishes you grew up on and some of the best of today's lighter fare.

DREAM ABOUT THOSE SWEETS 271

You'll love these old favorites and new classics. Every recipe is a hit with kids, friends, people at church and everybody at soccer. Try Hershey Bar Cake, Love Bites and the Snickerdoodles to hear the raves.

AIM FOR SERENDIPITY 313

Here are the special things you don't see everywhere. . . like Baked Potato Chips, Manifold Cooking and 200-Mile Pot Roast. You'll love this section.

5

Lone Star Legacy
Lone Star Legacy II
Changing Thymes

Lone Star Legacy is more than just a cookbook – it is a keepsake! Its more than 800 recipes are seasoned with cooking tips, spiced with Texas trivia, and frosted with breathtaking photos of Texas landmarks and landscapes. It has sold over 200,000 copies and was the first Texas cookbook selected for the Walter S. McIlhenny Community Cookbook Hall of Fame.

Following in the tradition of **Lone Star Legacy, Lone Star Legacy II** will capture your heart and tantalize your taste buds with over 800 new and exciting recipes. A collection of Mexican, French and German favorites, along with typical ranch cooking. Whether planning a backyard barbeque or a formal seated dinner, all recipes will help you capture the authentic flavors of Texas.

Austin Junior Forum's third presentation of about 500 extraordinary, family-tested recipes collected from past generations and present friends reflects the need for tasty, satisfying and balanced meals with less preparation time. This combination along with a nutritional analysis of every recipe, stunning photographs, easy-to-follow format, colorful anecdotes and cooking tips is a must have for the cooks of today.

TO ORDER:

To order copies of **Lone Star Legacy, Lone Star Legacy II** and **Changing Thymes,** you may call 800/661-2537 or write to the address below.

Austin Junior Forum Publications
P.O. Box 26628
Austin, Texas 78755

LONE STAR LEGACY	**$19.95**
LONE STAR LEGACY II	**$19.95**
CHANGING THYMES	**$19.95**
Shipping per book	**$6.00**

Thank you for your interest and support of our award-winning cookbooks.

Austin Junior Forum

About Austin Junior Forum

Austin Junior Forum (AJF), chartered in 1969, is a group of women supporting those in need across greater Austin, Texas, through gifts of time, talent and funds. The ongoing publication and sales of cookbooks has been one of the largest contributors to AJF's grants effort. **Lone Star Legacy, Lone Star Legacy II,** and **Changing Thymes** enable us to continue giving to those less fortunate in Austin. This selection of a few favorites of the recipes from each of these outstanding recipe collections allows our work to continue into the future.

Austin Junior Forum Publications

The Board of Austin Junior Forum Publications would like to thank those AJF members who graciously gave of their time and effort to make this collection possible.

Members of the AJF Publications Board:

Pamela Jones, Chairman
Melanie Legett, Operations Mgr.
Dawn McDaniel, Marketing
Sarah Fuquay, Asst. Treasurer
Shawn Butler, AJF President

Tricia Barbee, Orders Processing
Christine Skiles, Cookbook
  Demos
Kelly Elliott, Treasurer
Julie Cahoon, Publicity

Special thanks go to:

Kathy Marsh
Martha Hoffman
Linda Watson
Jessica Mace
Heather Anthony
Kelly Norwood
Jill Spencer
Bonnie & Ken Moyer

Mary Kay Hann
Mary Cheryl Dorwart
Sharon Wallace
Renee Mitchell
Lindy Jordan
Norma Bishop
Judy Strawmeyer
Phyllis Biggar

Nicole Kenisky
Shelli Hill
Sharon Butza
Barbara Roeling
Rebecca Ehlert
Chris Bussell
Fran Greve
Kathy Clay

BEST OF

Lone Star ★ Legacy

APPETIZERS & BEVERAGES

Spicy Avocado Dip

1   can (10 ounces) tomatoes with green chilies
1   envelope (1.25 ounces) onion soup mix
6   ounces cream cheese, softened
3   avocados, mashed

1   tablespoon minced onion
2   teaspoons Worcestershire sauce
Juice of 1 lemon
Salt to taste
Tostados

Drain tomatoes with green chilies and chop. Add remaining ingredients, and mix well. Serve with tostados. Yields 3½ cups.

Mrs. Marcus Bone (Beverly)
Lone Star Legacy II

Exotic Dip

¼   cup finely chopped pecans or walnuts
4   strips bacon, cooked and crumbled, divided
6   ounces cream cheese, softened

4   ounces Bleu cheese
½   cup mayonnaise
¼   teaspoon salt
¼   teaspoon white pepper
Crackers

Combine all ingredients, reserving one half of bacon to sprinkle on top. Serve with assorted crackers. Yields 2 cups.

Ada Smyth
Lone Star Legacy II

Spinach Salmon Dip

1	can (7¾ ounces) salmon
1	package (10 ounces) chopped frozen spinach, thawed and squeezed dry
1	cup mayonnaise
1	cup sour cream

½	cup chopped fresh parsley
1	tablespoon lemon juice
1	teaspoon grated onion
½	teaspoon dried dill weed
	Chips or vegetable dippers

Drain and flake salmon. Combine with remaining ingredients. Chill for several hours and serve with chips or crisp vegetables. Yields 5 cups of dip.

Mrs. Jim Rado (Vicki)
Lone Star Legacy II

Asparagus Dip

1	package (10 ounces) frozen chopped asparagus, cooked and drained
1	green onion, finely minced
8	ounces cream cheese, softened
8	ounces sour cream

½	teaspoon salt
¼	teaspoon white pepper
⅛	teaspoon garlic salt
⅛	teaspoon celery salt
½	teaspoon dill weed
	Vegetable dippers

Combine all ingredients in a food processor and blend until smooth. Chill and serve with your favorite vegetable dippers. Yields 2½ cups.

Ada Smyth
Lone Star Legacy II

"Hot" Guacamole Dip

1	cup mashed avocado
2	teaspoons finely chopped onions
2	teaspoons minced fresh jalapeños

1	small clove garlic, crushed
1	teaspoon vegetable oil
1	teaspoon cider vinegar
¼	teaspoon salt
	Tortilla chips

Combine all ingredients well. Chill. Serve with tortilla chips. Yields 1 cup.

Matt Martinez, Jr.
Lone Star Legacy II

Great Layered Taco Dip

3 ripe avocados
1 tomato, chopped
Salt and pepper to taste
1½ teaspoons lemon juice
¼ teaspoon garlic powder
2 tablespoons minced onion
Hot pepper sauce to taste
1 cup mayonnaise
1 cup sour cream
1 package (1½ ounces) taco seasoning

1 can (32 ounces) refried beans
4 tomatoes, chopped
1 bunch green onions, chopped
8 ounces Cheddar cheese, grated
1 can (4¼ ounces) chopped ripe olives
Tostados

Peel and mash avocados. Add 1 chopped tomato, salt, pepper, lemon juice, garlic powder, minced onion and hot pepper sauce and set aside. Mix mayonnaise, sour cream and taco seasoning and set aside. On large platter spread refried beans as first layer of dip. Next, spread the avocado mixture. Cover with the sour cream and mayonnaise mixture. Sprinkle with 4 chopped tomatoes, green onions and cheese; top with black olives. Serve with tostados. Serves 10.

Mrs. James Hurlbut (Marsha)
Lone Star Legacy II

Shrimp Con Queso Dip

1   (32 ounce) package
    pasteurized process
    cheese spread
1   (8 ounce) package
    cream cheese
1   (10¾ ounce) can cream of
    shrimp soup, undiluted
2   (10 ounce) cans tomatoes
    with green chilies
2   tablespoons dried onion
    flakes
½   teaspoon dried minced garlic

2   tablespoons cumin seed
1   teaspoon basil
½   teaspoon hot pepper
    sauce
½   teaspoon sugar
2   tablespoons Worcestershire
    sauce
1   pound cooked shrimp
    (about 2 cups), cut in
    bite-sized pieces

Combine all ingredients except shrimp in top of large double boiler. Heat, stirring frequently, until cheese is melted and mixture is well blended. Add shrimp to cheese mixture. Pour into chafing dish. Serve with large corn chips. Makes approximately 11 cups.

Dip may be frozen for up to 6 weeks.

Donna Earle Crain
Changing Thymes

Per tablespoon_____

Calories 29 Protein 1.85 g Carbohydrates .462 g Fat 2 g Cholesterol 11.5 mg Sodium 112 mg

Easy Black Olive Dip

Chill for several hours

1   (8 ounce) package cream
    cheese, softened
3   tablespoons lemon juice
½   teaspoon garlic salt
    or more to taste

¼ to ⅓ cup milk
1   (4 ounce) can black olives,
    drained and chopped

Combine cream cheese, lemon juice and garlic salt, beating until smooth. Add milk, a tablespoon at a time, until dip is desired consistency. Fold olives into dip; do not blend or puree. Chill for several hours or overnight. Serve with chips or crackers. Makes approximately 2 cups.

Linda Cook Uhl
Changing Thymes

Per tablespoon

Calories 30, Protein .64 g Carbohydrate .655 g Fat 3 g Cholesterol 8.05 mg Sodium 44.8 mg

Artichoke Hearts Supreme

5   tablespoons butter,
    divided
2½ tablespoons flour
1   cup whipping cream
½   teaspoon salt
Dash of cayenne pepper
1   tablespoon Worcestershire
    sauce
1   cup sherry

2   cans (14 ounces each)
    whole artichoke hearts,
    well drained
½   pound fresh mushrooms
2   tablespoons butter, melted
1   cup crab meat, drained
Parmesan cheese, grated
Paprika
Parsley

Melt 2½ tablespoons butter and add flour to make a roux. Add whipping cream, salt and pepper. When thick and smooth, add Worcestershire sauce. Remove from heat and add sherry. Place artichoke hearts in a shallow buttered baking dish and set aside. Sauté mushrooms in 2½ tablespoons melted butter; add crab meat and stir. Spread crab and mushroom mixture over artichoke hearts; cover with cream sauce. Top with Parmesan cheese and sprinkle generously with paprika and parsley. Bake at 375° for 20 minutes. Serves 10 to 12.

Mrs. Jim Nunnelly (Sandy)
Lone Star Legacy II

Antipasto Dip

1	(4 ounce) can ripe olives	2	green onions, chopped
1	(4 ounce) can green chilies	1	tablespoon olive oil
2	ripe tomatoes, chopped	1	teaspoon wine vinegar

Mix all ingredients together. Chill for 1 hour. Makes approximately 2¼ cups.

A quick, easy, tasty and versatile dip, it tastes good with garlic bread, may be used like salsa or as a topping for grilled fish or chicken breast and topped with Monterey Jack cheese.

Carla Fisher
Changing Thymes

Per tablespoon

Calories 8 Protein .135 g Carbohydrates .713 g Fat .5 g Cholesterol 0 mg Sodium 11.8 mg

Artichoke and Lemon Basil Dip

½	cup non-fat mayonnaise	2	tablespoons canola or olive oil
3	tablespoons water		
1	tablespoon lemon juice	2	sprigs celery leaves
1	teaspoon minced shallot or green onion	1	bay leaf
			Juice of ½ lemon
¼	cup chopped fresh parsley		Water
½	teaspoon Dijon mustard	2	large or 4 small artichokes
½	teaspoon dried basil		

Combine mayonnaise, 3 tablespoons water, lemon juice, shallot, parsley, mustard and basil. Chill until ready to serve as dip for artichokes. To steam artichokes, add oil, celery leaves, bay leaf and lemon juice to water in bottom of steamer. Steam artichokes for 45 to 50 minutes. Remove and chill before serving. Serves 4.

Pamela Jones
Changing Thymes

Per serving

Calories 67 Protein 4.24 g Carbohydrates 15.0 g Fat .2 g Cholesterol 6.31 mg Sodium 201.2 mg

Cold Artichoke Dip

1 package (0.8 ounces)
  buttermilk dressing mix
8 ounces cream cheese,
  softened
1 cup mayonnaise

1 can (14 ounces)
  artichoke hearts, drained
  and chopped
Crackers

Mix all dip ingredients together and chill. Yields 2½ cups. This is a very easy and good dip. Serve with crackers.

Mrs. John Perkins (Sandy)
Lone Star Legacy II

Artichoke Bacon Dip

1 can (14 ounces) artichoke
  hearts, well drained
½ cup mayonnaise
1 tablespoon minced onion
1 teaspoon lemon juice
⅛ teaspoon salt

Dash of white pepper
Dash of cayenne pepper
4 slices of bacon, fried
  crisp, drained and
  crumbled
Chips or crackers

Coarsely chop artichoke hearts and put into a medium sized mixing bowl. Add mayonnaise, onion, lemon juice, salt and peppers. Mix on medium speed of electric mixer for about 1 minute. Refrigerate for several hours. Just prior to serving, stir in crumbled bacon. Yields 2½ cups.

Serve as a dip with corn chips or as a spread with crackers. This dip may also be served warm and is best made a day ahead.

Mrs. Terry Arndt (Barbara)
Lone Star Legacy II

Blackeyed Pea Dip

4	cups blackeyed peas, cooked and drained	1	clove garlic, minced
5	canned jalapeños, chopped	½	pound sharp Cheddar cheese, grated
1	tablespoon jalapeño juice	½	pound margarine
½	medium onion, chopped		
1	can (4 ounces) green chilies, chopped		

Blend peas, jalapeños, juice, onion, chilies and garlic in blender. Heat cheese and margarine in microwave until melted and combine with blackeyed pea mixture. Serve hot from chafing dish with corn chips. Serves 16 to 20.

This is a New Year's Day version of refried beans!

Cookbook Committee
Lone Star Legacy

Hot Blackeyed Pea Dip

½	green bell pepper, chopped	1	teaspoon pepper
1	rib celery, chopped	1	teaspoon salt
1	tablespoon hot pepper sauce	¼	teaspoon nutmeg
½	cup catsup	2	cans (16 ounces each) blackeyed peas
3	chicken bouillon cubes	½	cup chopped tomatoes
¼	teaspoon cinnamon	1	teaspoon garlic powder
8	jalapeños, chopped	½	cup bacon drippings
1	onion, chopped	3	tablespoons flour
			Chips or crackers

In a large saucepan, combine bell pepper, celery, hot pepper sauce, catsup, bouillon cubes, cinnamon, jalapeños, onion, pepper, salt and nutmeg. Simmer for 20 minutes. Add blackeyed peas, tomatoes and garlic powder. Simmer 30 minutes. Blend flour with bacon drippings. Pour into cooked mixture and simmer 15 minutes. Serve with chips or crackers. Yields 1½ quarts.

This is powerfully hot, but wonderful! Adjust hot pepper sauce and jalapeños o taste.

Mrs. Clay Wilkins (Marion)
Lone Star Legacy II

Crab Meat Dip

2 cups mayonnaise	½ teaspoon celery seed
1 cup small curd cottage cheese	½ teaspoon caraway seed
¼ to ½ cup finely chopped onion	¼ teaspoon garlic salt
¼ teaspoon salt	½ tablespoon dry mustard
¼ teaspoon hot pepper sauce	½ teaspoon pepper
1½ tablespoons Worcestershire sauce	1 cup crab meat
	Potato chip dippers

Combine all ingredients together except crab meat and mix well. Set in refrigerator overnight. Just before serving add crab meat and mix well. Serve with potato chips. Yields 4 cups dip.

Mrs. Greg Gordon (Kathy)
Lone Star Legacy II

Oriental Crab Dip

1 (3 ounce) package reduced calorie cream cheese, softened	1 (8 ounce) can water chestnuts, drained and chopped
1 tablespoon reduced sodium soy sauce	Green bell pepper, chopped (optional)
1 (6 ounces) can crab meat, drained	Green onion, chopped (optional)

Combine all ingredients in a bowl. Mix well. Chill until ready to serve. Serve with your favorite crackers. Makes approximately 1¼ cups.

Kathy Gordon
Changing Thymes

Per tablespoon _____

Calories 25 Protein 2.34 g Carbohydrates 1.78 g Fat 1 g Cholesterol 9.94 mg Sodium 93.2 mg

Quick and Easy Crab Dip

1	(8 ounce) package cream cheese, softened	3	green onions, chopped
¼	cup margarine, melted	1	(6 ounce) can crab meat, drained
1	tablespoon lemon juice	¾	teaspoon garlic salt or to taste
2	tablespoons milk		

Cream together all ingredients in a medium bowl. Cover and chill for several hours to blend flavors. Remove from refrigerator 30 to 45 minutes before serving. Serve with chips or assorted crackers. Makes approximately 2¼ cups.

Decorate with parsley or a decorative vegetable to add pizzazz.

Barbara Stromberg Boyd
Changing Thymes

Per tablespoon

Calories 37 Protein 1.43 g Carbohydrates .321 g Fat 3.5 g Cholesterol 10.6 mg Sodium 47.1 mg

Raw Vegetable Dip

1	cup mayonnaise	½	cup chopped fresh parsley
1	cup sour cream		
2	tablespoons minced onion	1	tablespoon Dijon mustard
1	large clove garlic, minced		Raw vegetable dippers
1	teaspoon salt		
½	teaspoon pepper		

Blend all ingredients and refrigerate for 2 to 3 hours. Yields 2 cups.

Serve on a bed of iceburg lettuce as a dip for raw vegetables.

Mrs. James C. Doss (Charlene)
Lone Star Legacy II

Texas Garden Dip

1 package (10 ounces) frozen chopped spinach
1 can (14 ounces) artichoke hearts, drained
1 cup sour cream
1 teaspoon pepper
½ cup grated Parmesan cheese
3 tablespoons chopped green onion
Vegetable dippers or chips

Cook spinach according to package directions and drain well. Place all ingredients in blender. Blend at medium speed until well blended. Chill several hours or overnight. Serve with vegetables or chips. Yields 3 cups.

Mrs. B. Lynn Turlington (Jill)
Lone Star Legacy II

Ken's Picadillo Dip

½ pound hot bulk sausage
1 pound ground beef
1 teaspoon salt
Pepper to taste
1 can (16 ounces) tomatoes, cut up
3 green onions, chopped
1 jar (2 ½ ounces) chopped pimientos
¼ to ½ cup almond slices
1 clove garlic, finely chopped
1 can (6 ounces) tomato paste
2 jalapeños, seeded and chopped
½ to ¾ cup golden raisins
¼ teaspoon oregano

Mix meats together by hand. Put into a large pan and barely cover with water. Add salt and pepper. Stir meat until well blended. Simmer covered for 30 minutes. Add remaining ingredients and cook 15 minutes longer. Serve hot in a chafing dish with chips. Freezes well. For a change of pace, substitute cashews for almonds.

Featured in article in Los Angeles Times when originally published.
Mrs. Ken Moyer (Bonnie)
Lone Star Legacy

Green Chile Dip

8	ounces cream cheese, softened	1	tablespoon mayonnaise
1	can (4 ounces) chopped green chiles	½	tablespoon lemon juice

Mix all ingredients together thoroughly. Refrigerate. Remove from refrigerator about 30 minutes before serving. Serve with chips.

Mrs. Jim Lederer (Anne)
Lone Star Legacy

Andalé Dip

2	cans (4 ounces each) chopped green chilies	1	can (16 ounces) tomatoes, drained and chopped (reserve liquid)
2	cans (4 ounces each) chopped black olives	2	tablespoons wine vinegar
4 to 6 chopped green onions		1	tablespoon oil
			Salt and pepper to taste

Mix all ingredients together. If the mixture seems a little dry, add reserved tomato liquid. This dip needs to be a little soupy. Refrigerate for several hours or overnight to blend flavors. Serve with Doritos or tortilla chips. Yields a generous 2 cups.

Mrs. Ken Moyer (Bonnie)
Lone Star Legacy

Spinach Dip

1	package (10 ounces) frozen chopped spinach or 2 cups fresh cooked spinach, chopped	½	cup minced parsley
		½	cup minced onion
		1	teaspoon salt
1	cup sour cream	½	teaspoon celery salt
½	cup mayonnaise	¼	teaspoon pepper
		⅛	teaspoon nutmeg

Thaw spinach; place in a colander and press out excess water. Mix spinach with remaining ingredients. Cover and refrigerate at least 24 hours. May be prepared up to 3 days in advance. Serve as a dip for fresh vegetables. Yields about 3 cups.

Mrs. Jim Rado (Vicki)
Lone Star Legacy

Aunt Sophia's Almond Cheese Spread

¼ cup unblanched almonds, toasted and finely chopped	1 tablespoon chopped green onion (optional)
2 slices bacon, crisply cooked and crumbled	½ cup mayonnaise or mayonnaise-type salad dressing
1 cup (4 ounces) grated American cheese	

Combine almonds, bacon, cheese, onion and mayonnaise or salad dressing. Serve immediately or refrigerate and use as a sandwich spread or on crackers or vegetables. Makes approximately 1¾ cups.

This spread makes a great grilled cheese sandwich.

Cheryl Briggs Patton
Changing Thymes

Per tablespoon_____

Calories 69 Protein 2.24 g Carbohydrates .496 g Fat 6.5 g Cholesterol 10.3 mg Sodium 145 mg

Cheese Dip Olé

1 (10 ounce) can tomatoes with green chilies	½ teaspoon lemon juice
2 (8 ounces) packages low fat cream cheese, softened	¼ teaspoon Worcestershire sauce
1 (2 ounce) jar pimiento-stuffed green olives, drained	Salt and black pepper to taste

Combine all ingredients in blender container. Blend until smooth. Chill until ready to serve. Serve with tortilla chips. Makes approximately 2¾ cups.

Dip is quick to fix and works great with any Mexican dish.

Caryn Cluiss
Changing Thymes

Per tablespoon_____

Calories 26 Protein 1.16 g Carbohydrates .993 g Fat 2 g Cholesterol 5.77 mg Sodium 95.4 mg

23

Ken's Pico de Gallo

2	large tomatoes, diced	1	tablespoon oil
2	large onions, chopped finely	½	teaspoon white vinegar
3	medium tomatillos, chopped	1	teaspoon salt
		½	teaspoon pepper
2	serrano peppers (1½ inches each) finely chopped	⅓	cup cilantro leaves, finely chopped, optional

Mix all ingredients together. Can be served right away or chilled for several hours. It is best the same day because of the fresh tomatoes, but keeps well for several days. Cilantro is optional, and as a traditional herb of Mexico, is a delightfully authentic flavor, and a surprise as well. Yields 2 cups.

This recipe is wonderful with fajitas, but is also a tasty relish with any Mexican dish.

Mrs. Ken Moyer (Bonnie)
Lone Star Legacy II

Tuna Pâté

1	(8 ounce) package low fat cream cheese, softened	2	tablespoons snipped parsley
1	tablespoon grated onion	2	(7 ounce) cans water-pack tuna, drained and flaked
1	tablespoon chili sauce		
1	teaspoon Worcestershire sauce	2	tablespoons dry sherry
			Salt to taste

Combine cream cheese, onion, chili sauce, Worcestershire sauce and parsley, mixing until well blended. Add tuna and sherry and mix well. Season with salt. Shape tuna mixture into mound in serving bowl or press into 3-cup mold lined with plastic wrap. Invert on serving plate. Serve with raw vegetables or crackers. Makes approximately 3 cups.

Kari J. Tobias
Changing Thymes

Per tablespoon

Calories 27.1 Protein 2.48 g Carbohydrates .27 g Fat 1.5 g Cholesterol 7.68 mg Sodium 48 mg

Crab Dip Gourmet

1   (8 ounce) package cream
    cheese, softened
½   cup mayonnaise
¼   cup sherry
1   teaspoon Worcestershire
    sauce

Juice of 1 lemon
Salt and black pepper to taste
1   pound crab meat
Parsley sprigs for garnish
Paprika for garnish

Combine all ingredients except crab meat in chafing dish. Heat over low flame, stirring constantly, until well blended. Add crab meat to sauce, stirring gently to mix. Garnish with parsley and sprinkle with paprika. Serve with French bread cubes. Makes approximately 4 cups.

This recipe is guaranteed to please.

Mary Lauderman Tavcar
Changing Thymes

Per tablespoon_____

Calories 33 Protein 1.72 g Carbohydrates .313 g Fat 3 g Cholesterol 12 mg Sodium 45.1 mg

Betty's Sweet Potato Chips

¼ pound sweet potatoes
Ice water

Vegetable oil for deep frying
Powdered sugar or salt

Peel sweet potatoes. Cut cross-wise in very thin slices. Soak in ice water for a few hours or chill in cold water overnight. Drain sweet potato slices and blot with paper towel to dry. Deep fry in vegetable oil at 375° until crisp. Drain on paper towel. Sprinkle with powdered sugar or salt to taste. Serves 1.

Sweet potato chips are excellent with salad.

Donna Earle Crain
Changing Thymes

Per serving_____

Calories 172 Protein 1.87 g Carbohydrates 30.7 g Fat 5 g Cholesterol 0 mg Sodium 14.8 mg

Potato and Leek Frittata

May be served at room temperature as an appetizer

1 tablespoon butter	½ cup half and half
1 tablespoon olive oil	¼ teaspoon salt
1 cup cubed peeled potatoes	Freshly ground black pepper to taste
1 cup thinly sliced white portion of leeks, rinsed and dried	½ cup (2 ounces) freshly grated Gruyère or Swiss cheese
6 eggs, beaten, or 1½ cups egg substitute	1 tablespoon minced parsley

Heat butter and oil in non-stick skillet. Add potatoes and leeks and cook until tender and very lightly browned. Combine eggs, half and half, salt, black pepper, cheese and parsley, mixing thoroughly. Pour over potatoes and leeks. Cook over low heat, gently lifting bottom and edges until eggs begin to set. Cook, covered, over low heat for 2 to 3 minutes or until firm. To lightly brown top of frittata, place under broiler. Cut into wedges to serve. Serves 8.

For delicious variations, top with ½ cup chopped artichoke hearts, chopped spinach, chopped tender asparagus or thin tomato slices.

Jeanne Cassidy
Changing Thymes

Per serving

Calories 154 Protein 7.76 g Carbohydrates 6.4 g Fat 11 g Cholesterol 176 mg Sodium 161 mg

Creamy Vegetable Rollups

¼ cup (2 ounces) low fat cream cheese, softened
¼ cup low fat cottage cheese
¼ cup coarsely shredded carrot
2 tablespoons minced celery
1 tablespoon minced green onion
1 tablespoon minced green bell pepper

1 tablespoon chopped parsley
2 teaspoons diced pimiento
¼ teaspoon dried dillweed
⅛ teaspoon garlic powder
4 (6 inch) flour tortillas

Combine all ingredients except tortillas in bowl. Mix well. Chill, covered, for at least 2 hours. Spoon 3 tablespoons cheese mixture on each tortilla, spreading to edges. Roll up, jelly roll fashion. Cut into bite-sized slices and place on serving plate. Serves 8.

Dee Williamson
Changing Thymes

Per serving

Calories 77 Protein 4.59 g Carbohydrates 11.2 g Fat 1 g Cholesterol 2.81 mg Sodium 199 mg

Bryan's Fresh Salsa

2 cups chopped tomatoes
¼ cup chopped green onion
2 tablespoons diced onion
1 teaspoon diced fresh jalapeño pepper

2 tablespoons chopped fresh cilantro
2 cloves garlic, chopped
1 teaspoon fresh lime juice
¼ teaspoon salt

Combine all ingredients in medium bowl. Mix thoroughly. Serves 8.

Bryan Rumble Norton
Changing Thymes

Per serving

Calories 15.3 Protein .629 g Carbohydrates 3.41 g Fat .2 g Cholesterol 0 mg Sodium 77.7 mg

Marinated Mushrooms

Must prepare in advance

3	pounds mushrooms, cleaned and stems removed	4	teaspoons salt or to taste
2²/₃	cups vegetable oil	1	tablespoon freshly ground black pepper
2	cups garlic wine vinegar	4	cloves garlic, coarsely chopped
¼	cup chopped fresh parsley		
4	teaspoons sugar		

Combine mushrooms, oil, vinegar, parsley, sugar, salt, black pepper and garlic in large jar. Marinate the mushrooms in dressing for 2 days (but not more than 2 days). Drain mushrooms before serving. Serves 12.

Cheryl Briggs Patton
Changing Thymes

Per serving_____

Calories 249 Protein 2.45 g Carbohydrates 7.53 g Fat 25 g Cholesterol 0 mg Sodium 361 mg

Raspberry Cheese Ball

1	(8 ounce) package cream cheese, softened	¼	cup chopped walnuts
2	tablespoons sherry	¼	cup seedless raspberry preserves

Combine cream cheese, sherry and walnuts, mixing until well blended. Chill mixture for 30 minutes. At serving time, shape into a ball. Make a hollow on the top of the ball. Spoon preserves into hollow and around sides of ball. Serve with club crackers. Serves 24.

This is the Cookbook Committee's favorite cheese ball.

Donna Earle Crain
Changing Thymes

Per tablespoon_____

Calories 51 Protein .918 g Carbohydrates 2.73 g Fat 4 g Cholesterol 10.4 mg Sodium 29.4 mg

Queso Pesos

1	(32 ounce) package pasteurized process cheese spread	1	teaspoon garlic powder
2	(8 ounce) packages cream cheese, softened	1	jalapeño pepper, finely chopped
2	teaspoons cayenne pepper powder	2	cups chopped pecans
			Chili powder

Combine cheese spread and cream cheese, mixing until blended. Add cayenne, garlic powder, jalapeño pepper and pecans to cheese mixture, blending well. Shape cheese mixture into 1 × 10-inch logs. Roll in chili powder, coating completely. Wrap logs in wax paper. Store in refrigerator or freezer. Serve by cutting log into ¼ to ½-inch slices and serve on crackers. Makes approximately 8 cups.

To make a cheese ball, reserve ½ cup pecans, form a portion of the mixture into a ball and roll in pecans. Cheese logs may be stored in the refrigerator for several weeks or in the freezer for a longer period.

Ann Bommarito Armstrong
Changing Thymes

Per tablespoon_____

Calories 57 Protein 1.99 g Carbohydrates .613 g Fat 4.5 g Cholesterol 10.6 mg Sodium 112 mg

Cheese Straws

1	pound sharp Cheddar cheese, finely grated	1	teaspoon salt
1	cup unsalted butter, softened	1½	teaspoons hot pepper sauce
3	cups sifted flour	2	teaspoons cayenne pepper

Combine all ingredients. Put through a cookie press in ¼ inch wide strips or roll out on a slightly floured board ⅛ inch thick and cut into ¼ inch strips 3 to 5 inches long. Place on an ungreased cookie sheet and bake at 375° for 10 to 15 minutes. Yields 36.

These can be stored in a sealed container for several weeks.

Cookbook Committee
Lone Star Legacy II

Pepper Jelly Turnovers

1	jar (5 ounces) pasteurized processed cheese spread	2	tablespoons water
½	cup butter	1	jar (4 ounces) jalapeño jelly
1	cup flour		

Cut cheese and butter into flour. Quickly stir in water and shape into a ball. Chill overnight. Roll dough very thin and cut with biscuit cutter into 5 inch circles. Fill half with jalapeño jelly. Fold over and crimp edges with fork. Bake at 375° for 8 to 10 minutes. Yields 24 to 36.

Turnovers are also good filled with orange marmalade. They may be frozen and reheated before serving.

Mrs. Jim Rado (Vicki)
Lone Star Legacy II

Cocktail Shrimp

1	pound medium shrimp	½	pound sliced bacon, cut into thirds
1	bottle (8 ounces) French dressing		

Shell and devein shrimp. Place in bowl and add enough French dressing to cover. Marinate in refrigerator overnight. When ready to cook, wrap each shrimp with ⅓ piece of bacon and secure with toothpick. Arrange on broiler pan and bake at 400° for 20 minutes, turning once. Yields 35 to 50 pieces.

You can use Italian dressing instead of French and you can wrap with bacon and leave in the refrigerator to pop in oven shortly before guests come.

Mrs. Joe Bowles (Mary)
Lone Star Legacy II

Pickled Shrimp

2	tablespoons olive oil	8	whole cloves
1	pound shrimp, cooked, peeled and deveined	1	bay leaf
		2	teaspoons salt
1	cup white vinegar	1	teaspoon sugar
2	tablespoons water		Dash cayenne pepper
¼	cup sliced onion		

Pour oil over shrimp in a bowl. Combine the remaining ingredients in a saucepan and bring to a boil. Pour over shrimp while hot. Cool, then refrigerate 24 hours. Yields 40 to 50 pieces.

Mrs. Marcus Bone (Beverly)
Lone Star Legacy II

Really Different Hors D' oeuvres

4	ounces cream cheese	1	tablespoon dry Hidden Valley salad dressing mix
1	package (6 ounces) frozen crab meat or shrimp, thawed and drained		
		1	tablespoon mayonnaise
2	tablespoons fresh lemon juice	2	zucchini, thinly sliced
			Paprika to garnish

Heat cheese in 1 quart bowl on HIGH 30 seconds to 1 minute to soften. Add all ingredients but zucchini and paprika. Arrange zucchini slices on microwave proof serving dishes. Top each slice with a teaspoonful of crab mixture. Sprinkle with paprika. Cook on HIGH until zucchini is crisp-tender, about 1 to 2 minutes. Let cool slightly. Chill before serving. Yields about 40.

Mrs. Larry Hall (Jane)
Lone Star Legacy

Barbecued Meatballs

Meatballs:

1	cup milk	½	teaspoon garlic salt
3	pounds ground beef	½	teaspoon pepper
2	cups quick oats	2	teaspoons chili powder
2	eggs	2	teaspoons salt
1	onion, chopped		

Combine all ingredients together and mix well. Shape into 1½ inch balls and place in a greased baking dish.

Sauce:

2	cups catsup	1½	cups brown sugar
2	tablespoons imitation smoke flavor	½	teaspoon garlic salt
		½	cup chopped onion

Bring sauce ingredients to a boil. Pour over meatballs and bake at 350° for 1 hour. Yields 128 meatballs.

This recipe can be halved easily.

Mrs. Robert Vossman (Nancy)
Lone Star Legacy II

Saucy Meatballs

Meatballs:

2	pounds ground beef	1	egg, slightly beaten
1	large onion, grated	¾	teaspoon salt
1	handful oatmeal		

Combine all ingredients and shape into 50 to 60 small balls. Brown well in a large skillet or broil on both sides.

Sauce:

1	bottle (12 ounces) chili sauce	2	tablespoons fresh lemon juice
1	jar (10 ounces) grape jelly		

In a very large saucepan, combine all sauce ingredients. Drop meatballs into sauce. Simmer approximately 30 minutes. Serve from chafing dish with toothpicks. Yields 50 to 60 meatballs.

These freeze beautifully. When ready to use, defrost and reheat slowly.

Mrs. Sid Mann (Kathi)
Lone Star Legacy II

Artichoke Nibbles

2	jars (6 ounces each) marinated artichoke hearts	⅛	teaspoon pepper
1	small onion, finely chopped	⅛	teaspoon oregano
1	clove garlic, minced	⅛	teaspoon Tabasco
4	eggs, beaten	2	cups grated sharp Cheddar cheese
¼	cup fine bread crumbs	2	tablespoons minced parsley
¼	teaspoon salt		

Drain marinade from one jar of artichoke hearts into medium skillet. Drain second jar and discard marinade. Chop artichokes and set aside. Heat oil; add onion and garlic and sauté until limp, about five minutes. Combine eggs, bread crumbs, salt, pepper, oregano and Tabasco. Fold in cheese and parsley. Add artichokes and sautéed onions, blending well. Pour into a 9 inch square glass baking dish. Bake at 325° for 30 minutes. Allow to cool briefly before cutting into one inch squares. Can also be served cold. This dish may be prepared ahead of time and reheated 10 to 12 minutes.

Mrs. Don Panter (Carolyn)
Lone Star Legacy

Bacon Hors D'Oeuvres

1½	teaspoons dry mustard	3	eggs, beaten
1½	teaspoons cayenne	1	pound sliced bacon
3	teaspoons cider vinegar		Cracker or cornflake crumbs

Mix mustard, cayenne, and vinegar into a paste. Stir in beaten eggs. Cut bacon into fourths. Dip each individual bacon piece into egg mixture; then roll in crumbs. Bake at 350° for 15 to 18 minutes. Drain on paper towels. Store in the refrigerator in a covered dish. Reheat at 200° for 10 minutes. Serves 10 to 12.

The bacon can be cooked in the microwave, making this a super easy dish.

Mrs. Jim Schultz (Mary Kay)
Lone Star Legacy

Cheese Crisps

2	sticks butter	2	cups grated Cheddar cheese
2	cups flour	2	drops Tabasco

Mix all ingredients together and knead until smooth. Roll out and cut with biscuit cutter, or pinch into balls and then flatten. Bake on a greased cookie sheet at 400° for 15 to 18 minutes.

Mrs. Jim Rado (Vicki)
Lone Star Legacy

Texas Cheese Log

3	ounces cream cheese, softened	1	tablespoon Worcestershire sauce
½	pound Velveeta cheese, softened	1	teaspoon garlic salt
1	cup grated Cheddar cheese, softened	6	dashes Tabasco
		1	cup chopped pecans, optional
			Chili powder

Mix all ingredients together except chili powder, and form into a log or ball. Chill until firm. Roll in chili powder to cover. Serve with crackers. This cheese log can be frozen.

Mrs. Larry Hall (Jane)
Lone Star Legacy

Nachos y Pollo

2	whole chicken breasts, boned and skinned	1	cup chopped tomatoes
1½	teaspoons salt, divided	¼	teaspoon pepper
2½	teaspoons ground cumin, divided		Tortilla chips
1	onion, chopped	8	ounces Monterey Jack cheese, grated
2	tablespoons butter		Jalapeño pepper slices
1	can (4 ounces) chopped green chillies		Sour cream, optional

Place chicken with 1 teaspoon salt in a saucepan; cover with water and bring to a boil. Cover and reduce heat; simmer 6 to 8 minutes. Drain chicken, reserving broth. Place chicken with 1½ teaspoons cumin in food processor and process until coarsely ground. Set aside. Sauté onion in butter until tender and add chicken, ¾ cup reserved chicken broth, green chillies, tomato, 1 teaspoon cumin, ½ teaspoon salt and pepper. Simmer uncovered for 20 minutes or until liquid evaporates. Place tortilla chips on a cookie sheet and spoon 2 tablespoons of chicken mixture on each chip. Top with cheese and a jalapeño slice. Broil until cheese melts. Yields 36 nachos.

You can also put a dollop of sour cream on these nachos after they come out of the oven to enhance the flavor.

Mrs. Marcus Bone (Beverly)
Lone Star Legacy II

Jalapeño Cheese Balls

8 ounces cream cheese	1 medium onion
½ pound mild Cheddar cheese	2 to 3 cloves garlic
½ pound pimiento cheese	3 small dried hot peppers
½ pound sharp Cheddar cheese	Salt and pepper to taste
½ pound jalapeño cheese	Paprika
½ cup chopped pecans	Dried parsley flakes

Grind all ingredients except paprika and parsley in a meat grinder. Mix with hands and form into balls (any size you desire). Roll in paprika or dried parsley flakes or a combination of the two. Refrigerate until ready to serve. May be frozen.

Mrs. Robert Henderson (Dale)
Lone Star Legacy

Super Nachos

2	cans (16 ounces each) refried beans	2 to 3 cans (4 ounces each) taco sauce
1½	pounds ground meat	Chopped green onions
1	onion, chopped	Sliced ripe olives
	Salt and pepper to taste	Sour cream
1	can (4 ounces) chopped green chilies	Guacamole, frozen or homemade
3	cups grated Cheddar cheese	Tostado chips

Spread refried beans in a large oblong pan. Brown meat and onion. Drain; season with salt and pepper, and layer over beans. Sprinkle green chilies over meat; cover with grated cheese and taco sauce. Bake at 400° for 25 to 30 minutes. Remove from oven and spread with chopped green onions and sliced ripe olives. Before serving, garnish with sour cream and guacamole. Use tostado chips for dipping.

Mrs. Robert Henderson (Dale)
Lone Star Legacy

Cream Cheese Pastry Dough

1	cup butter	1	egg yolk
8	ounces cream cheese	2	teaspoons half and half cream
½	teaspoon salt		
2	cups flour		

Beat butter, cream cheese and salt until smooth and blended. Work in flour to form a smooth dough. Flatten dough to form a rectangle and wrap in foil. Chill overnight or several days. Divide dough and roll on floured pastry cloth with floured rolling pin or between two sheets of waxed paper. Shape as directed; chill before baking. Brush all tops with egg yolk beaten with cream. Bake in 350° oven unless otherwise specified. Filled turnovers and rolls freeze well. Preheat oven before removing appetizers from the freezer; bake without defrosting and add 5 to 10 minutes to the baking time. Watch carefully. The color should be a rich, golden brown.

Cookbook Committee
Lone Star Legacy

Appetizer Quiches

½ cup bacon or bacon bits
½ cup grated Swiss cheese
1 tablespoon dried parsley
2 eggs, well beaten
½ cup half and half cream
½ teaspoon salt
¼ teaspoon dry mustard

½ teaspoon Worcestershire sauce
1 tablespoon grated Parmesan cheese
Paprika
½ recipe cream cheese pastry

Shape dough into two dozen balls and press into tiny muffin pans. Layer bacon, cheese and parsley into unbaked dough. Beat eggs with cream, salt, dry mustard and Worcestershire sauce. Pour over bacon, cheese and parsley. Sprinkle with Parmesan cheese and paprika. Bake at 350° for 30 minutes or until brown on top. These may be frozen and then warmed in a 200° oven. Yields 2 dozen.

Mrs. Larry Hall (Jane)
Lone Star Legacy

Olive Cheese Puffs

½ pound Cheddar cheese, grated
1¼ cups flour

½ cup melted butter
1 jar (13 ounces) stuffed green olives

Mix cheese and flour until crumbly. Add melted butter. Take one teaspoon of dough; flatten and put olive inside. Roll into a ball. Place on cookie sheet and bake at 400° for 15 to 20 minutes. Yields approximately 48 appetizers.

Mrs. Bill Butler (Stephanie)
Lone Star Legacy

Jalapeño Cheese Squares

1	pound Longhorn Cheddar cheese, grated	2	eggs
1	pound Monterey Jack cheese, grated	1	can (13 ounces) evaporated milk
1	can (4 ounces) jalapeños, chopped	½	cup flour

Layer cheese and jalapeños in 9 inch square pan. Mix together eggs, milk and flour. Pour over top. Cook at 350° for 45 minutes. Cool slightly; cut into squares and serve.

Mrs. Jim Carney (Jean)
Lone Star Legacy

Cheese Stuffed Tortillas

8	ounces cream cheese, softened	1	can (14 ounces) chopped green chilies, drained
1	carton (8 ounces) sour cream	1	tablespoon chopped pimiento
1½	cups (5 oz.) grated sharp Cheddar cheese	1	teaspoon garlic salt
1	cup chopped ripe olives	1	tablespoon minced onion
		12	flour tortillas

Mix all ingredients together except tortillas. Spread on flour tortillas; roll up in jelly roll style. Chill several hours. Slice and serve. Yields 72 half inch slices.

Mrs. Reed McFadden (Penny)
Lone Star Legacy II

Green Chili Pie

1 to 2 cans (4 ounces each) whole green chilies	**4 eggs, beaten**
1 pound Monterey Jack cheese, grated	

Cut chilies in half lengthwise; remove seeds, rinse with water and pat dry. Lightly butter a 9 or 10 inch glass pie pan, or a 9 × 13 inch Pyrex dish. Line the prepared pan with green chilies; cover the bottom and halfway up the sides. Spread grated cheese making sure that the chilies are completely covered. Pour eggs evenly over the cheese. Bake at 275° for 45 minutes until a knife inserted in the center comes out clean. Cool slightly and cut in squares or pie wedges. Serve warm.

Mrs. Bob Edgecomb (Mary)
Lone Star Legacy

Crab Delights

1 can (6 ounces) crab meat, drained	**1 tablespoon lemon juice**
6 tablespoons mayonnaise	**½ cup grated Parmesan cheese**
½ teaspoon salt	**7 slices of bread**
1 tablespoon grated onion	**Paprika**

Mix together the crab meat, mayonnaise, salt, onion, lemon juice and Parmesan cheese. Spread on bread which has been trimmed and quartered. Sprinkle with paprika. Cook at 400° until bubbly brown. Yields 28.

This spread may be mixed early in the day and refrigerated. Spread on bread and brown just before serving.

Mrs. Lorne Parks (Dephanie)
Lone Star Legacy II

Baked Brie en Croûte

1	package puff pastry (2 sheets)	1	(6 to 8 ounce) jar apricot preserves, pureed
1	(10 to 12 inch) round Brie cheese	1	egg white, slightly beaten

Place 1 sheet of pastry on baking sheet. Center cheese round on pastry. Shave white coating from top of cheese. Spread preserves on top of cheese. Gently fold pastry edges over cheese, overlapping top approximately ½ inch. Lightly brush edges of pastry with egg white to seal. Place second pastry sheet on top of cheese. Trim to fit the top of cheese and press lightly to seal. Lightly brush edges with egg white to seal. Using excess pastry pieces, decorate the "Brie cake" with cut-out hearts, bells or other designs, attaching with egg white to seal. Freeze, covered, on baking sheet overnight or until ready to use. Without thawing, bake at 425° for 20 to 30 minutes or until golden and puffed. Serves 24.

If pastry-covered cheese is not frozen when placed in oven, the cheese will be very runny when served.

Cheryl Briggs Patton
Changing Thymes

Per serving_____

Calories 115 Protein 4.45 g Carbohydrates 8.35 g Fat 7.5 g Cholesterol 27.7 mg Sodium 134 mg

Good Times Cheese Roll

16	ounces processed cheese, softened	1	jar (2 ounces) diced pimientos
8	ounces cream cheese, softened	3	green onions, chopped
1	can (4 ounces) chopped green chillies, drained	1	teaspoon chopped jalapeños, optional
		½	cup chopped pecans
			Crackers

Carefully roll out processed cheese between 2 pieces of waxed paper into a rectangle approximately 11 × 17 inches; remove top layer of waxed paper. Beat cream cheese until spreading consistency. Spread cream cheese evenly on top of processed cheese like a frosting. Sprinkle green chilies, pimientos, green onions, jalapeños and pecans evenly over cream cheese. Roll jelly roll style, removing wax paper with each quarter turn, until mixture is enclosed. Place seam side down in dish. Refrigerate until ready to serve. Serves 24.

This makes a very festive and delicious holiday appetizer.

Mrs. Charley Batey (Gail)
Lone Star Legacy II

Herbed Cheese Spread

8	ounces cream cheese, softened	¼	teaspoon dill weed
8	ounces whipped cream cheese	¼	teaspoon marjoram
6	tablespoons butter	¼	teaspoon thyme
1	clove garlic, minced	¼	teaspoon celery salt
½	teaspoon oregano leaves	¼	teaspoon onion powder
¼	teaspoon basil	¼ to ½	teaspoon black pepper
			Assorted crackers

Blend cream cheeses and butter. Add garlic and mix well. Put all dry spices in mortar and grind with pestle. Add spices to cheese mixture and mix thoroughly. Refrigerate overnight to blend all flavors. Let warm slightly before serving. Serve as a spread with assorted crackers. Yields 2½ cups.

Keeps well and can be done ahead of time, as it gives flavors time to enhance each other. Can be frozen.

Mrs. Dudley Baker (Kathy)
Lone Star Legacy II

41

Sweet Brie

24	ounces Brie cheese	2	cups firmly packed brown sugar
1	cup chopped pecans		Crackers or ginger snaps

Remove top rind from cheese. Preheat broiler and place Brie in a 10 inch quiche dish or pie plate, and sprinkle with pecans. Cover the top and sides of the cheese with sugar, patting gently with fingertips. Do not worry if the sides are not completely covered. Broil on lowest rack until sugar bubbles and melts, about 5 minutes. Serve immediately with crackers or ginger snaps. Serves 10 to 12.

Mrs. Jim Rado (Vicki)
Lone Star Legacy II

Curried Chicken Balls

8	ounces cream cheese, softened	3	tablespoons chutney
4	tablespoons mayonnaise	1	teaspoon salt
1½	cups chopped almonds	2	teaspoons curry powder
1	tablespoon butter	1	cup grated coconut,
2	cups cooked, chopped chicken		toasted, optional

Blend cream cheese and mayonnaise. Sauté almonds in the butter until lightly browned. Add the almonds, chicken, chutney, salt and curry powder to the cream cheese mixture. Shape into walnut sized balls and roll in the coconut, if desired. Chill until ready to serve. Yields 5 dozen balls.

Mrs. Greg Gordon (Kathy)
Lone Star Legacy II

Soy Sauce Mushrooms

3	tablespoons melted butter, no substitute	2	tablespoons soy sauce
2	tablespoons Worcestershire sauce	1	pound fresh mushrooms, cleaned with stems intact

Melt butter in a skillet and add both sauces. Add mushrooms and sauté about 5 minutes or until tender.

Mrs. Don Bradford (Melinda)

For a little different taste, try sautéing your mushrooms with a little sherry or your favorite spirit.

Cookbook Committee
Lone Star Legacy

Shrimp Ceviche

1½	pounds raw shrimp, peeled and deveined	4	tablespoons olive oil
1	cup fresh lime juice	4	serrano chilies or 1 jalapeño, chopped
1	can (4 ounces) chopped green chilies	1	clove garlic, finely minced
½	cup chopped green onions with tops	1	jar (4 ounces) chopped pimientos, drained
2	large tomatoes, chopped		Fresh cilantro or parsley, chopped
1	teaspoon salt		

Marinate bite size shrimp in lime juice in a covered flat dish for 2 to 3 hours. Mix remaining ingredients except cilantro; add to shrimp and lime juice. Marinate at least 8 hours. Drain. Garnish with cilantro or parsley. Serve cold in a chilled bowl.

This appetizer is best if the Mexican limones are used for the fresh lime juice.

Mrs. Dudley Baker (Kathy)
Lone Star Legacy

43

Ceviche

1	pound raw, boneless cod	20	capers
8	ounces lime juice	1	tablespoon cumin
1	large onion, chopped	¼	cup olive oil
15	cherry tomatoes	1	tablespoon parsley
1	small jalapeño pepper, chopped	1	teaspoon oregano
			Salt and pepper to taste
30	pitted Spanish green olives, chopped		Chips

Place fish in a glass container and cover with lime juice for 3 hours or until fish has a white, flaky, cooked appearance. Drain off lime juice. Cut fish into bite sized pieces and add remaining ingredients and marinate for 2 to 4 hours. Serve with chips. Serves 8.

Mrs. Tom Hollis (Doris)
Lone Star Legacy II

Curry Mayonnaise

Wonderful with freshly steamed artichokes

1 cup reduced calorie mayonnaise	1	teaspoon tarragon vinegar
1 to 2 tablespoons minced onion	1½	teaspoons dry mustard
	1	teaspoon curry powder

Combine all ingredients, mixing until well blended. Chill until ready to serve. Serve as dip for freshly steamed artichokes, other fresh vegetables or boiled shrimp; or as a spicy sandwich spread. Makes approximately 1 cup.

Pamela Jones
Changing Thymes

Per tablespoon_____

Calories 38 Protein .154 g Carbohydrates 2.74 g Fat 3 g Cholesterol 3.74 mg Sodium 77.6 mg

Party Cracker Spread

8	ounces cream cheese	1	teaspoon dill weed
1	package (0.6 ounces) Italian salad dressing		Crackers or chips

Soften cream cheese to room temperature. Mix with salad dressing and dill weed. Serve with crackers or chips. Yields 1 cup spread.

Mrs. Rick Denbow (Susan)
Lone Star Legacy II

Spicy Empanadas

1½	recipes cream cheese pastry	2	medium tomatoes, peeled and chopped
1	pound ground beef	½	cup water
1	package (1½ ounces) spaghetti sauce mix	¼	cup grated Parmesan cheese
¼	cup minced onion	½	cup grated Cheddar cheese
1	teaspoon seasoned salt		

Make pastry and chill. Brown beef until crumbly. Stir in sauce mix, onion, salt, tomatoes and water. Simmer 15 minutes; remove from heat. Add cheeses; mix and cool. Divide pastry into fourths. Roll ⅛ inch thick and cut in 3 inch rounds. Stack leftover dough and reroll. Place 1 teaspoon filling in each round a little off center; moisten edges. Fold pastry over and press edges. Seal and crimp with floured fork. Bake at 350° for 20 minutes or until golden brown. Yields 7½ dozen.

Mrs. Larry Hall (Jane)
Lone Star Legacy

Italian Artichoke Hearts

Artichoke hearts must marinate for 8 hours

2 (16 ounce) cans artichoke hearts, drained and quartered
1 cup Italian salad dressing

¼ cup (1 ounce) grated Romano cheese
½ cup Italian-seasoned breadcrumbs

Marinate artichoke hearts in salad dressing for 8 hours. Combine cheese and breadcrumbs in bag. Drain artichoke hearts. Place in bag and shake to coat thoroughly with cheese and breadcrumb mixture. Place on baking sheet. Bake at 375° for 12 to 15 minutes. Makes approximately 56.

Jane Miller Sanders
Changing Thymes

Per piece_____

Calories 35 Protein .83 g Carbohydrates 3.52 g Fat 2 g Cholesterol .505 mg Sodium 101 mg

Banana Slush Punch

5 bananas	1 can (46 ounces)
1 can (12 ounces) frozen	pineapple juice
orange juice concentrate	Water
1 can (6 ounces) frozen	4 quarts club soda, ginger
lemonade concentrate	ale or lemon-lime drink,
2 to 3 cups sugar	chilled

Mash bananas thoroughly and add slightly thawed frozen juices. Sprinkle sugar over mixture. Add pineapple juice, stirring well to dissolve the sugar. Put into a gallon container and fill with water. Freeze to a slush. Put mixture into a two gallon punch bowl and add the mixers. If lemon-lime or ginger ale is used, use less sugar. This punch base can be frozen and kept indefinitely. Allow several hours for the mixture to reach the slush stage before serving. Yields 2 gallons.

This is a great punch. We've served it at all kinds of receptions and parties. It never fails to get compliments. In place of 2 quarts of the mixer, add champagne for a lovely morning punch. We have also used rum and vodka. This punch seems to go well with any liquor.

Mrs. Dudley Baker (Kathy)
Lone Star Legacy

Ruby Punch

4 cups cranberry juice	1 cup orange juice
cocktail	Fruit for garnish
1 cup pineapple juice	

Combine ingredients in punch bowl. Garnish with orange slices, pineapple chunks and sliced strawberries. Add ice ring or Giant Ice Cubes. Yields 6 cups.

Mrs. Robert Vossman (Nancy)
Lone Star Legacy II

47

"Texas" Strawberry Wine Punch

1	pint strawberries	½	teaspoon almond extract
2	cups Texas rosé	1	lemon
½	cup sugar	1	bottle (1½ liters) chilled
1	can (6 ounces) pineapple		Texas Burgundy
	juice concentrate		

Wash and hull strawberries; crush coarsely. Combine with rosé, sugar, undiluted pineapple juice and almond extract. Grate rind from lemon; squeeze juice; add to rosé mixture along with empty lemon shell. Cover and refrigerate overnight. Strain liquid, discarding lemon pulp. Pour over ice and add Burgundy just before serving. Yields 16 (3 ounce) servings.

If you cannot find Texas wines, you may substitute wines of other origins, but Texas wines are the best.

Mrs. John Perkins (Sandy)
Lone Star Legacy II

Citrus Mint Tea

7	regular tea bags	2¼	cups pineapple juice
7	sprigs mint	1	(6 ounce) can frozen
1	cup sugar		lemonade concentrate,
4	cups boiling water		thawed, undiluted
3¾	cups water		Mint Sprigs for garnish

Place tea bags, mint and sugar in large container. Pour boiling water over tea mixture and steep for 30 to 45 minutes. Remove tea bags and mint sprigs. Add 3¾ cups water, pineapple juice and lemonade. Garnish individual servings with mint sprigs. Makes approximately 10 cups.

Beverly Woldhagen James
Changing Thymes

Per 1 cup serving

Calories 141 Protein .231 g Carbohydrates 36.2 g Fat .1 g Cholesterol 0 mg Sodium 12 mg

Texas "Tea"

2	ounces vodka	3	ounces triple sec
2	ounces gin	3	ounces sweet and sour
2	ounces rum		syrup
2	ounces tequila	3	ounces cola

Mix all beverages together and serve over ice in tall tea glasses. Serves 2.

This is the best tea in Texas.

Mrs. Denman Smith (Sandra)
Lone Star Legacy II

Iced Tea Cooler

1	cup sugar	4	cans (6 ounces each) cold
6	cups strong tea		water
2½	cups pineapple juice		Sprigs fresh mint, to garnish
1	can (6 ounces) frozen lemonade concentrate		

Dissolve sugar in hot tea and cool. Add other ingredients and mix well. Chill. Serve as a punch or over ice in tall glasses. Serves 15 to 20.

Great with hot gingerbread!

Mrs. Don Panter (Carolyn)
Lone Star Legacy

Hot Cranberry Cider

3	quarts apple cider	6	sticks cinnamon
1	quart cranberry juice cocktail	1	teaspoon whole allspice
¼	cup sugar	2	cups rum, optional
3	oranges, pierced with a fork	1	teaspoon bitters, optional
16	cloves	¼	cup sugar, optional

Place cider, cranberry juice and sugar in a large (30 cup) percolator. Put pierced oranges, cloves, cinnamon and allspice in the top basket and perk as for coffee. After cider has perked add the rum, bitters and additional sugar, if desired. Yields 32 (4 ounce) servings.

Mrs. Jerry Hunt (Gail)
Lone Star Legacy

Zippy Cranberry Cooler

6	**cups cranberry juice**	**3**	**(6 ounce) cans frozen**
6	**cups cold water**		**lemonade concentrate,**
5¼	**cups ginger ale**		**undiluted**

Combine cranberry juice, water and lemonade, mixing well. Just before serving, stir in ginger ale and add ice cubes. Makes approximately 20 cups.

Kathy Marsh
Changing Thymes

Per 1 cup serving

Calories 105 Protein .077 g Carbohydrates 27 g Fat .1 g Cholesterol 0 mg Sodium 8.68 mg

Nostalgia's
Cranberry Punch

9	**cups pineapple juice**	**2**	**tablespoons whole cloves**
9	**cups cranberry juice**	**½**	**teaspoon salt**
4½	**cups water**	**1**	**cup brown sugar**
4	**cinnamon sticks**		

Use a large (30 cup) coffee pot. Put spices and sugar in basket and place juices and water into percolator. Perk 45 minutes. Yields 40 (4 ounce) servings.

Mrs. Craig Smith (Sherrie)
Lone Star Legacy II

Mock Champagne

1	(6 ounce) can frozen lemonade concentrate, undiluted	2	cups cold water
		1¾	cups ginger ale
¾	cup pineapple juice	1¾	cups sparkling water
1	(6 ounce) can frozen white grape juice, undiluted		

Combine all ingredients in 2-quart pitcher. Makes approximately 8 cups.

Mary Francis
Changing Thymes

Per ½ cup serving_____

Calories 64 Protein .25 g Carbohydrates 16.2 g Fat .1 g Cholesterol 0 mg Sodium 4.78 mg

Texas Sunrise

4	cups cran-raspberry juice	2	cups club soda
2	cups pineapple juice	1	lime
2	cups orange juice	1	cup whole strawberries

Combine cran-raspberry, pineapple and orange juices in punch bowl or large pitcher. Add club soda. Cut lime into thin round slices, discarding ends. Float some or all of slices in punch. Stir in strawberries. Add ice, if desired, and serve. Makes approximately 10 cups.

Sally Guyton Joyner
Changing Thymes

Per ½ cup serving_____

Calories 62 Protein .361 g Carbohydrates 15.5 g Fat .1 g Cholesterol 0 mg Sodium 6.58 mg

51

Strawberry Smoothie

1	cup skim or 2% milk	2	teaspoons vanilla extract
1	cup plain non-fat or regular yogurt	2	cups fresh or frozen strawberries
2	tablespoons sugar		

Combine milk, yogurt, sugar and vanilla in blender container. Process until smooth. Gradually add strawberries, blending until smooth and thickened. Makes approximately 4 cups.

Nancy Norin Jordt
Changing Thymes

Per 1 cup serving

Calories 117 Protein 5.65 g Carbohydrates 19.3 g Fat 2 g Cholesterol 6.17 mg Sodium 74.5 mg

Peach Champagne Punch

1	can (32 ounces) peach nectar	1	bottle (16 ounces) rum
1	can (12 ounces) frozen orange juice concentrate	2	bottles (33.8 ounces each) club soda
1	can (6 ounces) frozen limeade concentrate	2	bottles champagne

Mix all ingredients together except champagne and refrigerate. At serving time, mix all ingredients in punch bowl and add champagne. Crushed ice or an ice ring may be used. Any remaining punch may be frozen for use later. Yields 50 (4 ounce) servings.

Mrs. Denman Smith (Sandra)
Lone Star Legacy II

White Sangria

1	gallon white wine	1	cup lemon juice
2	cups triple orange liqueur with cognac brandy	2	oranges, thinly sliced
1	can (12 ounces) frozen orange juice concentrate	2	lemons, thinly sliced
		1 to 2	bottles champagne or club soda

Mix all ingredients except champagne or club soda and chill well. Add champagne just before serving. Yields 24 (6 ounces) servings.

Mrs. Denman Smith (Sandra)
Lone Star Legacy II

Traditional Eggnog

12 egg yolks	1 fifth rum
1 cup sugar	4 cups whipping cream
4 cups milk	Freshly grated nutmeg

Beat egg yolks until fluffy. Add sugar gradually, beating until very light and thick. Add milk and rum. Chill until very cold, at least 5 to 6 hours. Whip cream and fold in. Chill for 1 hour before serving. Sprinkle with grated nutmeg. Yields 20 servings.

Nancy Young Chandler
Lone Star Legacy II

Lake Austin Cooler

1 glass tea, unsweetened	Ice
1 jigger Peppermint Schnapps	

Fill tall glass with ice. Add one jigger Peppermint Schnapps and fill with tea. Serves one. To make full use of our wonderful Texas sun, place 1 gallon of water, 3 family size tea bags into a gallon jar. Secure lid and place in sun for 3 to 4 hours. This tea with the Peppermint Schnapps is a real refreshing drink when spending the day on Lake Austin.

Nancy Young Moritz
Lone Star Legacy

Skip and Go Barefoot

1 can (6 ounces) frozen limeade concentrate, thawed	6 ounces vodka
	6 ounces beer

Empty can of limeade into blender and fill ¾ full of crushed ice. Add vodka and beer and blend until smooth. Serves 4.

Fantastic way to break the ice.

Mrs. Randy Hagan (Robin)
Lone Star Legacy

Tarzan's Frozen Tonic

1	can (6 ounces) frozen limeade concentrate, thawed	2	ounces gin or vodka
		2	ounces rum
		2	ounces tequila

Place all the ingredients in a blender. Fill ¾ full with crushed ice and blend until thick and frozen. Serves 6 to 8.

Guaranteed to make you swing from trees.

Mrs. John Carrell (Jane)
Lone Star Legacy

Mimosa

1	quart freshly squeezed orange juice, chilled	1	fifth champagne, chilled

Mix and pour into stemmed glasses. Serves 10 to 12.

As sweet and refreshing as the blossom it's named for.

Cookbook Committee
Lone Star Legacy

Mexico Wallop

1	quart tequila	2	quarts fresh fruits, cubes or balls
1	bottle champagne		Sugar to taste
4	bottles sauterne		

Sweeten to taste; chill thoroughly, and add ice cubes just before serving. Place in large punch bowl and serve in sherbet cups.

Marian Carlson Hidell
Lone Star Legacy

Mexican Martinis

¼ cup dry vermouth
1 fresh hot red or jalapeño
   pepper, split lengthwise

1 quart vodka or gin

Combine vermouth and pepper in a quart canning jar. Add vodka to top of jar. Cover with air tight lid and refrigerate 6 hours. Taste mixture to gauge strength of pepper flavor. Remove pepper or continue steeping up to 6 more hours. Yields 1 quart.

Marcus Bone
Lone Star Legacy II

Mexican Fizz

1½ ounces tequila
Dash grenadine
¼ cup orange juice

1½ ounces lemon juice
Ice

Mix all ingredients together and shake well with ice. Pour into 2 stemmed champagne glasses and enjoy. Serves 2.

Mrs. Denman Smith (Sandra)
Lone Star Legacy II

Border Buttermilk

1 can (6 ounces) frozen
   limeade concentrate

6 ounces tequila
   Ice to fill blender

Pour all ingredients into a blender and blend on high until ice is crushed and mixture is frothy. Serves 4.

This is famous in the valley to welcome newcomers.

Mrs. Dudley Baker (Kathy)
Lone Star Legacy II

Election Day Punch

8	cups cranberry juice	2	cups vodka
1	(6 ounce) can frozen orange juice concentrate, thawed, undiluted		Large block of ice
		1¾	cups club soda
¼	cup sugar		Orange and lemon slices

Combine cranberry juice, orange juice and sugar in a punch bowl and stir until sugar is dissolved. Stir in vodka and add large block of ice. Carefully pour club soda over punch. Garnish with orange and lemon. Makes approximately 12 cups.

Sandy Wyatt Niederstadt
Changing Thymes

Per ½ cup serving_____

Calories 110 Protein .169 g Carbohydrates 15.7 g Fat .1 g Cholesterol 0 mg Sodium 5.41 mg

Apricot Sours

1	(6 ounce) can frozen lemonade concentrate, undiluted	1	cup apricot brandy
		1¾	cups water
1	(6 ounce) can frozen orange juice concentrate, undiluted		

Mix all ingredients in a blender container until well blended. Serve over ice. Makes approximately 4 cups.

Sandy Wyatt Niederstadt
Changing Thymes

Per ½ cup serving_____

Calories 138 Protein .572 g Carbohydrates 18.1 g Fat .1 g Cholesterol 0 mg Sodium 3.05 mg

Holiday Wassail Bowl

4	cups cranberry juice	2	cups Triple Sec or cock-
2	(6 ounce) cans frozen orange juice concentrate, undiluted	½	tail Grand Marnier liqueur
			teaspoon allspice
4	cups water	18	whole cloves
2	tablespoons sugar	2	bottles white wine
			Cranberries for garnish (optional)

Bring all ingredients except wine to a simmer. Add wine and heat through, but do not boil. Chill for several hours. Serve in a punch bowl with a decorative ice ring, whole fresh cranberries and holly sprig. Makes approximately 17½ cups.

Kathy Marsh
Changing Thymes

Per ½ cup serving_____

Calories 121 Protein .309 g Carbohydrates 15.7 g Fat .1 g Cholesterol 0 mg Sodium 5.62 mg

Lake Austin Ice Tea

2	(6 ounce) cans frozen lemonade concentrate, undiluted	1	cup sugar or to taste
		6	cups water
		2	cups strongly-brewed tea
1	(6 ounce) can frozen orange juice concentrate, undiluted	1½	cups bourbon

Combine all ingredients in 1-gallon container. Blend well. Serve in tall glasses over crushed ice. Makes approximately 13 cups.

Sandy Wyatt Niederstadt
Changing Thymes

Per 1 cup serving_____

Calories 193 Protein .391 g Carbohydrates 32.8 g Fat .1 g Cholesterol 0 mg Sodium 6.24 mg

Texas Tickle

1	(6 ounce) can frozen lemonade concentrate undiluted	½	cup apricot brandy
		2	medium peaches, unpeeled and sliced
¾	cup vodka		Cracked ice

Combine all ingredients except ice in the container of an electric, blender, process until smooth. Gradually add ice, processing until mixture reaches desired consistency. Makes approximately 2½ cups.

Nanci Norin Jordt
Changing Thymes

Per ½ cup serving_____

Calories 212 Protein .346 g Carbohydrates 19.9 g Fat .1 g Cholesterol 0 mg Sodium 1.92 mg

Café Glacé

This recipe was stolen from J. Waddy Bullion from Dallas, Texas. Like kisses and watermelons, secret formulas and recipes that are stolen tend to taste better! J. Waddy is my father-in-law (I also have other names for him). He is an attorney specializing in corporate income tax work for oil companies. While on assignment in Venezuela, he chanced to sample this concoction (observing some ancient culture's fertility rites) in an obscure little Maracaibo (Hilton) Bar. It is so good, even those who don't like coffee will succumb. Collect 1 jigger day-old stale coffee, 1 jigger cheap brandy or expensive cognac (depending on whom you want to impress) and 1 pint vanilla ice cream. Chunk it all together in a blender and mix on high until smooth. Lock the door, close the drapes and serve in elegant clear glasses. Serves 2 to 4 adults.

Ed L. Mears III
Lone Star Legacy II

French 75

2 bottles white champagne

½ to 1 bottle (25 ounces) cognac or brandy

1 bottle (33.8 ounces) lemon-lime carbonated drink

1 bottle (33.8 ounces) club soda

1 bottle (6 ounces) maraschino cherries

1 orange, sliced

Ice

Mix all beverages and maraschino cherries in punch bowl. Add ice. Garnish with orange slices. Yields 25 (4 ounce) servings.

Mrs. Jim Rado (Vicki)
Lone Star Legacy II

BEST OF

Lone Star ★ Legacy

SALADS & SALAD DRESSINGS

Corn-Black Bean Salad

Chill for several hours to capture the full flavor

4	cups cooked black beans	½	cup minced cilantro or parsley
2	cups canned or frozen corn		Chopped fresh jalapeño pepper to taste (optional)
1	large red bell pepper, diced		Salt and black pepper to taste
1	large purple onion, chopped		Chopped avocados and tomatoes (optional)

Dressing:

2	cloves garlic, minced		Juice of 1 small lime
½ to ¾ cup vinaigrette dressing			

Combine beans, corn, bell pepper, onion, cilantro and jalapeño pepper. If canned beans are used, rinse and drain. Prepare dressing by mixing garlic, vinaigrette and lime juice. Add dressing to vegetables. Chill for several hours before serving. Just before serving, add avocado and tomato. Makes approximately 8 cups.

This salad is great served with grilled meat, fish or quesadillas.

Jeanne Cassidy
Changing Thymes

Per ½ cup serving_____

Calories 115 Protein 4.65 g Carbohydrates 16.3 Fat 4 g Cholesterol 0 Sodium 159 mg

Cilantro Corn Salad

3 (10 ounce) packages
frozen corn, thawed
¾ cup chopped red bell
pepper

½ cup chopped fresh
cilantro
¼ cup chopped green onion
Salt to taste

Dressing:
⅓ cup vegetable oil
⅓ cup white wine vinegar
2 tablespoons Dijon
mustard

½ teaspoon black pepper
1 tablespoon minced
jalapeño pepper

Combine corn, bell pepper, cilantro and green onion. Prepare dressing by combining oil, wine vinegar, mustard, black pepper and jalapeño pepper, whisking until well blended. Add dressing to vegetable mixture, stirring to coat thoroughly. Season with salt. Chill, covered, before serving. Makes approximately 5 cups.

Pamela Jones
Changing Thymes

Per ½ cup serving———————————————————————

Calories 140 Protein 2.53 g Carbohydrates 17.2 g Fat 8.5 g Cholesterol 0 Sodium 380 mg

Wilted Watercress Salad

3 hard cooked eggs, sliced
2 pounds fresh watercress
½ pound bacon

¼ cup wine vinegar
Salt and pepper

Wash watercress well; tear into large sprigs, drain and put into salad bowl. Cook bacon crisp; drain on paper towel and crumble; set aside. Reheat bacon drippings until very hot; pour over watercress and toss. Drain extra drippings back into skillet to heat and pour over cress again until cress begins to wilt. Add vinegar, bacon bits, salt and pepper and toss. Garnish with sliced hard cooked eggs. Serves 10 to 12.

Good for company.

Mrs. Don Bradford (Melinda)
Lone Star Legacy II

Betsy's Vegetable Salad

Prepare a day in advance

1	head cauliflower, cut in bite-sized pieces	2	yellow squash, sliced
1	bunch broccoli, flowerets only	¼	cup sliced black olives
		1½	cups (6 ounces) grated Cheddar cheese

Dressing:

1	(12 ounce) carton cottage cheese	1	envelope ranch style dressing mix
1	cup mayonnaise		

Combine cauliflower, broccoli, squash and olives. Prepare dressing by blending cottage cheese, mayonnaise and dressing mix in a food processor until smooth. Add enough dressing to vegetables to coat thoroughly. Chill, covered, overnight. Just before serving, sprinkle cheese on salad. Serve with remaining dressing, if desired. Makes approximately 8 cups.

Donna Earle Crain
Changing Thymes

Per ½ cup serving_____

Calories 177 Protein 6.43 g Carbohydrates 3.41 g Fat 16 g Cholesterol 22.5 mg Sodium 387 mg

Broccoli Sunflower Salad

2	bunches broccoli, chopped	6	slices bacon, cooked and crumbled
1	cup sunflower seeds		
½	cup raisins		

Dressing:

1	cup mayonnaise	2	tablespoons cider vinegar
2	tablespoons sugar		

Prepare dressing by blending mayonnaise, sugar and vinegar. Combine dressing and broccoli, mixing well. Add sunflower seeds, raisins and bacon to broccoli, tossing to mix. Makes approximately 6 cups.

Great to serve with pork or chicken.

Jane Miller Sanders
Changing Thymes

Per ½ cup serving_____

Calories 260 Protein 5.44 g Carbohydrates 12.7 g Fat 22.5 g Cholesterol 13.6 mg Sodium 168 mg

Green and White Salad

Chill overnight

1   small bunch broccoli,
     cut in flowerets
1   small head cauliflower,
     cut in flowerets
¼   cup chopped onion
1½   cups sliced celery
1   (2 ounce) jar pimiento-
     stuffed green olives,
     drained and sliced

3   hard-cooked eggs,
     chopped
Salt and black pepper to taste
Cayenne pepper to taste

Dressing:
1   cup mayonnaise
1   teaspoon fresh lemon
     juice

1   teaspoon dill weed

Steam broccoli and cauliflower, using small amount of water, until crisp tender. Drain and chill. Prepare dressing by blending mayonnaise, lemon juice and dill weed in large bowl. Add broccoli, cauliflower, onion, celery, olives and eggs to dressing, tossing gently to coat all ingredients. Season with salt, black pepper and cayenne pepper. Chill overnight. Makes approximately 8 cups.

Nanci Norin Jordt
Changing Thymes

Per ½ cup serving————————————————————

Calories 128 Protein 2.21 g Carbohydrates 2.79 g Fat 12.5 g Cholesterol 47.9 mg Sodium 215 mg

Watercress Cucumber Salad

1 cup coarsely chopped watercress
½ cup sliced purple onion
1 medium cucumber, cut lengthwise in quarters and sliced

1 small head Boston bib lettuce, torn in bite-sized pieces

Dressing:
½ cup low-fat sour cream
2 tablespoons lemon juice
2 tablespoons skim milk
2 teaspoons dill weed

1 teaspoon sugar
¼ teaspoon salt
¼ teaspoon black pepper

Combine watercress, onion, cucumber and lettuce in large bowl, tossing gently. Chill until ready to serve. Combine all dressing ingredients, blending thoroughly. Chill until ready to serve. Just before serving, drizzle 2 to 3 tablespoons dressing over salad. Toss to mix. Serve remaining dressing with salad. Serves 8.

Jane Miller Sanders
Changing Thymes

Per serving of_____

Calories 11 Protein .738 g Carbohydrates 2.3 g Fat .1 g Cholesterol 0 Sodium 3.71 mg

Per tablespoon of dressing _____

Calories 14 Protein .369 g Carbohydrates 1.02 g Fat 1 g Cholesterol 3.34 mg Sodium 43.4 mg

Beautiful Vegetable Salad

Chill at least 24 hours before serving

¾ cup white wine vinegar	5 stalks celery, cut into sticks
¼ cup water	1 green bell pepper, sliced
½ cup vegetable oil	1 purple onion, sliced
2 tablespoons sugar	1 (3¼ ounce) can green olives, drained
½ teaspoon black pepper	2 or 3 jalapeño peppers
½ teaspoon oregano	1 (15 ounce) can baby corn, drained
1 head cauliflower, cut in bite-sized pieces	
5 carrots, sliced	

Combine vinegar, water, oil, sugar, black pepper and oregano in large saucepan. Bring to a boil. Add cauliflower, carrots, celery sticks, bell pepper, onion, olives, jalapeño peppers and corn to vinegar mixture. Bring to a boil and cook for 5 minutes. Let stand until cool. Store in glass jars. Chill at least 24 hours before serving. Drain before serving. Makes approximately 12 cups.

Nice to serve at a buffet or as a change from a tossed salad.

Martha Rife
Changing Thymes

Per ½ cup serving_____

Calories 78 Protein1.09 g Carbohydrates 8.25 g Fat 5 g Cholesterol 0 Sodium 154 mg

Greek Salad

May be prepared several hours in advance

½ medium-sized purple
   onion, thinly sliced
1 pound fresh spinach,
   rinsed, stems removed
   and torn
½ cup (4 ounces) crumbled
   feta cheese

½ cup coarsely chopped
   walnuts
½ cup Greek olives, pitted
   and cut in halves

Layer, in order listed, onion, spinach, cheese, walnuts and olives in salad bowl. Cover and chill until ready to serve. Just before serving, toss with favorite dressing. Serves 8.

Basil Vinaigrette, page (99), is especially good on this salad.

LaNyce Whittemore
Changing Thymes

Per serving_____

Calories 92 Protein 4.61 g Carbohydrates 4.21 g Fat 7.1 g Cholesterol 12.6 mg Sodium 203 mg

Santa Fe Citrus Salad

5   cups loosely-packed torn
    romaine lettuce
1   cup sliced purple onion
1   cup thinly sliced peeled
    jícama
¼   cup chopped cilantro

1   cup pink grapefruit
     sections
1½ cups fresh orange
     sections (about 4
     medium-sized
     oranges)

Dressing:
¼   cup fresh orange juice
1½ tablespoons vegetable oil

1   teaspoon sugar
½   teaspoon ground cumin

Combine lettuce, onion, jícama and cilantro in large bowl. Prepare dressing by blending orange juice, oil, sugar and cumin. Drizzle dressing over salad. Add grapefruit and orange sections and toss gently. Serve immediately.

Pamela Jones
Changing Thymes

Per serving_____

Calories 72 Protein 1.59 g Carbohydrates 11.3 g Fat 3 g Cholesterol 0 Sodium 4.53 mg

Strawberry Spinach Salad

1	pound fresh spinach, rinsed, stems removed and torn	1	pint fresh strawberries, hulled and cut in halves
1	cup diagonally sliced celery	1	cup sugar
		1	cup chopped pecans

Poppy Seed Dressing:

¼	cup sugar	2	scallions, chopped
1	teaspoon salt	1	cup vegetable oil
1	teaspoon dry mustard	1½	tablespoons poppy seed
⅓	cup vinegar		

Combine spinach, celery and strawberries. Prepare caramelized pecans by slowly cooking sugar and pecans in skillet over low heat until all sugar has melted onto pecans and they are browned; DO NOT OVERCOOK. Immediately place pecans on wax paper and let stand until cool. Prepare dressing by blending sugar, salt, mustard, vinegar and scallions in food processor. Gradually add oil, processing to mix well. Stir in poppy seeds. Chill until ready to use. Add pecans and Poppy Seed Dressing to salad, tossing gently to mix. Serves 10.

Donna Earle Crain
Changing Thymes

Per serving of salad_____

Calories 177 Protein 2.48 g Carbohydrates 26.1 g Fat 8.5 g Cholesterol 0 Sodium 46.8 mg

Per 1 tablespoon dressing_____

Calories 186 Protein .313 g Carbohydrates 5.06 g Fat 19 g Cholesterol 0 Sodium 178 mg

Avocado Grapefruit Salad

1	head bibb or romaine lettuce	2	cans (11 ounces each) Mandarin oranges, drained
2	avocados, sliced	1	small red onion, sliced in rings
3	Ruby Red grapefruit, sectioned and membranes removed or 2 cans (16 ounces) grapefruit sections, drained		Prepared poppy seed dressing or celery seed dressing

Line salad bowl with salad greens. Tear some greens into bite size pieces. Add avocado, grapefruit and orange slices. Lightly toss with prepared dressing of your choice. Place onion rings on top of salad to add color and flavor. Serves 6 to 8.

Mrs. Dudley Baker (Kathy)
Lone Star Legacy

Marinated Fresh Asparagus

¼	cup lemon juice	1	tablespoon capers
⅓	cup olive oil	1	tablespoon chopped parsley
½	cup oil		
½	teaspoon salt	1	pound fresh asparagus, cooked
	Dash of pepper		Salad greens
½	teaspoon dry mustard		Tomatoes to garnish
1	tablespoon, chopped pimiento		

Combine lemon juice, oils, salt, pepper and mustard, stirring until well blended. Add pimiento, capers and parsley. Place cooked asparagus in a shallow 1½ quart casserole and pour marinade over all; cover and chill two hours. Drain asparagus and reserve marinade as needed for dressing for salad greens. Serve on a bed of lettuce, garnished with tomatoes.

Mrs. D. D. Baker, Jr. (Agnes)
Lone Star Legacy

69

Wilted Spinach Salad a la Villa Demos

1	pound spinach	¼	cup sugar
1	pound bacon, thick sliced	3	ounces Italian dressing
1	medium onion, sliced thin	3	ounces white vinegar
8	ounces fresh mushrooms, sliced thin		Seasoned croutons

Wash spinach and drain; then refrigerate at least 1 hour. Fry bacon until crisp; drain and crumble. In large skillet, sauté onion in ½ cup bacon drippings. Add sugar, dressing and vinegar. Pour over spinach which has been tossed with bacon and mushrooms. Top with croutons and serve immediately. Serves 6.

This is the famous salad served at the Villa Demos Restaurant in Acapulco.

Mrs. Robert Kelly (Margaret)
Lone Star Legacy

Spinach Salad

6	slices bacon, cooked and crumbled	2	hard cooked eggs, sliced
1	tablespoon bacon drippings		Small onion, peeled and cut into rings
4	tablespoons olive oil	1	cup fresh mushrooms, sliced
3	tablespoons red wine vinegar		Salt and pepper
1	pound fresh spinach		

In a small jar or bowl combine bacon drippings, olive oil and vinegar. Mix well and set aside. Place spinach, eggs, onion, mushrooms, and bacon in a salad bowl. Season with salt and pepper. Sprinkle with dressing and toss well.

Mrs. Larry Hall (Jane)
Lone Star Legacy

Cu-Cu Salad

1	small package (3 ounces) lime gelatin	¼	cup chopped onion
1	cup hot water	1	cup cottage cheese
1	cup grated cucumbers	½	cup mayonnaise
		½	teaspoon salt

Mix gelatin with water; stir until blended. Add remaining ingredients and mix well. Refrigerate overnight in a 9 × 13 inch glass dish. Serves 6.

This is nice because you don't have to wait for gelatin to firm up before adding the other ingredients. Quick and easy to do ahead.

Mrs. Robert West (Linda)
Lone Star Legacy

Romaine Salad

4	strips crisp fried bacon, reserve drippings	¼	teaspoon pepper
¾	cup oil	½	teaspoon salt
¼	cup vinegar	1	tablespoon sugar
¼	cup bacon drippings	1	head romaine lettuce
1	egg	3	slices bread, crusts removed
¼	teaspoon dry mustard	¼	cup oil
		1	clove minced garlic

Blend ¾ cup of oil, vinegar, bacon drippings, egg, and spices in a blender for 1 minute. Refrigerate for at least one hour. Serve over torn romaine lettuce pieces, and top with crumbled bacon and home-made croutons. Cut prepared bread in cubes for croutons. In ¼ cup oil, sauté one clove garlic; add bread and coat with oil. Remove from heat and let stand one hour. Toast in 350° oven until brown. Serves 8.

Mrs. Jette Campbell (Sally)
Lone Star Legacy

Layered Salad

Salad greens
Green pepper, chopped
Celery, chopped
Green onions, chopped
Fresh mushrooms, sliced
Water chestnuts, sliced
Olives, well drained and
    chopped
1 to 2 packages (10 ounces
    each) frozen peas
1   cup mayonnaise
1   carton (8 ounces) sour
    cream

1 to 2 tablespoons sugar,
    optional
1   package (.04 ounces)
    dry Ranch dressing
    mix, optional
2   cups grated cheese,
    Cheddar or Swiss
Parmesan cheese, grated
8 to 10 slices bacon,
    cooked and crumbled

The first layer should be your favorite salad greens or a mixture of several, such as spinach, romaine, bibb, or red leaf lettuce. Tear into bite size pieces. Greens should equal about 1½ heads. Place in a large straight sided, clear bowl. Next, layer any combination of the following: green pepper, celery, onions, mushrooms, water chestnuts, and olives to equal 1½ to 2 cups. The third layer should be frozen peas. For the fourth layer, combine mayonnaise and sour cream. If you like it sweet add sugar. If not add the dry Ranch dressing mix to the mayonnaise-sour cream mixture. Spread dressing evenly on top, making sure edges are sealed. Next sprinkle cheese, Cheddar or Swiss. Cover generously with Parmesan and top with crumbled bacon. Do not mix. Cover tightly with plastic wrap. Refrigerate overnight. Serves 10 to 12.

Mrs. Ken Moyer (Bonnie)
Lone Star Legacy

El Matt's Guacamole Salad

1   cup mashed avocado
¼   teaspoon salt
¼   teaspoon garlic powder
1   teaspoon cider vinegar

1   teaspoon vegetable oil
½   cup chopped tomatoes,
    optional

Blend all ingredients together well. Chill before serving. If using tomatoes, add ⅛ teaspoon more salt. Yields 1½ cups.

Matt Martinez, Jr.
Lone Star Legacy II

Mushroom Salad

½   pound mushrooms, sliced
¼   cup minced fresh parsley
¼   garlic clove, minced
⅓   cup salad oil
2½ tablespoons white wine
     vinegar

1½ tablespoons mayonnaise
½   teaspoon salt
⅛   teaspoon dry mustard
⅛   teaspoon pepper
6 to 8 lettuce leaves, washed
     and chilled

Wash mushrooms; trim off stems and slice fairly thick. Combine mushrooms and parsley. Chill. Combine garlic, salad oil, wine vinegar, mayonnaise, salt, mustard and pepper in a blender or food processor and blend well. Just before serving toss dressing with mushrooms and spoon salad onto lettuce leaves. Serves 4.

Mrs. Sid Mann (Kathi)
Lone Star Legacy II

Sprouts 'N Bean Salad

½   cup sugar
½   cup white vinegar
½   cup oil
Garlic salt to taste
Salt and pepper to taste
1   can (16 ounces) seasoned
     cut green beans

1   can (16 ounces) bean
     sprouts
1   jar (2 ounces) pimiento
     slices
1   package (1½ ounces)
     slivered almonds

Heat sugar, vinegar, oil, garlic salt, salt and pepper in a saucepan until sugar is dissolved. Mix green beans, bean sprouts, pimiento and slivered almonds in a bowl and cover with sauce. Marinate in the refrigerator for half a day or at least 2 hours. Serves 4 to 6.

Mrs. Bob Edgecomb (Mary)
Lone Star Legacy II

Ruth's Bean Salad

1   can (16 ounces) Italian cut
green beans
1   can (16 ounces) wax beans
1   can (16 ounces) kidney,
beans
1   medium red onion, sliced
1   jar (4 ounces) sliced
pimientos
1   can (8 ounces) water
chestnuts, sliced
1   can (14½ ounces)
artichoke hearts
¾   cup sugar
¾   cup vinegar
Salt to taste
Tabasco to taste
1   teaspoon dill seed
1   package Garlic-Cheese
salad dressing mix

Drain all beans well. Add remaining vegetables and mix well. For dressing, boil sugar and vinegar until well blended. Add salt, Tabasco, garlic, dill seed, and dry salad mix. Put in a large jar or covered bowl and refrigerate. Stir occasionally. Keeps indefinitely. Serves 8 to 10.

Mrs. Jim Schultz (Mary Kay)
Lone Star Legacy

Walnut and Green Bean Salad

Salad:
1½ pounds fresh green beans   Ice water
1   teaspoon salt

Cook green beans in salted water until tender crisp, about 4 minutes. Cool in ice water immediately; drain and pat dry.

Dressing:
¾   cup oil
½   cup fresh mint leaves
¼   cup tarragon vinegar
¾   teaspoon salt
½   teaspoon minced garlic
¼   teaspoon white pepper
1   cup crumbled Feta cheese
1   cup diced red onion
1   cup chopped, toasted
walnuts

Combine oil, mint, vinegar, salt, garlic and pepper in food processor until smooth. Mix in crumbled Feta cheese. Toss green beans with dressing and onion. Top with toasted walnuts. Chill until serving time or overnight. Serves 6.

Mrs. Denman Smith (Sandra)
Lone Star Legacy II

Three Bean Salad

2	cans (16 ounces each) cut green beans	⅔	cup cider vinegar
1	can (16 ounces) wax beans	⅓	cup sugar
1	can (16 ounces) red kidney beans	1	teaspoon salt
½	purple onion, sliced	½	teaspoon pepper
⅔	cup oil	2	dashes dry mustard
		4	slices bacon, fried

The day before you plan to serve, drain beans and place in a glass bowl. Add onion. Mix oil, vinegar, sugar, salt, pepper and mustard together and pour over bean mixture. Cover and refrigerate. Just before serving, crumble bacon and toss. Serves 10.

Mrs. Sid Mann (Kathi)
Lone Star Legacy II

Black Eyed Pea Salad

3	cans (15 ounces each) black eyed peas	1	can (10¾ ounces) tomato soup
1	can (15 ounces) carrots	¾	cup sugar
1	cup chopped onion	¾	cup white vinegar
1	clove garlic, crushed	5	tablespoons Worcestershire sauce
1	jar (2 ounces) sliced pimiento	⅓	cup oil

Drain, wash and dry black eyed peas. Add remaining ingredients. Mix well and chill until ready to serve. Serves 12 to 15.

Jerry A. Hunt
Lone Star Legacy II

Marinated Pea Salad

1 can (12 ounces) shoe peg
corn, drained
1 can (16 ounces) French
style green beans, drained
1 can (8½ ounces) English
peas, drained
1 cup chopped celery
1 green pepper, chopped
1 small onion, chopped

1 jar (2 ounces) pimientos,
drained and chopped
½ cup oil
½ cup cider vinegar
1 cup sugar
Salt
Paprika
½ teaspoon garlic salt

Combine all ingredients. Refrigerate for one or two days. Serves 12.

Mrs. John C. Waller (Elsie)
Lone Star Legacy

Chilled Dilled Peas

1 cup sour cream
1 small bunch fresh chives,
snipped, or 4 green
onions with tops, minced
2 tablespoons fresh
snipped dill or 1
tablespoon dried dill weed

1 teaspoon curry powder
Salt and freshly ground black
pepper to taste
1 (16 ounce) package
frozen petite green peas,
thawed

Combine sour cream, chives or green onion, dill, curry powder, salt and black pepper. Add peas and gently mix. Chill thoroughly or overnight. Serve chilled. Makes approximately 3 cups.

Jeanne Cassidy
Changing Thymes

Per ½ cup serving ——————————————————

Calories 147 Protein 5.52 g Carbohydrates 13.5 g Fat 8.5 g Cholesterol 17 mg Sodium 197 mg

Moroccan Tomato Salad

3	tomatoes	6	hot cherry peppers
3	ribs of celery		Salt to taste
½	cup chopped parsley	¼	teaspoon cayenne pepper
⅓	cup capers	1	teaspoon paprika
2	green bell peppers	¼	cup olive oil

Core the tomatoes and cut unto ½ inch cubes. Place in a salad bowl. Trim the celery and coarsely chop. Add to tomatoes along with parsley and capers. Trim bell peppers and cherry peppers; chop and add to salad bowl. Blend together salt, cayenne pepper, paprika and olive oil and pour over salad. Toss to blend well and serve at room temperature. Serves 6.

Mrs. Cecil Smith (Diana)
Lone Star Legacy II

Fire and Ice Tomatoes

6	large tomatoes, skinned and quartered	1	teaspoon sugar
1	large green bell pepper, cut into strips	⅛	teaspoon red pepper
		⅛	teaspoon black pepper
1	large red onion, sliced	2	teaspoons salt
¾	cup cider vinegar	¼	cup water
1½	teaspoons celery salt	1	cucumber, thinly sliced, optional
1½	teaspoons mustard seed		

Toss tomatoes, green pepper and onion in a large glass bowl. Combine remaining ingredients except cucumber and bring to a boil for 1 minute. While still hot, pour over vegetables. Chill for several hours or overnight. At serving time the cucumber may be added if desired. Serves 12 to 14.

Mrs. Jack Frucella (Mary Nell)
Lone Star Legacy II

77

Spicy Tomato Salad

5	medium tomatoes, sliced ¼ inch thick
½	cup olive oil
2	tablespoons wine vinegar or lemon juice
1	tablespoon basil, crushed
¼	teaspoon salt
	Freshly ground pepper
2	tablespoons sliced green onions or shallots
1 to 2	tablespoons parsley, chopped

Arrange tomato slices in a glass serving dish. Combine remaining ingredients and pour over tomatoes. Chill until cold. Serves 6.

Mrs. Jack Dempsey (Estelle)
Lone Star Legacy

Grandma's Tomato Aspic

3	envelopes unflavored gelatin
4	cups vegetable cocktail juice, divided
1	teaspoon salt
½	teaspoon onion powder
⅛	teaspoon garlic powder
1	teaspoon Worcestershire sauce
	Dash hot pepper sauce
1	cup diced celery
1	cup sliced green olives
	Lettuce
1	avocado, to garnish
	Juice of ½ lemon

Place gelatin in 2 cups vegetable cocktail juice. Heat remaining juice; add softened gelatin to dissolve. Add seasonings and allow to cool. Add celery and olives and pour into a ring mold. Refrigerate until set. At serving time, unmold on a bed of lettuce. Garnish with avocado slices dipped in lemon juice. Serves 10 to 12.

Marinated tiny shrimp also make a pretty and tasty accompaniment. I love this aspic! It is Dudley's grandmother's recipe, and it is not as sweet as most.

Mrs. Dudley Baker (Kathy)
Lone Star Legacy II

Salad Cocktail

Gouda cheese	**Apple**
Green and red peppers	**Celery**

Cut all ingredients into small bite size pieces and combine in a bowl. Proportions can vary to taste. Add lemon and oil dressing spiked with a little salt and toss until coated lightly. Serve on bed of Boston lettuce.

This is a favorite salad served in the Cumberland Hotel in London.
Mrs. Randy Hagan (Robin)
Lone Star Legacy

Texas Coleslaw

1	large cabbage, trimmed, quartered and cored	1	cup sugar
1	medium green pepper, cut into large chunks	1	teaspoon salt
		1	teaspoon dry mustard
1	medium onion, peeled and cut into chunks	1	teaspoon celery seeds
		1	cup cider vinegar
		2/3	cup oil

Chop cabbage, green pepper and onion into very fine pieces. Place in large bowl and toss to mix. Mix sugar, salt, mustard and celery seeds in 4 cup measure. Add vinegar and oil and bring to boil on HIGH. Stir until sugar is dissolved. Pour over cabbage and toss well. Cool to room temperature; cover and refrigerate. Keeps well. Serves 6 to 8.

Mrs. Larry Lerche (Gail)
Lone Star Legacy

Corn Bread Salad

8   cups crumbled corn bread
1   medium-sized onion, chopped
1   green bell pepper, chopped
2   tomatoes, chopped
1   (16 ounce) package bacon, cooked and crumbled
1½ cups low-fat mayonnaise-type salad dressing

About 15 to 20 minutes before serving, combine crumbled corn bread, onion, bell pepper, tomatoes, bacon and salad dressing, tossing lightly but thoroughly. If mixed too far in advance, corn bread will become soggy. Makes approximately 13 cups.

I love to take this to luncheons and have people guess what is in it. They guess potatoes and seafood but never cornbread.

Donna Earle Crain
Changing Thymes

Per ½ cup serving_____

Calories 143 Protein 3.83 g Carbohydrates 15.8 g Fat 7.5 g Cholesterol 19.5 mg Sodium 357 mg

French Dijon Salad

Vegetable:
2 to 3 cups red potatoes, cooked and diced
½   pound fresh green beans, cooked

Mix potatoes with green beans. Chill.

Dressing:
2 to 3 tablespoons olive oil
3   ounces wine vinegar
1   teaspoon salt
¼   teaspoon white pepper
2   tablespoons Dijon mustard

Romaine lettuce
2   tomatoes, cut in wedges
12 ripe olives, pitted
Capers to taste

Mix olive oil, vinegar, salt, pepper and mustard. Pour over potatoes and beans and toss. Arrange romaine lettuce on a salad plate and mound salad in center. Surround with tomato wedges and top with olives and capers. Serves 4 to 6.

For a variety add tuna to potato mixture.

Mrs. Randy Hagan (Robin Roberts)
Lone Star Legacy II

Grandma's Hot German Potato Salad

3 pounds new potatoes	⅓ cup water
½ pound bacon, cooked and crumbled reserving drippings	3 to 4 tablespoons sugar
	¾ cup chopped celery
	¾ cup chopped onion
1 tablespoon flour	Salt and pepper to taste
⅔ cup plus 1 tablespoon cider vinegar	3 hard cooked eggs
	Paprika for garnish

Gently cook the potatoes in boiling water until just tender. Drain and set aside. Meanwhile, return ½ cup bacon drippings to the skillet over low heat and add 1 tablespoon flour, stirring until dissolved. Add vinegar and water, stirring constantly, and simmer for about 1 minute or until thickened. Turn heat off and add sugar, stirring until dissolved. When the potatoes are just cool enough to handle, slice ⅓ of them into a large casserole; add ⅓ each of the celery, onion and bacon. Sprinkle lightly with salt and pepper and drizzle several spoonsful of dressing over the top. Repeat this process two more times, reserving 3 spoonsful of dressing. Slice the eggs over the top and drizzle the remaining dressing over the eggs. Sprinkle lightly with paprika for garnish. Serve warm. Serves 8 to 10.

Mrs. Terry Arndt (Barbara)
Lone Star Legacy II

Rice and Fresh Mushroom Salad

1 package (7 ounces) instant rice	1 cup chopped celery
	½ pound mushrooms sliced
5 chicken bouillon cubes	1 jar (4 ounces) diced pimiento, drained
1 cup chopped onion	
1 cup chopped green bell pepper	1 bottle (8 ounces) creamy Italian dressing

Cook rice according to package directions, except omit the salt and add bouillon cubes. Let cool. Combine rice and remaining ingredients. Stir well and chill. Serves 8 to 10.

Barbara Beall Stanley
Lone Star Legacy II

Grandma's Sauerkraut Salad

Must chill overnight

1	(21 ounce) can sauerkraut	1	(2 ounce) jar diced
1	large onion, minced		pimiento, drained
2	cups diced celery	1	carrot, grated (optional)

Dressing:

½	cup vegetable oil	¾	cup sugar
½	cup vinegar	1	teaspoon celery seed

Combine sauerkraut, onion, celery, pimiento and carrot. Blend together all dressing ingredients. Add dressing to vegetables, mixing well. Chill, covered, overnight. Makes approximately 6 cups.

A German tradition served with pork as a New Year's Day kickoff in hopes of bringing prosperity and good fortune all year long.

Marry Lauderman Tavcar
Changing Thymes

Per ½ cup serving

Calories 150 Protein .852 g Carbohydrates 17.4 g Fat 9 g Cholesterol 0 Sodium 347 mg

Artichoke Rice Salad

1	package (8 ounces) chicken flavored rice mix	2	jars (6 ounces each) artichoke hearts, reserve
4	green onions, thinly sliced		liquid
½	green pepper, chopped	¾	teaspoon curry powder
12 to 24	pimiento stuffed olives, sliced	⅓	cup mayonnaise

Cook rice mix as directed (no butter). Cool and add onions, pepper and olives. Drain artichoke hearts, reserving liquid. Cut artichokes in half or less. Combine liquid, a little at time, with curry powder and mayonnaise. Use only enough liquid to moisten. Add to rice mixture and marinate for several hours.

For a one-dish meal, 1 cup of chopped chicken, ham, or turkey can be added.

Mrs. Dudley Baker (Kathy)
Lone Star Legacy

Cat's Spaghetti Salad

1 (8 ounce) package spaghetti, cooked	½ cup sliced cherry tomatoes
1 large squash, diced	1 medium cucumber, sliced
1 large zucchini squash, diced	½ cup chopped mushrooms,
	⅓ cup minced parsley

Dressing:

½ cup low-fat Catalina salad dressing	1 teaspoon garlic powder
½ cup low-fat French salad dressing	½ teaspoon lemon pepper or black pepper
3 tablespoons low-fat Italian salad dressing	

Prepare dressing by blending salad dressings, garlic powder and pepper. Add dressing to spaghetti, tossing to coat thoroughly. Add squash, tomatoes, cucumber, mushrooms and parsley, tossing gently. Chill before serving. Makes approximately 8 cups.

Mary Francis
Changing Thymes

Per ½ cup serving

Calories 95 Protein 2.34 g Carbohydrates 17.4 g Fat 2 g Cholesterol 1.46 mg Sodium 217 mg

Fettuccine Salad

1	(16 ounce) can corn, drained and liquid reserved	1	cup (4 ounces) grated Parmesan cheese
4	quarts water	2	cups fat-free mayonnaise
1	tablespoon salt	½	bunch green onions, minced
1	(16 ounce) package fettuccine pasta	1	red bell pepper, diced
2	chicken bouillon cubes, crushed	1	tablespoons black pepper
		1	teaspoon garlic or more to taste

Combine corn liquid, water and salt in stock pot. Bring to a boil. Break fettuccine strands and drop into boiling water. Reduce heat and simmer for 5 to 7 minutes, stirring constantly. Pour into colander and rinse fettuccine with cool water. Chill until ready to use. Combine bouillon cubes, corn, cheese, mayonnaise, onion, bell pepper, black pepper and garlic in microwave-safe container. Cook at 100 percent power briefly, just until warm. Stir to blend. Pour sauce over cold fettuccine in large bowl and mix thoroughly. Chill before serving. Makes approximately 12 cups.

For a complete meal, top salad portions with sliced grilled chicken.

Barbara Bump
Changing Thymes

Per ½ cup serving_____

Calories 74 Protein 3.17 g Carbohydrates 12.5 g Fat 1.5 g Cholesterol 3.33 mg Sodium 714 mg

Greek Pasta Salad

1	(12 ounce) package rotelle pasta	¼	cup toasted pine nuts
1	small green bell pepper, cut crosswise in thin strips	¼	cup sliced black olives
1	small yellow bell pepper, cut crosswise in thin strips	1	(8 ounce) package feta cheese, cubed
1	small red bell pepper, cut crosswise in thin strips	2	tablespoons chopped basil
1	medium tomato, cut in thin wedges	¼	teaspoon crushed dried oregano

Dressing:

²/₃	cup olive oil	2	tablespoons grated Parmesan cheese
3	tablespoons red wine vinegar	1¼	teaspoons salt
2	tablespoons chopped basil	¼	teaspoon black pepper
2	tablespoons chopped green onion		

Prepare pasta according to pack age directions. Drain and set aside to cool. Prepare dressing by combining oil, vinegar, basil, green onion, cheese, salt and black pepper in food processor. Process until smooth. Combine pasta, bell peppers, tomato, nuts and olives in large bowl. Add dressing to salad, tossing to coat thoroughly. Roll cubed cheese in basil, add to salad and toss to mix. Sprinkle oregano on salad surface. Serve at room temperature. Makes approximately 8 cups.

Linda Cook Uhl
Changing Thymes

Per ½ cup serving_____

Calories 176 Protein 4.4 g Carbohydrates 8 54 g Fat 14.5 g Cholesterol 13.2 mg Sodium 354 mg

West Lynn Pasta Salad

1	(16 ounce) package rotini pasta	1	cup sliced black olives
1	cup diced red bell pepper	1	cup toasted pecan pieces
1	cup thinly sliced green onion	1	cup coarsely chopped artichoke hearts

Dressing:

½	cup olive oil	3	cloves garlic
¼	cup red wine vinegar	1	(½ ounce) bunch fresh basil
¼	cup tamari (naturally brewed soy sauce)		

Prepare pasta according to package directions. Drain, rinse to cool and let drain again for 5 minutes. Combine pasta, bell pepper, green onion, olives, pecans and artichoke hearts, mixing well. Combine all dressing ingredients in blender container. Blend until garlic is pureed. Add dressing to pasta mixture and toss until thoroughly coated. Makes approximately 13 cups.

West Lynn Café
Changing Thymes

Per ½ cup serving

Calories 145 Protein 3.14 g Carbohydrates 15.7 g Fat 8 g Cholesterol 0 Sodium 165 mg

Spaghetti Salad

¾	cup mayonnaise	½	cup green olives, chopped
2	cloves garlic, crushed	1	can (10 ounces) Ro-Tel tomatoes and green chilies, drained and chopped
¼	cup chopped onion		
½	teaspoon cumin seeds, crushed	1	package (10 ounces) spaghetti, cooked and rinsed
Salt to taste			
¼	cup diced celery		

Mix mayonnaise, garlic, onion, cumin seeds, salt, and tomatoes. Add a little juice if too thick. Toss with spaghetti, celery, and olives until well coated. Serves 8 to 10.

Mrs. Don Panter (Carolyn)
Lone Star Legacy

Vermicelli Salad

1	package (12 ounces) vermicelli	½	cup chopped green onion
3	teaspoons lemon juice	½	cup chopped pimiento
3	teaspoons oil	½	cup chopped ripe olives
½	cup chopped celery		Mayonnaise to moisten
½	cup chopped green bell pepper		Salt and pepper to taste

Cook pasta according to package directions. Drain, but do not rinse. When cool enough to handle, place in a bowl and add lemon juice and salad oil. Blend and cover tightly. Refrigerate overnight. Add vegetables the next day. Moisten with mayonnaise, and season with salt and pepper. Blend and refrigerate several hours or overnight. Serves 12.

This is a great change from potato salad.

Mrs. Linden Welsch (Phyllis)
Lone Star Legacy II

Party Pasta Salad

1	package (12 ounces) macaroni shells	1	can (6 ounces) sliced ripe olives, drained
2	jars (6 ounces each) marinated artichoke hearts, drained and juice reserved	½	cup tarragon vinegar
		½	cup artichoke liquid
		1 to 1½	cups Caesar salad dressing
1	package (5 ounces) pepperoni, thinly sliced	1	cup grated Parmesan cheese, divided
1	onion, finely chopped		Salt and pepper to taste

Cook pasta per directions on package or until tender. Drain and put into a large bowl to cool. Cut artichokes into bite sized pieces. When pasta is cool, add pepperoni, artichoke pieces, onion and ripe olives. Combine tarragon vinegar and artichoke liquid with Caesar salad dressing. Mix well and pour over pasta mixture; add ¾ cup Parmesan cheese and stir well. Sprinkle remainder of Parmesan cheese on top. Serves 12 to 14.

This salad can be done a day ahead to allow flavors to mix.

Mrs. Steve McMillon (Mary Beth)
Lone Star Legacy II

Fancy Chicken Salad

3	cups cold cooked chicken, diced		Seedless grapes, sliced, optional
1	cup finely chopped celery	1	teaspoon salt
½	cup sliced almonds	1	cup mayonnaise
2½	tablespoons parsley, minced	½	cup whipping cream, whipped

Combine chicken, celery, almonds, parsley, grapes, salt and mayonnaise. Fold in whipping cream. Chill until ready to serve. Serves 8.

Mrs. John Perkins (Sandy)
Lone Star Legacy

Chicken, Broccoli and Pasta Salad

4	skinless, boneless chicken breast halves, cooked	3	cups broccoli flowerets, steamed and chilled
1	(8 ounce) package rotelle pasta, cooked and drained		

Dressing:

½	cup toasted coarsely chopped walnuts	1	tablespoon lemon juice
1	cup mayonnaise	2	teaspoons coarsely chopped garlic
½	cup basil leaves		
½	cup (2 ounces) freshly grated Parmesan cheese		

Tear chicken into narrow strips. Combine chicken, pasta and broccoli in large bowl. Prepare dressing by blending walnuts, mayonnaise, basil, cheese, lemon juice and garlic in food processor, processing until smooth. Add dressing to chicken mixture, tossing to moisten all ingredients. Chill thoroughly before serving. Makes approximately 8 cups.

To toast walnuts, bake at 350° for 5 to 7 minutes.

Linda Cook Uhl
Changing Thymes

Per ½ cup serving _____

Calories 278 Protein 20.5 g Carbohydrates 6.92 g Fat 19 g Cholesterol 58.2 mg Sodium 185 mg

Almond Curry Chicken Salad

3 cups cubed cooked chicken	Fresh lemon juice to taste
1 tart apple, chopped	1 cup mayonnaise
2 teaspoons chopped onion	⅓ teaspoon salt
½ cup chopped celery	Dash of black pepper
½ cup grape halves	Dash of seasoned salt
½ cup slivered almonds, toasted	⅓ teaspoon curry powder
	Lettuce leaves

Combine chicken, apple, onion, celery, grapes and almonds. Blend lemon juice, mayonnaise, salt, black pepper, seasoned salt and curry powder together. Fold into chicken mixture. Serve on lettuce leaves. Makes approximately 6½ cups.

Marilyn Markham
Changing Thymes

Per ½ cup serving

Calories 228 Protein 10.9 g Carbohydrates 4.52 g Fat 19 g Cholesterol 36.2 mg Sodium 187 mg

Maude's Taco Salad

1 pound ground beef	4 green onions, chopped
1 package (1.5 ounces) taco seasoning	1 bag (1¾ ounces) corn chips
1 can (15 ounces) kidney beans, drained and rinsed	1 can (2¼ ounces) ripe olives
1 head of lettuce	1 bottle (8 ounces) sweet and spicy French dressing
2 avocados, chopped	
2 tomatoes, chopped	

Brown ground beef in skillet; drain and add taco seasoning and kidney beans. Wash lettuce and break into bite sized pieces and place in bowl. Add avocados, tomatoes, onions, corn chips and olives to lettuce, then add meat mixture. Toss with dressing. Serves 6.

Mrs. Randy Hagan (Robin Roberts)
Lone Star Legacy II

Stuffed Tomatoes

16 ounces tuna or crab meat
1 cup finely diced celery
½ cup grated onion
Salt and pepper to taste

Mayonnaise
8 regular tomatoes or 100
   cocktail tomatoes
Parsley to garnish

Mix thoroughly tuna or crab meat, celery, onion, salt and pepper. Add enough mayonnaise to make a thick paste. Cut out inside of tomatoes and fill with the mixture. Top with parsley.

Mrs. Marcus Bone (Beverly)
Lone Star Legacy

Southwestern Chicken Salad

3 cups chopped cooked
   chicken
1 cup chopped celery
4 slices bacon, cooked and
   crumbled
1 (4 ounce) can chopped
   green chilies, drained

1 cup peanuts, chopped
½ cup fat-free mayonnaise
Salt and black pepper to taste
½ head lettuce, chopped
Tortilla chips or melon slices
   (optional)

Combine chicken, celery, bacon, chilies, peanuts and mayonnaise, tossing to mix well. Season with salt and black pepper. Chill until ready to serve. Arrange lettuce on individual salad plates. Place ½ cup chicken mixture on lettuce. Serve with chips or melon. Makes approximately 6 cups.

Barbara Bump
Changing Thymes

Per ½ cup serving_____

Calories 165 Protein 14.5 g Carbohydrates 5.49 g Fat 10 g Cholesterol 30.2 mg Sodium 343 mg

Shrimp Avocado Salad

May be prepared 1 day in advance

1   (10 ounce) package frozen
    cooked shrimp, thawed
    and drained
2   cups cooked rice
2   avocados, peeled and
    chopped
Lemon juice
¾   cup chopped onion
2   tablespoons chopped
    pimiento

1   large tomato, seeds
    removed and diced
½   cup chopped black olives
½   cup chopped green olives
Salt to taste
1   tablespoon plus
    1 teaspoon fat-free
    mayonnaise

Combine shrimp and rice. Chill. Sprinkle avocado with lemon juice, tossing to coat avocado. Combine avocado, onion, pimiento, tomato and olives. Add vegetables to shrimp and rice mixture. Season with salt. Add mayonnaise to salad, stirring lightly. Chill until ready to serve. Salad maybe prepared a day in advance. Makes approximately 6 cups.

Ann Bommarito Armstrong
Changing Thymes

Per ½ cup serving_____

Calories 139 Protein 6.84 g Carbohydrates 14.2 g Fat 6.5 g Cholesterol 46.1 mg Sodium 222 mg

Avocado Imperial

1½ cups crab claw meat
1   tablespoon grated onion
1   teaspoon chopped parsley
1   teaspoon chopped chives
Pinch of tarragon
2   tablespoons lime juice,
    divided

1   avocado, halved and
    seeded
½   cup mayonnaise
¼   cup whipping cream,
    whipped
⅓   cup chili sauce

Combine crab meat, onion, parsley, chives, tarragon and 1 tablespoon lime juice. Halve avocado, remove seed and sprinkle with remaining tablespoon of lime juice. For sauce combine mayonnaise, whipped cream and chili sauce. To serve spoon crab meat mixture into avocado halves and top with sauce. Serves 2.

Ada Smyth
Lone Star Legacy II

South Seas Salad

6	large fresh tomatoes	2	tablespoons red wine vinegar
2	cups cooked diced shrimp	1/2	teaspoon salt
1½	cups chilled cooked rice	1/4	teaspoon dry mustard
½	cup chopped celery	1/4	teaspoon paprika
¼	cup diced ripe olives	1	small clove garlic, minced
1	tablespoon fresh snipped parsley		Fresh lettuce
¼	cup salad oil		

With tomato stem end down, cut each into six wedges, cutting to but not through base. Spread wedges slightly apart and carefully scoop out pulp. Dice and drain this pulp. Combine tomato pulp, shrimp, rice, celery, olives and parsley Blend oil and vinegar with spices. Pour over shrimp mixture and toss slightly. Fill tomato wedges with this mixture and serve on a bed of lettuce. Serves 6.

This is a really nice dish for a luncheon . . . very showy.

Mrs. Ken Moyer (Bonnie)
Lone Star Legacy

Cool Crab Salad

1   (7½ ounce) can crab meat,
    drained and cartilage
    removed
1   cup (4 ounces) diced
    Swiss cheese
2   hard-cooked eggs, chopped

⅓   cup chopped sweet pickle
¼   cup chopped celery
2   tablespoons chopped
    green bell pepper

Dressing:
½   cup sour cream
1½ tablespoon lemon juice
2   tablespoons chopped onion
¼   teaspoon sugar

¼   teaspoon salt
Dash of black pepper
½   teaspoon dill weed

Combine crab meat, cheese, eggs, pickle, celery and bell pepper in large bowl. Prepare dressing by blending sour cream, lemon juice, onion, sugar, salt, black pepper and dill weed. Add dressing to salad, gently tossing to mix. Chill until ready to serve. Makes approximately 3 cups.

Rosemary Bennett Douglass
Changing Thymes

Per ½ cup serving

Calories 209 Protein 16.4 g Carbohydrates 8.43 g Fat 12.5 g Cholesterol 131 mg Sodium 464 mg

Tuna Parmesan Salad

1	(12 ounce) package medium shell macaroni	½	cup chopped green onion
2	(6⅛ ounce) cans water-packed tuna	½	cup chopped red bell pepper
1	(10 ounce) package frozen chopped broccoli, thawed		Lettuce leaves Fruit slices for garnish

Dressing:

1	cup mayonnaise	1	teaspoon hot pepper sauce
2	tablespoons low-fat milk		
⅓	cup grated Parmesan cheese	1	teaspoon lemon pepper
		½	teaspoon garlic powder

Prepare macaroni according to package directions. Drain, rinse with cold water and set aside to cool. Prepare dressing by blending mayonnaise, milk, cheese, hot pepper sauce, lemon pepper and garlic powder, mixing well. Combine macaroni, tuna, broccoli, onion and bell pepper, tossing to mix. Add dressing and blend thoroughly. Chill, covered, stirring occasionally. Serve individual portions on lettuce leaves and garnish with fruit slices. Makes approximately 12 cups.

Barbara Bump
Changing Thymes

Per ½ cup serving

Calories 115 Protein 5.76 g Carbohydrates 5.42 g Fat 8 g Cholesterol 11.2 mg Sodium 134 mg

Marvelous Whole Apple Salad

9	small Rome Beauty apples, peeled and cored	3	cinnamon sticks
2	cups sugar	8	ounces cream cheese, softened
2	cups water		Milk
1	teaspoon red food coloring		Chopped walnuts or pecans

Put apples in a 9 × 9 inch pan and pour syrup over the apples. Simmer over very low heat 10 minutes. Turn apples over and simmer 10 more minutes. Cool in the pan. Turn apples over again and refrigerate in the pan. Whip cream cheese with a little milk. With a pastry bag, squirt cream cheese in center of apples; top with nuts.

Mrs. Val Judd (Nancy)
Lone Star Legacy II

Custard Fruit Salad

4 eggs, beaten	1 pound miniature
1 can (20 ounces) pineapple chunks, drained, reserving juice	marshmallows
	1 cup whipping cream
	1 teaspoon vanilla extract
1 cup sugar, divided	2 to 3 bananas, sliced
1 teaspoon vinegar	1 cup chopped pecans, optional
2 tablespoons flour	
Dash of salt	

Make a custard by combining eggs, reserved pineapple juice, ½ cup sugar, vinegar, flour and salt, and cooking over low heat until mixture coats a spoon. Remove from heat and let cool. Whip the cream, gradually adding vanilla and ½ cup sugar, beating until soft peaks form. Pour half the custard into a large bowl, then add in layers half the bananas, half the pineapple chunks, half the marshmallows, and half the whipped cream. Repeat layers, ending with whipped cream. Sprinkle top with chopped pecans, if desired.

Mrs. Mark Veltri (Pam)
Lone Star Legacy II

Frozen Peach Salad

1 jar (28½ ounces) spiced peaches, reserve juice	1 cup evaporated milk, chilled
1½ cups miniature marshmallows	1 cup chopped pecans
	1 tablespoon lemon juice
2 tablespoons sugar	
4 ounces cream cheese, softened	

Mash peaches and stir in marshmallows. Combine sugar, ¼ cup peach juice and cream cheese. Beat until fluffy. Add peaches and marshmallows. Whip milk and add to peach mixture. Add pecans and lemon juice. Freeze in individual molds or an 8 × 12 inch dish. Serves 8 to 10.

Mrs. Orland Patton (Alice)
Lone Star Legacy II

Holiday Cherry Salad

1 (3 ounce) package raspberry gelatin	⅓ cup mayonnaise
1 cup boiling water	1 (8 ounce) can crushed pineapple, undrained
1 (22 ounce) can cherry pie filling	1 cup whipping cream, whipped
1 (3 ounce) package lemon gelatin	1½ cups miniature marshmallows
1 cup boiling water	Chopped pecans for garnish (optional)
1 (3 ounce) package cream cheese, softened	

Dissolve raspberry gelatin in 1 cup boiling water. Stir pie filling into dissolved gelatin liquid. Pour into 2-quart baking dish. Chill until partially firm. Dissolve lemon gelatin in 1 cup boiling water. Combine cream cheese and mayonnaise, beating until smooth. Gradually add lemon gelatin to cream cheese mixture, mixing well. Stir pineapple into cream cheese mixture. Fold in whipped cream, then marshmallows. Spread pineapple mixture on raspberry gelatin layer. Chill until firm. Sprinkle pecans on salad. Serves 12.

This has become a favorite at our house for Christmas and Easter.

Rosemary Bennett Douglass
Changing Thymes

Per serving_____

Calories 245 Protein 2.39 g Carbohydrates 35.1 g Fat 11.5 g Cholesterol 25 mg Sodium 126 mg

Cranberry Cherry Salad

1 can (20 ounces) white cherries, halved and pitted	1 can (16 ounces) whole cranberry sauce
1 scant cup reserved cherry juice	2 tablespoons lemon juice
1 small package cherry gelatin	3 ounces cream cheese, diced small
	½ cup chopped pecans

Heat cherry juice to boiling; add gelatin and stir until dissolved. Blend in cranberry sauce and lemon juice. Chill until partly set. Fold in cherries, cream cheese, and pecans. Pour into ring or other mold. Serves 8.

Mrs. B. L. Turlington (Jill)
Lone Star Legacy

Mandarin Orange Salad

1	carton (8 ounces) sour cream	1	can (20 ounces) crushed pineapple, drained
1	small package (3 ounces) orange gelatin	1	carton (8 ounces) whipped topping, thawed
1	can (11 ounces) Mandarin slices, drained		

Mix sour cream and powdered gelatin thoroughly. Add drained fruit to sour cream mixture. Stir in whipped topping. May be served immediately or can be refrigerated for later use. Serves 8.

Variation: Use strawberry jello, strawberries, and bananas.

Mrs. Ron Garrick (Bonnie)
Lone Star Legacy

Bing Sherry Salad

1	can (16½ ounces) pitted bing cherries, drained (reserve juice)	3	tablespoons unflavored gelatin
2	cups orange juice	¾	cup chopped pecans
1½	cups sherry		Whipped topping or mayonnaise to garnish
1	cup sugar		

Mix cherry juice with 1½ cups of the orange juice, sherry, and sugar; bring to a boil. Soak gelatin in remaining ½ cup orange juice. Dissolve in hot fruit syrup. Chill mixture until partially set; pour into a mold or a 9 inch square pan. Stir in cherries and nuts and distribute evenly. When congealed, top with whipped topping or mayonnaise. Serve 12.

Mrs. Rober West (Linda)
Lone Star Legacy

Strawberry Nut Salad

2	small packages strawberry gelatin	3	medium bananas, mashed
1	cup boiling water	1	cup coarsely chopped walnuts or pecans
2	packages (10 ounces each) frozen sliced strawberries, thawed, reserve juice	1	pint sour cream
			Lettuce for garnish
1	can (1 pound 4 ounces) crushed pineapple, drained		

Combine gelatin with boiling water, stirring until dissolved. Fold in strawberries, pineapple, bananas and nuts. Pour one half of the strawberry mixture into an oblong baking dish. Refrigerate until firm. About 1½ hours later evenly spread top with sour cream. Gently spoon on remainder of strawberry mixture. Cut into squares and serve on a bed of lettuce. Serve 10 to 12.

Mrs. Larry Strickland (Linda)
Lone Star Legacy

Mango Salad

2	small packages orange gelatin	1	can (29 ounces) mangos and juice
1	small package lemon gelatin	8	ounces cream cheese, cut into 8 pieces
1	cup boiling water		Juice of 1 to 2 limes

Dissolve orange and lemon gelatins in boiling water, in large bowl. Mixture will be sticky. Blend mangos with juice; pour one-half into gelatin mixture, stirring to mix. In blender add cheese one at a time until well blended. Pour into gelatin mixture, stirring well. Add lime juice to taste. Pour into ring mold or 9 × 13 dish, and chill. Serves 10 to 12.

This is a cool, delicious tropical treat. If mangos are unavailable in your area, you can substitute one large can of peaches or apricots.

Mrs. Bob Edgecomb (Mary)
Lone Star Legacy

Apricot Mango Mousse

1	(6 ounce) package apricot gelatin	1	(16 ounce) can apricots, undrained
1	envelope unflavored gelatin	1	(8 ounce) package cream cheese, softened
2	cups boiling water		
1	(15 ounce) can mangos, undrained		Kiwi slices for garnish

Dissolve apricot and unflavored gelatin in boiling water. Using food processor, blend mangos, apricots and cream cheese thoroughly. Add gelatin and mix well. Pour gelatin mixture into individual parfait dishes or 8-cup mold. Chill until firm. Garnish with kiwi slices. Serves 14.

Cookbook Committee
Changing Thymes

Per ½ cup serving_____

Calories 140 Protein 2.96 g Carbohydrates 20.6 g Fat 6 g 17.8 mg Sodium 82.5 mg

99

Basil Vinaigrette

2	large cloves garlic, minced	½	teaspoon salt
1	tablespoon dried basil or 3 tablespoons chopped fresh basil	½	teaspoon freshly ground black pepper
2	teaspoons sugar	¼	cup sherry wine vinegar
		½	cup olive oil

Combine garlic and basil in food processor. Add sugar, salt, black pepper and wine vinegar. With chopping blade running, gradually add oil in steady stream. May be prepared at least 1 day in advance. Dressing may be stored in refrigerator for up to 1 week. Makes 1 cup.

Fantastic served on fresh tomatoes from the garden or with a mixture of favorite salad greens, mushrooms and herbs. For a clear vinaigrette, place garlic and basil in a bowl, add other ingredients and whisk to blend. Flavored oils and vinegars may be substituted.

LaNyce Whittemore
Changing Thymes

Per tablespoon_____

Calories 64 Protein .072 g Carbohydrates 1.08 g Fat 7 g Cholesterol 0 Sodium 66.8 mg

Dijon Salad Dressing

3	tablespoons Dijon mustard	1	teaspoon sugar
¾	cup low-fat plain yogurt	1	clove garlic, minced
½	teaspoon salt	1	tablespoon capers, drained
	Pinch of black pepper		
3	tablespoons lemon juice		

Combine mustard, yogurt, salt and black pepper. Add lemon juice, sugar, garlic and capers to yogurt mixture, whisking to blend. Serve on green salads. Makes 1¼ cups.

Pamela Jones
Changing Thymes

Per tablespoon_____

Calories 9 Protein .615 g Carbohydrates 1.26 g Fat .5 g Cholesterol .559 mg Sodium 90.1 mg

Caesar Dressing

1	cup salad oil	4	tablespoons lemon juice
2	cloves garlic, finely chopped	½	cup Parmesan cheese
½	teaspoon ground pepper	2	tablespoons Worcestershire
½	teaspoon salt		sauce
1	egg		

Soak garlic in oil for 30 minutes. Blend all ingredients in blender for a few seconds.

Mrs. Marcus Bone (Beverly)
Lone Star Legacy

Honey Lime Dressing

1	cup sugar	⅓	cup lime juice
½	cup honey	⅓	cup water
2	tablespoons dry mustard	2	cups corn oil
1	tablespoon ground ginger		

Blend all ingredients, except oil, in blender. Slowly add corn oil and blend. Yields 1 quart.

This is great on fresh fruit.

Mrs. Jim Rado (Vicki)
Lone Star Legacy

Lemon Herb Dressing

⅔	cup vegetable oil	1	teaspoon salt
⅓	cup lemon juice	½	teaspoon basil
2	tablespoons red wine vinegar	½	teaspoon tarragon
2	teaspoons chopped parsley		

Mix all ingredients together well. Serve over tossed green salad. Yields 1¼ cups dressing.

Mrs. Jim Rado (Vicki)
Lone Star Legacy II

BEST OF

Lone Star Legacy

SOUPS & SANDWICHES

Corn and Crab Meat Soup

¼ cup chopped onion	4 cups milk
¼ cup butter	1 cup half and half cream
2 tablespoons flour	Salt and pepper to taste
½ teaspoon curry powder	1 carton (16 ounces) crab
4 cups fresh or frozen corn	meat

Sauté onion in butter until soft. Add flour and curry powder and cook 1 minute. Add corn; cook 5 minutes. Stir in milk and cream, salt and pepper and bring to a boil. Stir in crab meat and serve. Serves 8 to 10.

Mrs. Marcus Bone (Beverly)
Lone Star Legacy II

Cheesy Corn Soup

⅓ cup chopped green bell pepper	1 chicken bouillon cube
¼ cup chopped onion	1 cup boiling water
2 tablespoons margarine	1 can (8¾ ounces) cream style corn
8 ounces cream cheese, cubed	½ teaspoon salt
1 cup milk	Dash of pepper

Sauté bell pepper and onion in margarine. Add cream cheese and milk. Heat slowly stirring until smooth. Dissolve bouillon cube in water; stir into cream cheese mixture. Add remaining ingredients. Heat through. Serves 4.

Mrs. Ken McGinnis (Susan)
Lone Star Legacy II

Corn Chowder

2	cups water	2	cups skim milk
2	cups diced potatoes	1	cup fresh tomatoes
½	onion, chopped		chopped
4	ribs celery, diced		Salt and white pepper to
¾	teaspoon basil		taste
1	bay leaf	2	ounces Cheddar cheese,
1	can (17 ounces) cream		grated
	style corn		

Combine water, potatoes, onion, celery, basil and bay leaf and bring to a boil. Simmer until potatoes are tender. Remove bay leaf and add corn, milk, tomatoes and heat thoroughly; do not boil. Add salt, pepper and cheese, stirring until cheese is·melted and soup thickens. Serves 8.

This soup only has about 125 calories per serving.

Mrs. Jim Schultz (Mary Kay)
Lone Star Legacy II

Mexican Corn Soup

4	cups fresh corn kernels	2	cups milk or cream
¼	cup chopped onion	1	cup grated Cheddar cheese
2	tablespoons butter	1	can (4 ounces) green
2	tablespoons flour		chilies, chopped, optional
	Salt and pepper to taste		Tortilla chips
2	cups chicken broth	½	cup crisp bacon, crumbled

Sauté corn and onion in butter until tender. Add flour, salt and pepper; cook 1 minute. Gradually add broth, alternating with milk or cream, until thickened. Add Cheddar cheese and green chilies; do not over heat. Serve soup in individual bowls, stirring in 4 or 5 tortilla chips; garnish with crumbled bacon.

Mrs. George Dolezal (Sharon)
Lone Star Legacy

Corn Shrimp Soup

5 tablespoons oil	1 can {10 ounces} tomatoes
5 tablespoons flour	and green chilies
1 onion, chopped	3 cans (17 ounces each)
1 cup shallots, chopped	whole kernel corn
3 cloves garlic, minced	1 can (17 ounces) cream
1 green bell pepper,	style corn
chopped	5 quarts water
2 celery ribs, chopped	Salt and pepper to taste
4 tablespoons chopped	2 pounds shrimp, peeled and
parsley	deveined
1 can (17 ounces) stewed	
tomatoes, chopped	

Heat oil in soup pot. Make a roux by adding flour and cooking until brown. Add onion, shallots, garlic, bell pepper, celery and parsley. Cook 10 minutes or until onion is tender. Add stewed tomatoes and tomatoes with chilies. Cook 10 minutes longer, stirring constantly. Add all corn and stir until well mixed with seasonings. Add water, salt and pepper. Simmer 1 hour, stirring occasionally. Add shrimp. Simmer 30 minutes longer. Serves 10 to 12.

Carolyn Moore
Lone Star Legacy II

Carmelita's Tortilla Soup

1	(2 to 3 pound) chicken or 6 chicken breast halves	8	cups chicken broth
1½	large onions, diced	2	large tomatoes, chopped
1	(4 ounce) can diced green chilies, drained	2	cloves garlic, mashed
			Salt to taste
1	tablespoon vegetable oil		Ground cumin to taste
2	fresh serrano peppers, finely chopped		Juice of 2 limes
		8	corn tortillas, cut in strips
1	(10 ounce) can tomatoes with green chilies, undrained	¼	cup (1 ounce) grated Monterey Jack cheese (optional)

Boil chicken in 3 quarts of water until tender. Remove chicken and set aside. Strain broth and set aside Discard skin and bones from chicken. Chop into bite-sized pieces and add to broth. Sauté onion and green chilies in oil until tender. Stir in serrano peppers. Reheat broth and chicken. Add sautéed vegetables, tomatoes and garlic. Season with salt and cumin. Stir in lime juice. Simmer soup until thoroughly heated, adding tortilla strips just before serving. Ladle soup into individual bowls and sprinkle each serving with cheese. Makes approximately 12 cups.

Cheryl Briggs Patton
Changing Thymes

Per ½ cup serving_____

Calories 83 Protein 8.48 g Carbohydrates 7.35 g Fat 2 g Cholesterol 19.2 mg Sodium 489 mg

Cheesy Chicken Vegetable Soup

1	(3 pound) chicken, cut up	2	cups diced potatoes
9	cups water	1	cup cooked rice
½	teaspoon salt	4	chicken bouillon cubes
½	teaspoon black pepper	1	(16 ounce) package
½ to ¾ cup chopped onion			pasteurized process
2	cups diced celery		cheese spread, cut in
2	cups diced carrots		chunks,

Combine chicken, water, salt, black pepper, onion and celery in stock pot. Simmer, covered, for 45 minutes or until chicken is tender. Remove chicken from broth. Remove and discard skin and bones. Coarsely chop chicken and return to broth. Add carrots, potatoes, rice and bouillon. Simmer, covered, for 1¼ to 1½ hours, stirring occasionally. Add cheese to soup. Stirring gently, heat until cheese is melted. Makes approximately 18 cups

Barbara Stromberg Boyd
Changing Thymes

Per ½ cup serving_____

Calories 150 Protein 10.4 g Carbohydrates 4.73 g Fat 10 g Cholesterol 40.3 mg Sodium 370 mg

Chunky Minestrone

1½ cups chopped onion
2 medium carrots, sliced
1 clove garlic, minced
2 teaspoons olive oil
½ cup uncooked long grain rice
1 teaspoon Italian seasoning
3 cups water
1 (29 ounce) can chopped tomatoes, undrained
2 (10½ ounce) cans beef consommé
2 tablespoons ketchup

2 medium zucchini squash, cut in halves lengthwise, then sliced
1 (15½ ounce) can garbanzo beans, drained
1 (10 ounce) package frozen chopped spinach, thawed and drained
¼ teaspoon salt
¼ teaspoon black pepper
2/3 cup (2 2/3 ounces) freshly grated Parmesan cheese

Sauté onion, carrots and garlic in olive oil in stock pot over medium-high heat for 3 minutes. Add rice, Italian seasoning, water, tomatoes, consommé and ketchup to vegetables. Bring to a boil, reduce heat and simmer, covered, for 20 minutes. Add zucchini, garbanzo beans, spinach, salt and black pepper to vegetables. Cook for 5 minutes. Ladle soup into individual bowls and sprinkle with Parmesan cheese. Makes approximately 15 cups

Vicki Ashley Atkins
Changing Thymes

Per ½ cup serving

Calories 67 Protein 4.08 g Carbohydrates 9.93 g Fat 1.5 g Cholesterol 1.75 mg Sodium 229 mg

Baked Potato Soup

4	large baking potatoes	4	green onions, chopped, divided
²/₃	cup butter or margarine		
²/₃	cup all-purpose flour	12	slices bacon, cooked and crumbled, divided
6	cups milk		
¾	teaspoon salt	1¼	cups (5 ounces) shredded Cheddar cheese, divided
½	teaspoon black pepper		
		1	cup sour cream

Pierce potato skins several times with fork. Bake at 400° for 1 hour or until tender. Let stand until cool. Cut potatoes into halves lengthwise, scoop out pulp and set aside; discard skins. Melt butter in heavy saucepan over low heat. Add flour, stirring until smooth. Cook for 1 minute, stirring constantly. Gradually add milk. Cook over medium heat, stirring constantly, until mixture is thickened and bubbly. Add potato pulp, salt, pepper and 2 tablespoons green onion, ½ cup bacon and 1 cup cheese. Cook until thoroughly heated. Stir in sour cream. Ladle soup into individual bowls and garnish with remaining onion, bacon and cheese. Chopped tomatoes and chopped jalapeño peppers may also be used. Makes approximately 12 cups.

Potato skins may be left on potatoes. Add extra milk for thinner consistency if desired. Low-fat milk and low-fat sour cream may be substituted.

Gwen Waldin Irwin
Changing Thymes

Per ½ cup serving

Calories 186 Protein 5.77 g Carbohydrates 12.7 g Fat 12.5 g Cholesterol 35.2 mg Sodium 242 mg

Cheesy Chowder

1 (16 ounce) package bacon, chopped
2 medium-sized onions, chopped
3 or 4 carrots, coarsely chopped
3 medium potatoes, peeled and diced
2½ to 3 cups chicken broth

1 cup milk
3 cups (12 ounces) grated American cheese
3 to 4 tablespoons all-purpose flour
Salt and freshly ground black pepper to taste
Chopped parsley for garnish

Fry bacon in 4-quart saucepan until crisp. Remove bacon and set aside. Retain 2 tablespoons bacon drippings in saucepan. Add onion and sauté until translucent. Add bacon, carrots, potatoes and broth. Bring to a boil, reduce heat and simmer, covered, for 15 minutes or until potatoes are tender. Stir in milk. Combine cheese and flour, tossing to coat cheese. Add to soup and stir until cheese is melted. Season with salt and black pepper. Ladle soup into individual bowls and garnish each serving with parsley. Makes approximately 12 cups.

This is a wonderful soup for a cold winter's night (if Texas ever has any!).

Cheryl Briggs Patton
Changing Thymes

Per ½ cup serving

Calories 121 Protein 5.79 g Carbohydrates 6.63 g Fat 8 g Cholesterol 17.7 mg Sodium 431 mg

New England Clam Chowder

¼ cup diced bacon
¼ cup minced onion
1 can (10½ ounces) cream of potato soup
¾ cup milk

2 cans (7 ounces each) minced clams, undrained
1 tablespoon lemon juice
⅛ teaspoon pepper

In a large saucepan sauté bacon and onions until bacon is crisp and onion tender. Drain bacon grease. Stir in soup and milk; heat thoroughly, stirring occasionally. Stir in undrained clams, lemon juice and pepper. Heat well. Serves 4.

Mrs. Marcus Bone (Beverly)
Lone Star Legacy II

Oyster Chowder

4	potatoes, peeled and diced	2	pints oysters
1	teaspoon salt	2	cups half and half cream
1	cup water	4	tablespoons butter
1	cup chopped celery	¼	teaspoon cayenne pepper
1	medium onion, chopped		Salt and pepper to taste
1	cup corn, cut from 2 ears fresh corn	½	pound bacon, crisply fried and crumbled

Cook potatoes in salted water about 8 minutes. Add celery, onion and corn. Cover and cook another 10 minutes. Add oysters, cream, butter and cayenne. Simmer for 30 minutes until oysters are cooked. Add salt and pepper to taste. Top with crumbled bacon. Serves 8.

Mrs. Denman Smith (Sandra)
Lone Star Legacy II

Cheddar Cheese Soup

6	tablespoons margarine	8 to 10 ounces Cheddar cheese, grated
3	chopped green onions	Salt and pepper to taste
3	stalks celery, chopped	
2	carrots, grated	3 drops Tabasco sauce
2	cans chicken broth	8 ounces sour cream
4	cans potato soup	

Sauté onions, celery, and carrots in margarine. Add chicken broth and simmer 30 minutes. Add potato soup, cheese, salt and pepper, Tabasco, and sour cream. Simmer 15 minutes. Do not boil. Makes 10 cups.

Mrs. Chris Williston (Janice)
Lone Star Legacy

Basic Gumbo

¾ cup oil
¾ cup flour
2 onions, chopped
3 tablespoons butter
4 cups sliced fresh okra
3 cup chopped fresh
 tomatoes
2 green bell peppers,
 chopped
3 ribs celery, chopped
4 cloves garlic, minced
2 tablespoons butter
¼ teaspoon dried thyme
2 quarts boiling water
2 chicken bouillon cubes

1 to 2 tablespoons crushed
 dried pepper
4 tablespoons salt
2 bay leaves
2 teaspoons Worcestershire
 sauce, optional
1 teaspoon ground allspice
1 teaspoon ground black
 pepper
1 teaspoon hot pepper
 sauce, optional
Cooked meat of your choice
Filé powder
Hot cooked rice

Mix oil and flour in small heavy saucepan and cook over low heat 30 to 45 minutes, stirring frequently, until roux is the color of mahogany. In a large Dutch oven or kettle, sauté onion in butter until soft, about 5 minutes. Stir in okra and sauté 3 to 5 minutes. Stir in tomatoes, bell peppers and celery and simmer 20 to 30 minutes. Add remaining ingredients except filé powder and rice and rice and simmer covered about 1½ hours, stirring frequently. At this point you may add cooked chicken, shrimp, crayfish, oysters, sausage or fish filets and simmer for 15 minutes more. Ladle into serving bowls and top each with a scoop of rice. Pass filé powder and hot pepper sauce. Serves 8.

Mrs. Don Bradford (Melinda)
Lone Star Legacy II

Calabacita con Puerco

1	medium-sized pork loin roast, boned and cubed		Dried red pepper to taste
3	tablespoons oil		Salt and pepper to taste
3	ears of corn	1	can (8 ounces) tomato sauce
1	large onion, chopped		Water
4	cloves garlic, minced	4	medium Mexican green squash or zucchini, chopped
1	teaspoon cumin		
2	teaspoons chili powder		

Brown pork in oil, then drain. While pork is cooking, cut corn off cobs and scrape cobs. To the pork add corn, onion, garlic, spices, tomato sauce and enough water to cover. Bring to a boil, then simmer for 45 to 50 minutes. Add squash and additional water to cover, if necessary, and simmer another 30 minutes or until squash is tender. Serves 6 to 8.

Like any soup, calabacita is better warmed up — the only trouble is there's usually none left to reheat! This dish can also be made with chicken.

Ken and Susan McGinnis
Lone Star Legacy II

Crab Bisque

¼	pound butter or margarine	4	tablespoons flour
½	cup finely chopped onion	2	cups milk
½	cup finely chopped green pepper	1	teaspoon salt
¼	cup finely chopped parsley	1	teaspoon white pepper
2	cups sliced fresh mushrooms	2	cups half and half cream
		3	cups chopped crab
		3	tablespoons sherry, optional

Heat butter and sauté onion, green pepper, parsley, and mushrooms until soft. Add flour and stir to dissolve. Add milk, salt, and pepper and simmer until thickened and well blended. Add cream and crab and simmer for 15 minutes. Can be served immediately, but flavor is enhanced when refrigerated overnight and then reheated. Add sherry just before serving.

Mrs. Denman Smith (Sandra)
Lone Star Legacy

No-Name Soup

1 package (10 ounces) frozen broccoli or 1½ cups fresh	2 cans chicken broth
4 to 5 new potatoes	Salt and pepper to taste
1 bunch green onions	Sour cream as garnish

Cook vegetables with salt and pepper in broth until tender. Purée in blender. Serve hot with a tablespoon of sour cream on top of each bowl. Serves 6 to 8.

This is an East Texas "country" dish. It has no name and no known origin but is quick and great for last minute company.

Mrs. Tom Hollis (Doris)
Lone Star Legacy

French Country Lentil Soup

1 (16 ounce) package dried lentils	4 (10½ ounce) cans beef consommé
1 large onion, chopped	2 cloves garlic, minced
2 tablespoons olive oil	3 tablespoons brown sugar
4 carrots, coarsely grated	²/₃ cup dry red wine
1 teaspoon fines herbes	½ cup chopped parsley
1 (29 ounce) can tomatoes chopped with juice	Salt and black pepper to taste

Rinse lentils. Soak in water to cover for several hours or over night. Drain. Sauté onion in olive oil in stock pot for 5 minutes. Add lentils, carrots, fines herbes, tomatoes, consommé, garlic and brown sugar to onion. Simmer for 45 minutes to 1 hour or until lentils are tender. Add wine and parsley. Season with salt and black pepper. Simmer for 5 minutes, adding water if needed for desired consistency. Makes approximately 10 cups.

Great with French bread and a glass of red wine. Favorite dried herbs may be substituted for fines herbes, or a combination of thyme, oregano, rosemary, sage and basil to measure 1 teaspoon.

Jeanne Cassidy
Changing Thymes

Per ½ cup serving_____

Calories 131 Protein 9.67 g Carbohydrates 19.1 g Fat 1.5 g Cholesterol 0 mg Sodium 490 mg

Black Bean Soup with Poblano Cream

2	cups dry black beans	2	medium carrots, diced
1	ham hock	3	stalks celery, diced
4	cups beef broth	6	cloves garlic, diced
2	medium-sized onions, diced	1	poblano chili pepper
1	green bell pepper, seeds removed and diced	1	cup low-fat sour cream
		¼	cup red wine (optional)

Soak beans according to package directions. Drain well. Combine beans, ham hock and broth in stock pot. Cook until beans are tender. Discard ham hock. Add onion, bell pepper, carrots, celery and garlic to beans. Simmer for about 1 hour or until vegetables are tender. Add red wine 10 minutes before serving. Remove stem, seeds and membrane of poblano pepper. Purée the pepper. Mix with sour cream. Ladle soup into individual serving bowls and garnish each with 1 teaspoon sour cream mixture. Makes approximately 8 cups.

Featured in American Cowboy Magazine

Linda Simmons
Changing Thymes

Per ½ cup serving_____

Calories 109 Protein 6.32 g Carbohydrates 14.6 g Fat 3 g Cholesterol 9.24 mg Sodium 223 mg

Dave's Fabulous Garlic Soup

6	beef bouillon cubes	1	tablespoon flour
8	cups boiling water	½	teaspoon pepper
20	fresh garlic cloves		Pinch of salt
2	tablespoons butter	6	egg yolks, beaten
1	bunch green onions, minced		

In a large bowl or saucepan, combine bouillon cubes and water, stirring until cubes are dissolved. Peel garlic and mince. In a heavy saucepan over low heat, lightly brown garlic in butter with minced green onions, stirring constantly so as not to burn. Add flour and stir until slightly browned. Add broth and pepper; simmer 30 minutes to an hour. Just before serving, slowly add egg yolks, stirring constantly. Serve with toasted French bread that has been topped with Monterey Jack cheese. Serves 6.

This is a wonderful cure for whatever ails you and a great substitute for chicken soup! The 20 garlic cloves make is so good. Top off with caesar croutons.

Mrs. David King (Priscilla)
Lone Star Legacy II

Texas Country Bean Soup Mix

1	pound dried yellow split peas	1	pound Great Northern beans
1	pound dried black beans	1	pound dried split peas
1	pound dried red beans	1	pound dried blackeyed peas
1	pound dried pinto beans		
1	pound dried navy beans	1	pound barley pearls
1	pound dried kidney beans		

Combine all of above beans. Mix well. Yields 20 cups. *Divide into 10 portions (2 cups each).*

This is wonderful included in a Christmas Gift Basket along with a recipe for Texas Country Bean Soup.

Mrs. Steve McMillon (Mary Beth)
Lone Star Legacy II

Texas Country Bean Soup

2	cups Texas Country Bean Soup Mix	1	can (16 ounces) tomatoes with juice, chopped
2	quarts water	1	can (10 ounces) tomatoes with green chilies and juice
2	pounds ham, diced and divided		
1	onion, chopped	4	carrots, diced
2	cloves garlic, minced	2	ribs celery, chopped
½	teaspoon salt		

Wash and soak beans overnight; drain. Put beans into 2 quarts fresh water with 1 pound diced ham, onion, garlic and salt. Bring to a boil; reduce heat and cover. Simmer for 2 to 2½ hours. Add remaining ingredients and simmer 30 more minutes. Yields 2 quarts.

For a change add diced chicken instead of ham and ½ cup red wine. This is good served with hot cornbread and a salad on a cold day.

Mrs. Steve McMillon (Mary Beth)
Lone Star Legacy II

Carrot Curry Soup

1	medium onion, chopped	2	teaspoons sugar
2	tablespoons butter	¾	teaspoon curry powder
5 to 6	carrots, peeled and chopped	½	teaspoon salt
4 to 5	cups chicken broth	¼	teaspoon white pepper
2	tablespoons lemon juice	¼	teaspoon dill weed
		3	tablespoons dry sherry

Sauté onion in butter in a large skillet. Add carrots, broth, lemon juice, sugar, curry powder, salt, pepper and dill weed. Reduce heat and cook until carrots are tender-crisp. Pour into blender and purée until smooth. Stir in sherry; cover and chill. Serves 8.

Mrs. Marvin Sentell (Julie)
Lone Star Legacy II

Tim's Potato Soup

5	medium potatoes, peeled and cubed	¼	teaspoon white pepper
3	medium onions, chopped	1	cup chicken broth
5	ribs celery with leaves, diced	1	can (10¾ ounces) cream of chicken soup
1½	tablespoons butter	4	cups half & half cream
2	teaspoons salt		Chopped parley to garnish

Boil potatoes until tender. In the meantime, sauté onions and celery in butter until tender; do not brown. Drain potatoes. Add remaining ingredients, except parsley, potatoes and return to heat. Stir constantly until mixture comes to a boil. Reduce heat and simmer 2 minutes. Mash some of the potatoes in the soup to thicken the texture. Ladle into bowls and garnish with a pat of butter and chopped parsley. Serves 10 to 12.

Mrs. Tim Mizner (Carol)
Lone Star Legacy II

Lentil and Brown Rice Soup

5	cups chicken broth	1	rib celery, chopped
3	cups water	3	cloves garlic, minced
1½	cups lentils, rinsed	½	teaspoon basil
1	cup brown rice	½	teaspoon oregano
1	can (32 ounces) tomatoes. undrained	¼	teaspoon thyme
3	carrots, cut into ¼ inch pieces	1	bay leaf
		½	cup minced fresh parsley
1	onion, chopped	2	tablespoons cider vinegar
			Salt and pepper to taste

In a heavy kettle combine the chicken broth, water, lentils, rice and coarsely chopped tomatoes and juice. Add carrots, onion, celery, garlic, basil, oregano, thyme and bay leaf. Bring liquid to a boil. Simmer covered, stirring occasionally, for 45 to 55 minutes, or until the lentils and rice are tender. Stir in parsley, vinegar, salt and pepper. Discard bay leaf. The soup will be thick and will thicken as it stands. Thin the soup, if desired, with additional hot chicken stock or water. Yields 14 cups, serving 6 to 8.

Mrs. Ernest Butler (Sarah)
Lone Star Legacy II

French Onion Soup

3   large white onions, sliced
2   tablespoons margarine
1   tablespoon flour
4   cloves garlic, minced
¼   teaspoon oregano
½   teaspoon thyme
½   teaspoon paprika

4   cups water
2   cups beef broth
1   cup chicken broth
4   slices French bread, optional
1   cup grated Swiss cheese

Brown onion in margarine. Add flour, garlic and spices. Sauté for 3 minutes. Add water, beef and chicken broth. Boil 20 minutes, stirring occasionally. To serve, place bread in bowls, ladle soup to cover, top with cheese and run under broiler till cheese is melted and bubbly. Serves 4.

Great with roast beef or pastrami sandwiches.

Betsey Bishop
Lone Star Legacy II

Vegetable Beef Soup

2 to 3 pounds soup bones
2   large onions, quartered
Salt and pepper
¾   pound fresh green beans, snapped
1   pound carrots, peeled and sliced

1   stalk celery, sliced, and leaves
2   cans (14½ ounces each) tomatoes
1½ to 2 pounds round steak, cubed
1 to 1½ cups shell macaroni

Place soup bones, onions, salt and pepper into a large pan and cover with 3 to 4 quarts water. Cook slowly 4 to 6 hours. Refrigerate overnight. Add green beans, carrots, celery and tomatoes to broth and simmer 1½ to 2 hours. Add meat and simmer an additional 2 to 3 hours. Add macaroni and cook until done. Adjust seasonings to taste. Yields 4 to 5 quarts.

Mrs. Larry Crain (Pat)
Lone Star Legacy II

Quick and Tasty Soup

2	cups water	¼	cup chopped broccoli
2	teaspoons chicken	¼	pound tofu, cubed
	bouillon granules	2	tablespoons picante sauce
¼	cup chopped green onion		Dash of white vinegar
¼	cup chopped celery	1	egg, beaten

Bring water to a boil and add chicken bouillon, onion, celery, broccoli, tofu, picante sauce and vinegar. Simmer until vegetables are crisp tender. Swirl in egg just before serving. Serves 2.

This soup is filling and low calorie. Any combination of vegetables you have on hand will work, such as cabbage, mushrooms, bean sprouts or snow peas.

Mrs. Denman Smith (Sandra)
Lone Star Legacy II

Fireside Chili

2	pounds chili meat	2	cloves garlic, finely
1	pound ground beef		chopped
2	tablespoons bacon	3	heaping tablespoons chili
	drippings		powder
1	pint hot water	1	tablespoon oregano
1	can (10½ ounces) tomato	1	tablespoon cumin
	purée	1	teaspoon paprika
1	teaspoon Tabasco	1	teaspoon ground mustard
1	chili pepper pod or more	¼	teaspoon cayenne pepper
	to taste	1	teaspoon salt
2	large onions, finely		
	chopped		

Brown meats; add bacon drippings and cook 5 minutes. Add hot water, tomato purée, Tabasco, pepper, onion and garlic; simmer 30 minutes. Add rest of the ingredients and simmer slowly for 1 to 2 hours. Serves 6 to 8.

Serve with crackers, raw onion, grated sharp Cheddar cheese and plenty of ice cold Texas beer.

Mrs. Lawrence Christian (Joyce)
Lone Star Legacy

Cucumber Yogurt Soup

4	cups seeded and chopped cucumbers	1	clove garlic, crushed
2	cups water	3	fresh mint leaves
2	cartons (8 ounces each) plain yogurt	¼	teaspoon dried dill weed
2	tablespoons honey		Salt and white pepper to taste

Combine all ingredients in a large bowl and mix. Pour into a blender and blend until smooth. Cover and chill for several hours. Serves 8.

Mrs. Greg Gordon (Kathy)
Lone Star Legacy II

Cheese and Olive Sandwiches

1	cup pimiento stuffed olives. chopped	3	green onions, finely chopped
¾	cup grated Monterey Jack cheese	¾	cup grated Cheddar cheese
½	cup mayonnaise	½	teaspoon chili powder
	Salt to taste	6	English muffins

Combine all ingredients except muffins and mix well. Spread on muffins and bake at 400° until bubbly. Serve hot. Serves 6.

For a change of taste, you may substitute ripe olives and add a dash of curry powder.

Mrs. Marcus Bone (Beverly)
Lone Star Legacy II

Olive Nut Sandwiches

8	ounces cream cheese, room temperature	½	teaspoon onion powder
			White pepper to taste
½	cup mayonnaise	24	bread slices, buttered
½	cup chopped green olives		lightly
½	cup chopped pecans		

Blend cream cheese and mayonnaise. Add olives, pecans, onion powder, pepper, and mix well. Trim crusts off bread. Spread with sandwich spread mixture. Cut into halves or thirds. Cover tightly in refrigerator until ready to serve. Serves 12.

Louise Holt
Lone Star Legacy

Pimiento Cheese

1	package (8 ounces) Cheddar cheese, grated	3	pimientos, chopped fine
			Dash black pepper
1	teaspoon grated onion	1	tablespoon salad dressing
1	teaspoon finely chopped parsley		

Combine all ingredients with enough salad dressing to attain spreading consistency desired.

Mrs. Daniel O'Donnell (Sharon)
Lone Star Legacy

Sandy's Pimiento Cheese

2	cups grated Cheddar cheese	½	cup chopped green bell pepper
2	cups grated processed cheese	½	cup chopped pecans
1	jar (4 ounces) diced pimiento	½	cup mayonnaise
		2	loaves wheat bread

Mix together cheeses, pimiento, bell pepper, pecans and mayonnaise. Spread bread with pimiento cheese and you are ready to eat. Trim crust for party sandwiches. Yields 40 finger sandwiches.

Mrs. John Perkins (Sandy)
Lone Star Legacy II

Town Lake Sandwiches

1	tablespoon low-fat cream cheese, softened	⅛	cucumber, peeled and thinly sliced
1	sandwich roll, cut lengthwise in half	¼	cup bean sprouts
1	ounce turkey pastrami or turkey ham	¼	avocado, peeled and sliced

Spread cream cheese on bottom half of roll. Roll up pastrami and place on cream cheese. Add cucumber, bean sprouts and avocado. Cover with top of roll. Serves 1.

Sandwich can be stored in sealed container until served.

Ann Bommarito Armstrong
Changing Thymes

Per sandwich

Calories 334 Protein 15.6 g Carbohydrates 35.4 g Fat 15.5 g Cholesterol 23.7 mg Sodium 621 mg

Sandwiches Del Rio

4   slices rye, light wheat or
    white bread
2   tablespoons mayonnaise
2   ripe avocados, peeled and
    thinly sliced
1   medium-sized onion,
    thinly sliced

1   (4 ounce) can whole green
    chilies, drained and cut
    in strips
1 or 2 tomatoes, sliced
8   slices bacon, crisply
    cooked
4   ounces thinly sliced
    Cheddar cheese

Spread bread with mayonnaise. Layer each slice with avocado, onion, chilies, tomato and 2 strips bacon. Top with cheese slices. Broil for about 5 minutes or until cheese is melted. Serves 4.

Mary Lou Cindrich
Changing Thymes

Per sandwich

Calories 395 Protein 14.6 g Carbohydrates 19.6 g Fat 30 g Cholesterol 44.6 mg Sodium 922 mg

Swiss Sandwich Loaf

3   cups (12 ounces) shredded
    Swiss cheese
2/3 cup chopped tomato
1/2 cup chopped green onion

2/3 cup mayonnaise
1   (7 inch) round loaf
    pumpernickel

Combine cheese, tomato, onion and mayonnaise. Slice bread crosswise to form 11 slits; do not cut completely through bottom of loaf. Spread filling in alternate slits. Wrap loaf in aluminum foil. Bake at 325° for about 30 minutes or until cheese is melted. Separate into 6 sandwiches. Serves 6.

Loaf may be left intact and separated just before serving. The filling is also very good for grilled sandwiches.

Barbara Bittner
Changing Thymes

Per sandwich

Calories 272 Protein 10.8 g Carbohydrates 17.2 g Fat 18 g Cholesterol 31.9 mg Sodium 357 mg

Calzones

1	cup low-fat ricotta cheese	2	teaspoons oregano
1	cup (4 ounces) shredded mozzarella cheese	1	(10 count) can refrigerated biscuits
¼	pound cooked ham, finely chopped		

Combine ricotta and mozzarella cheese, ham and oregano. Separate biscuits. Place each between sheets of wax paper and roll to form 6-inch circles. Spoon cheese mixture into center of each biscuit. Lightly moisten edges of dough with water. Fold each (like a turnover) to form semi-circle, a "calzone." Press edges with fork tines to seal. Place on baking sheet prepared with vegetable cooking spray. Bake at 400° for 10 to 12 minutes or until golden brown. Serve immediately. Serves 10.

These can be assembled in advance, stored in refrigerator and baked just before serving. Leftovers can be refrigerated and reheated.

Jane Miller Sanders
Changing Thymes

Per serving

Calories 172 Protein 8.98 g Carbohydrates 14.2 g Fat 4 g Cholesterol 21.8 mg Sodium 548 mg

Mini Pizzas

1	pound hamburger meat	1	jar (10¾ ounces) pizza sauce
2	cans (10 count each) biscuits	1	cup Cheddar cheese, grated

Brown hamburger meat and drain. Add pizza sauce to meat and stir in Cheddar cheese. Roll each biscuit very thin. Place 2 tablespoons of meat mixture on each biscuit, and bake at 350° for 10 minutes, or until brown and bubbly. Serves 20.

These make cute little appetizers, if the biscuits are cut in half.
Mrs. Charles Cantwell (Winn)
Lone Star Legacy

Hot Ham Sandwiches

½ cup butter, melted
2 tablespoons mustard
½ teaspoon Worcestershire
    sauce
1 teaspoon minced onion
1 tablespoon poppy seeds

8 sandwich buns, split
1 pound thinly sliced ham
1 (8 ounce) package sliced
    Swiss, Cheddar or
    American cheese

Combine melted butter, mustard, Worcestershire sauce, onion and poppy seed, mixing well. Spread on buns. Layer ham and cheese on buns. Wrap for freezing. Freeze. To serve, bake sandwiches in foil at 350° for 20 minutes. Serves 8.

Carla Fisher
Changing Thymes

Per sandwich

Calories 406 Protein 21.4 g Carbohydrates 25 g Fat 24 g Cholesterol 80.9 mg Sodium 1671 mg

Barbecue Beef

3 to 4 pounds chuck roast
2 beef bouillon cubes
½ teaspoon rosemary
1 teaspoon oregano
1 teaspoon garlic powder
1 teaspoon savory salt
1 teaspoon salt

1 teaspoon pepper
1 can (6 ounces) tomato
    paste
Water to cover
2 cups barbeque sauce
Toasted buns

Place roast, bouillon cubes, spices and tomato paste in Dutch oven. Cover with water. Bring to boil; simmer covered for four hours. Uncover and simmer four more hours. Add barbecue sauce and cook uncovered until tender and falling apart. Remove bones and fat and serve beef on toasted buns. Serve 6 to 8.

Mrs. Daniel O'Donnell (Sharon)
Lone Star Legacy

Basil Burgers

1½ pounds ground sirloin beef	6 slices provolone cheese
¼ cup basil pesto	6 slices tomato
1 large clove garlic, minced	Thin purple onion slices
¼ cup oil-packed sun-dried tomatoes, drained and minced	6 bagels, onion rolls or seed buns, split
Salt and freshly ground black pepper to taste	

Combine beef, pesto, garlic, tomatoes, salt and black pepper. mixing thoroughly. Shape into four patties. Brush grill rack with oil. Grill burgers to desired doneness, topping with cheese slices as cooking is completed. Serve burgers, topped with tomato slices and onion, on bagels, rolls or buns. Serves 6

Jeanne Cassidy
Changing Thymes

Per burger_____

Calories 602 Protein 38 g Carbohydrates 44.2 g Fat 30 g Cholesterol 90.6 mg Sodium 825 mg

Tavern Sloppy Joes

1½ pounds ground beef	2 tablespoons bar-b-que sauce
½ cup catsup	
2 teaspoons prepared mustard	½ cup chopped onion
1 teaspoon white vinegar	1 tablespoon Worcestershire sauce

Mix all ingredients together and cook in a crock pot for 3 to 4 hours on high. For the last ½ hour remove cover. Serve on hamburger buns. Serves 6.

Mrs. Doug Lapham (Debbie)
Lone Star Legacy II

BEST OF

Lone Star ★ Legacy

BREADS &
BRUNCH

Butter Crescent Rolls

1 package yeast	3 eggs, beaten
1 cup warm water	¾ teaspoon salt
1 cup melted butter, divided	4½ cups flour
½ cup sugar	

Dissolve yeast in warm water in a large mixing bowl. Add ½ cup melted butter, sugar, eggs and salt; stir well. Gradually add flour, mixing well. Cover and let rise 4 hours in a warm, 85°, draft-free place. Divide dough into 2 equal parts. Knead each part 4 or 5 times on lightly floured board. Roll into 12 inch circles and brush with remaining melted butter. Cut each circle into 12 wedges. Roll up each wedge, beginning at wide end. Place on lightly greased cookie sheets and let rise 1 hour in a warm, draft-free place. Bake at 400° for 10 minutes or until light brown. Yields 24 rolls.

These freeze beautifully. After thawing, place in preheated 350° oven 2 to 3 minutes. This will crisp the rolls as though they were freshly baked.

Mrs. Ron Bruney (Carol)
Lone Star Legacy II

Very Easy White Bread

2 packages yeast	2 teaspoons salt
¼ cup warm water	1 tablespoon shortening
2 cups warm milk	6 cups flour
4 tablespoons sugar	

Soften yeast in warm water. Combine warm milk, sugar, salt and shortening. Add yeast and mix well. Add 2 cups of flour at a time. Knead about 5 minutes, adding more flour until the dough does not stick to your fingers. Put dough into 2 greased loaf pans. Let rise until double in size, about 1 hour. Bake at 350° for 40 to 45 minutes. Yields 2 loaves.

Mrs. Hal Williamson (Gayle)
Lone Star Legacy II

My Favorite Cheese Bread

1	cup margarine	¼	teaspoon garlic powder
12	ounces Cheddar cheese, grated	¼	teaspoon paprika
½	cup grated Parmesan cheese	½	teaspoon seasoned salt
1	teaspoon Worcestershire sauce	1	loaf French bread, sliced in half lengthwise

Have all ingredients at room temperature. Mix together all ingredients except bread. Broil bread slices on 1 side until brown; remove from broiler. Spread cheese mixture on the other side of the bread; broil until bubbly. Watch carefully. Yields 12 slices of bread.

Mozzarella cheese may be used instead of Cheddar cheese. The cheese mixture freezes well. This is wonderful at barbecues.

Mrs. David King (Priscilla)
Lone Star Legacy II

Buttermilk Rolls

1½	packages yeast	½	teaspoon baking powder
¼	cup warm water	½	teaspoon baking soda
1	cup buttermilk	3	cups flour
3	tablespoons sugar	1	teaspoon salt, optional
3	tablespoons oil		Melted butter

Dissolve yeast in warm water. In large mixing bowl mix buttermilk, sugar, oil, baking powder and baking soda. Add yeast after it is dissolved. Add enough flour to make a stiff dough. Let rise until double in size. Punch down and then shape as desired. Place in greased muffin tins and let rise until doubled. Bake at 400° for 8 to 10 minutes. Yields 18 rolls.

After baking, brush the tops with melted butter.

Linda Kelley
Lone Star Legacy II

Old South Refrigerator Rolls

1	cup mashed potatoes	1	yeast cake
1	cup potato water	1	cup lukewarm water
1	cup sugar	1	tablespoon salt
1	cup shortening	4	cups flour, sifted
2	eggs		

Combine mashed potatoes, potato water, sugar and shortening. Beat in eggs 1 at a time and cream well. Dissolve yeast cake in 1 cup lukewarm water and add to potato mixture. Add salt to the first sifter of flour. Add enough flour to the potato mixture to make a stiff handling dough. Put into a large bowl, cover tightly, and place in refrigerator. Pinch off dough as needed. Roll, cut and let rise. Bake at 450° for 10 to 12 minutes. Yields 16 rolls.

Barbara Beall Stanley
Lone Star Legacy II

Breads and Sweet Breads

Sour Dough Bread Starter

¼	cup milk	¼	cup warm water
½	cup water	2	teaspoons sugar
2	teaspoons vegetable oil	1½	teaspoons salt
1	package yeast	1½	cups flour

Combine milk, water and oil; bring to a boil. Cool to lukewarm. Dissolve yeast in water. Add with sugar and salt to cooled milk mixture. Cover. Let stand 12 to 18 hours to sour. Add flour and stir well. Yields 2½ cups.

Mrs. Ernest Butler (Sarah)
Lone Star Legacy II

131

Sour Dough French Bread

½	cup milk	1½	tablespoons sugar
1	cup water	2½	teaspoons salt
1½	tablespoons oil	4¾	cups flour
1	package yeast	2	tablespoons starter dough
¼	cup warm water		

Combine milk, water and oil and bring to a boil. Cool to lukewarm. Dissolve yeast in water and add with sugar and salt to cooled milk mixture. Place flour in a large bowl; pour milk into well made in center of flour; add starter and blend well. *Do not knead.* Place in a greased bowl; cover and let rise until double. Turn onto lightly floured board. Divide into half. Roll each into a 15 × 10 inch rectangle. Roll the oblong up tightly towards you. Taper ends by rolling. With scissors make cuts ¼ inch deep diagonally along loaf 2 inches apart. Let rise uncovered until double. Bake at 425° for 15 minutes. Reduce heat to 350° and bake 15 to 20 minutes. Brush top with ¼ teaspoon salt dissolved in ½ cup water and bake another 5 minutes. Cool in a drafty place for crisp crust. Yields 2 loaves.

Mrs. Ernest Butler (Sarah)
Lone Star Legacy II

Heavenly Biscuits

5	cups flour	1	cup shortening
¼	cup sugar	2	cups buttermilk
1	teaspoon baking soda	1	package yeast
3	teaspoons baking powder	¼	cup very warm water
¾	teaspoon salt		

Sift together flour, sugar, soda, baking powder and salt. Cut in shortening and add buttermilk. Mix yeast with water and add to mixture. Roll out dough and cut with biscuit cutter; place in greased pan. Let rise 30 minutes. Bake at 400° for 15 minutes. Yields 48.

Mrs. Rick Denbow (Susan)
Lone Star Legacy II

Grandmother's Buttermilk Biscuits

2	cups flour	½	teaspoon baking soda
1	teaspoon salt	6 to 7	tablespoons shortening
4	teaspoons baking powder	1	cup buttermilk

In a mixing bowl sift dry ingredients together. Cut shortening into flour mixture; gradually add buttermilk. Turn out onto a floured board and knead a few times. Roll dough out to ½ to ¾ inch thickness and cut with a biscuit cutter. Place biscuits with sides touching on a cookie sheet and bake at 450° for 12 to 15 minutes. Yields 12 biscuits.

My grandson loves these biscuits and makes them all the time.

Mrs. Jack Allen Bone (Joyce)
Lone Star Legacy II

Texas Beer Bread

3	cups self rising flour	1	egg, beaten
¼	cup sugar	1	tablespoon water
1	can Lite beer		Melted butter

Mix flour and sugar in bowl. Add beer; watch it foam, and mix just until blended. Pour into buttered loaf pan, preferably glass. Combine egg with water and brush top of loaf. Let rise 10 minutes. Bake at 350° for 40 to 45 minutes. Brush top with butter while hot.

Great for last minute.

Don Bradford
Lone Star Legacy

Good Texas Cornbread

1	cup yellow cornmeal	1	cup buttermilk
½	cup flour	½	cup milk
1	teaspoon salt	1	egg
1	tablespoon baking powder	¼	cup margarine, melted
½	teaspoon baking soda		

Mix together cornmeal, flour, salt, baking powder and baking soda. Stir in remaining ingredients. Pour into greased muffin tins and bake at 425° for 20 to 25 minutes. Yields 12 muffins.

Mrs. Bob Edgecomb (Mary)
Lone Star Legacy II

Mexican Cornbread

1	cup stoneground cornmeal	1	can (4 ounces) diced green chilies, drained
1	cup flour		
½	cup milk or dry milk	1	cup water
2	tablespoons sugar	⅓	cup oil
4	teaspoons baking powder	2	eggs
½	teaspoon salt	1	tablespoon butter or bacon drippings
4	ounces grated Cheddar cheese		

Combine cornmeal, flour, milk or dry milk, sugar, baking powder and salt in a bowl. Stir in cheese and chilies. Beat together water, oil and eggs. Stir into dry ingredients until just blended. Melt butter or bacon drippings in an 8 inch pan. Pour batter into pan and bake at 375° for 30 to 35 minutes. Yields 16 (2 inch) squares.

This recipe does work with either milk or dry milk and also freezes well.

S. D. Jackman
Lone Star Legacy II

Creamed Cornbread

1	can (17 ounces) cream style corn	2	eggs, beaten
1	cup cornmeal	½	teaspoon baking soda
1	cup butter, melted	2	cups grated sharp Cheddar cheese
¾	cup buttermilk	2	jalapeño peppers, diced
1	onion, finely chopped		

In a large bowl combine creamed corn, cornmeal, melted butter, buttermilk, onion, eggs and baking soda. Mix well. Place half of batter into a 9 inch greased baking dish. Cover evenly with 1 cup of cheese, then all of the diced peppers. Cover with remaining batter and cheese. Bake at 350° for 1 hour. Let cool 15 minutes, then cut into squares. Serves 9.

Mrs. Marcus Bone (Beverly)
Lone Star Legacy II

Beer Puppies

4	cups stone ground cornmeal	1	medium onion, minced
2	cups flour	1	egg
1	tablespoon baking powder	¼	cup chopped parsley
1¼	teaspoons salt	1½	teaspoons pepper
2 to 2½ cups beer		3	quarts peanut oil

Sift cornmeal, flour, baking powder and salt into bowl. Add beer, onion, egg, parsley and pepper. Stir quickly until moist; do not over stir. If batter seems too thick, add ½ cup beer. Preheat oven to 250°. Heat oil in an electric skillet to 365°. Drop batter by rounded teaspoons into hot oil and cook until brown, about 2 minutes. Drain and keep warm in oven. Serve hot. Yields 6 dozen.

Mrs. Marcus Bone (Beverly)
Lone Star Legacy II

Hush Puppies

²⁄₃	cup yellow cornmeal		Pinch soda
¹⁄₃	cup flour	1	small onion, minced
1	teaspoon sugar		Pinch salt
1	teaspoon baking powder	¼	cup milk

Mix dry ingredients. Add milk until mixture is pasty. Drop by spoonfuls into hot fat. Cook until golden brown; drain. Serve hot. Yields 12.

Mrs. Larry Keith (Virginia)
Lone Star Legacy

Jambalaya Cornbread Muffins

3	tablespoons butter	1	teaspoon salt
½	cup finely chopped green bell pepper	2	eggs
½	cup finely chopped green onions	2	cups buttermilk
1	cup yellow cornmeal	1	cup finely chopped, cooked ham
1¼	cups flour	1	cup finely crumbled, cooked bulk sausage
2	teaspoons baking soda		

Melt butter in a skillet and sauté bell pepper and onion until soft and clear but not brown. Remove from heat. In a large bowl sift together dry ingredients. In a smaller bowl beat eggs and stir in buttermilk. Add the egg mixture to the flour mixture all at once, stirring only until mixed. Carefully fold in ham, sausage, bell pepper and onion. Spoon into well greased muffin tins, filling ²⁄₃ full. Bake at 400° for 30 minutes or until nicely browned. Serve with hot butter. Yields 12.

Mrs. Charles Smith (Jeannie)
Lone Star Legacy II

Polenta

1	cup yellow cornmeal divided	2	packages dry yeast
2	tablespoons sugar	1¼	cups warm water
2	teaspoons salt	2	tablespoons chopped parsley
8	slices bacon, cooked, crumbled and drippings reserved	2	tablespoons chopped chives
1	cup boiling water	4	cups flour

Combine ¾ cup cornmeal, sugar, salt and 2 tablespoons bacon drippings. Pour boiling water over cornmeal mixture. In another large bowl sprinkle yeast over warm water and stir to dissolve. Let rest a few minutes, then add to cornmeal mixture. Stir in crumbled bacon, parsley and chives. Slowly add flour one cup at a time until well blended and smooth. Place bowl in a warm place, cover and allow to rise one hour or until doubled. Punch dough down and beat with a wooden spoon. Divide dough between two quart casseroles which have been greased and sprinkled with some of the reserved cornmeal. Let rise an additional 30 minutes. Sprinkle top with more of the cornmeal. Bake at 350° for 55 to 60 minutes or until golden brown. Remove from casseroles and cool on a wire rack. Yields 2 rounds.

Mrs. Denman Smith (Sandra)
Lone Star Legacy II

Broiled Parmesan Toast

French bread, thinly sliced	½ cup finely chopped onion
Butter or margarine	1 teaspoon Worcestershire sauce
½ cup mayonnaise	Paprika
¼ cup grated Parmesan cheese	

Spread French bread slices completely with butter and place on cookie sheet. Mix together mayonnaise, cheese, onion and Worcestershire sauce. Spread mixture on buttered bread, then sprinkle with paprika. Broil in oven until golden brown. Serve immediately. Serves 8 to 10.

This could also be placed on smaller slices and be served as an appetizer.

Mrs. Tom Russell (Ann)
Lone Star Legacy II

Robin's Whole Wheat Tortillas

2	cups whole wheat flour	1	tablespoon shortening
1	teaspoon salt	2/3	cup cold water
1½	teaspoons baking powder		

Sift dry ingredients into a medium mixing bowl. Cut in shortening and add enough cold water to make a stiff dough. Knead on a lightly floured board. Make small balls; pat thin. Bake on a soapstone or lightly greased griddle. Yields 12.

It helps to have a tortilla press for gringos who have trouble patting them thinly enough! A standard tortilla is 6 inches in diameter.

Mrs. Randy Hagan (Robin Roberts)
Lone Star Legacy II

Homemade Flour Tortillas

4	cups flour	2/3	cup shortening
2	teaspoons salt	1	cup plus 3 tablespoons hot
1/8	teaspoon baking powder		water

Combine flour, salt and baking powder, stirring well. Cut in shortening with a pastry blender until mixture resembles coarse meal. Gradually stir in water, mixing well. Shape dough into 1½ inch balls; roll each on a floured surface into a 6 inch circle. Cook tortillas in an ungreased skillet over medium heat about 2 minutes on each side or until lightly browned. Pat tortillas lightly with spatula while browning the second side if they puff during cooking. Serve hot. Yields 24.

Mrs. J. Edward Reed (Marian)
Lone Star Legacy II

Applesauce Muffins

2	teaspoons baking soda	2	cups flour
1½	cups applesauce, heated	1	teaspoon cinnamon
⅔	cup margarine, melted	½	teaspoon ground cloves
1	cup sugar	½	teaspoon allspice

Add soda to hot applesauce. Mix in melted margarine. Mix all dry ingredients together and add to applesauce mixture. Pour into greased muffin tins and bake at 350° for 10 to 12 minutes. For a variation you may add 1 cup raisins that have been plumped in simmering water and/or 2 cups finely chopped pecans. Yields 12.

Mrs. Mark White (Linda Gayle)
Lone Star Legacy II

Holiday Cranberry Muffins

1	cup raw cranberries, chopped	¼	teaspoon salt
		¼	cup sugar
½	cup sugar	1	egg, beaten
2	cups flour	¾	cup buttermilk
¾	teaspoon baking soda	¼	cup shortening, melted

Let cranberries stand overnight in ½ cup sugar. Combine dry ingredients. Add liquid ingredients all at once. Stir until moistened. Add cranberries and stir. Fill greased muffin pans two-thirds full. Bake in a 400° oven for 20 minutes. Yields 18 muffins.

Cookbook Committee
Lone Star Legacy

Sour Cream Muffins

1	egg	2	teaspoons baking powder
1	cup sour cream	½	teaspoon baking soda
2	tablespoons butter, melted	½	teaspoon salt
2	cups sifted flour	¼	cup milk
¼	cup sugar		

Beat egg and sour cream until light and fluffy. Add melted butter. Sift flour, sugar, baking powder, baking soda, and salt together. Add to egg mixture with milk. Stir only until dry ingredients are dampened. Fill 12 greased muffin tins one half full. Bake at 400° for 20 minutes or until muffins are golden brown.

Ellie Winetroub
Lone Star Legacy

Six Week Muffins

5	teaspoons baking soda	4	cups flour
2	cups boiling water	1	teaspoon salt
1	cup shortening	4	cups All Bran
2	cups sugar	2	cups 40% Bran
4	eggs	2	cups chopped dates,
1	quart buttermilk		raisins or both

Add soda to boiling water; cool. Cream shortening and sugar; add eggs and soda mixture. Add remaining ingredients; mix well. Store covered in the refrigerator. Do not stir again. Spoon into muffin tins. Bake at 375° for 25 minutes. Keeps up to six weeks.

Mrs. Elof Soderburg (Mary)
Lone Star Legacy

Peach Flip

2 packages dry yeast	½ cup hot, scalded milk
½ cup warm water	2 teaspoons salt
½ cup sugar	3 unbeaten eggs
½ cup margarine	5 to 5½ cups flour

Soften yeast in warm water. Combine in mixing bowl sugar, margarine, scalded milk and salt. Stir to melt butter. Cool to lukewarm. Blend in eggs and softened yeast. Gradually add flour to form stiff dough. Knead on floured board until smooth and satiny, 3 to 5 minutes. Place in greased bowl; cover. Let rise in warm place until light and doubled in size, 1 to 1½ hours.

Filling:

⅔ cup sugar	1 cup peach or apricot
2 teaspoons cinnamon	preserves
2 tablespoons soft butter	1 cup chopped walnuts

Combine sugar and cinnamon; set aside. On a floured board, roll out half of the dough to a 20 × 10-inch rectangle. Spread with half of the butter and half of the preserves. Sprinkle with half of the cinnamon-sugar mixture and half of the walnuts. Roll up starting with the 20-inch side. Seal edge. Place seam side down on greased cookie sheet; bring ends together and seal to make a ring. Cut slits two-thirds of the way through the roll, 1½ inches apart. Repeat with remaining dough. Cover and let rise in warm place about 30 minutes. Bake at 350° for 20-25 minutes until golden brown. Yields 2 rings.

Variation: This recipe can also be used to make sweet rolls. Prepare as directed, but instead of shaping dough into rings, cut dough into 1¼-inch slices and place in greased muffin tins. Let rise and bake as directed. Yields 30-36 rolls.

Frosting:

1 cup powdered sugar	Chopped walnuts or sliced
1 teaspoon vanilla	almonds to garnish
2 tablespoons milk	

Combine all ingredients and drizzle over rings; garnish with nuts, if desired.

Donna Haverkamp
Lone Star Legacy II

Deep South Ginger Muffins

¾	cup butter	½	cup buttermilk
½	cup sugar	1	teaspoon soda
2	eggs	½	cup dark molasses
⅛	teaspoon cinnamon	½	cup chopped nuts
1	teaspoon ginger	½	cup raisins
⅛	teaspoon allspice	2	cups flour

Mix ingredients in order given. Put into well greased muffin tins or cup cake liners. Bake at 400° about 10 minutes. Yields 24.

Batter may be stored in refrigerator.

Mrs. Wayne Davison (Cindi)
Lone Star Legacy

Buñuelos

4	eggs	1	teaspoon salt
½	cup milk		Oil
¼	cup butter, melted		Sugar
3	cups flour		Cinnamon
1	tablespoon sugar		

Beat eggs; add milk and melted butter. Stir in flour, sugar and salt to make a dough that is easily handled without sticking. Make into walnut sized balls. Roll each ball out on a floured surface until it is the shape of a tortilla. Fry in hot oil until golden brown. Combine sugar and cinnamon and sprinkle on each buñuelo. Serve warm. Yields approximately 5 to 6 dozen.

Traci Lerche
Lone Star Legacy II

Donut Balls

3	cups pancake mix	2	eggs, beaten
1½	teaspoons cinnamon	2	tablespoons oil
⅓	cup sugar	¾	cup milk
½	teaspoon nutmeg		Powdered sugar

Combine pancake mix, cinnamon, sugar and nutmeg. Add eggs, oil and milk, stirring only until blended. If dough is too stiff, add 1 more teaspoon of milk. Drop batter into deep 325° oil and fry for 2 to 2½ minutes or until brown. Drain on paper towels and dust with powdered sugar. Yields 24.

Mrs. Leo Mueller (Nancy)
Lone Star Legacy II

Nutty Cheese Spread

1	(8 ounce) package cream cheese, softened	½	cup firmly-packed brown sugar
1	teaspoon vanilla	½	cup chopped nuts
¼	cup sugar		

Combine all ingredients and blend well. Chill for at least 1 hour before serving. Makes 1½ cups.

Serve with slices of apple, pear or banana or with English muffins or bagels. Also good on banana bread.

Sherrie Smith
Changing Thymes

Per 1 tablespoon serving

Calories 70 Protein .905 g Carbohydrates 5.77 g Fat 5 g Cholesterol 10.4 mg Sodium 29.1 mg

Cinnamon Pull Aparts

½   cup chopped nuts
3   cans (10 count) biscuits
1   teaspoon cinnamon
½   cup sugar
1   stick margarine
1   cup brown sugar

Grease bundt pan. Place nuts in bottom. Cut biscuits into quarters. Roll in cinnamon sugar mixture. Arrange in pan. Melt margarine and brown sugar. Pour over sugared biscuits. Bake at 350° for 30 to 40 minutes. Remove from pan. Serves 8 to 10.

Mrs. Jim Schultz (Mary Kay)
Lone Star Legacy

Perfect Gingerbread

2   cups flour
½   cup sugar
1½ teaspoons ginger
½   teaspoon cinnamon
2   teaspoons baking powder
Scant teaspoon soda
¼   teaspoon salt
¾   cup molasses
1   cup buttermilk
1   egg
¼   cup melted shortening
1 to 2 teaspoons vanilla

Put all dry ingredients in sifter. Put wet ingredients in mixing bowl. Sift dry ingredients into the mixing bowl. Beat until smooth. Pour into greased 9 × 5 loaf pan. Bake at 350° for about 1 hour.

Delicious served plain. I also like a topping of whipped cream with bananas. Pecans may be added if desired.

Mrs. Don Panter (Carolyn)
Lone Star Legacy

Pumpkin Bread

3	cups sugar	3½	cups flour
1	cup oil	2	teaspoons baking soda
4	eggs	1½	teaspoons salt
2	cups canned pumpkin	2½	teaspoons cinnamon
¾	cup water	2½	teaspoons nutmeg

In large mixing bowl combine sugar, oil, eggs, and pumpkin. Sift dry ingredients together and add to sugar mixture, alternating with water. Pour batter into a lightly greased bundt pan or into four ungreased one pound coffee cans, filling half full. Bake at 350° for hour.

For a heartier cake, add 1 cup pecans and/or 1 cup raisins just before pouring into bundt pan. Slice bread rounds and serve with orange cream cheese for a sweet sandwich.

Mrs. Bob Edgecomb (Mary)
Lone Star Legacy

Apple Raisin Bread

3	cups all-purpose flour	1¼	cups vegetable oil
1½	teaspoons baking soda	4	eggs, beaten
½	teaspoon baking powder	1	tablespoon plus
1½	teaspoons salt		1 teaspoon vanilla
2	teaspoons cinnamon	3	cups chopped apples
1	teaspoon ground cloves	⅔	cup raisins
2½	cups sugar	½	cup chopped nuts

Generously grease bottoms only of two 9 × 5 × 3-inch loaf pans. Beat all ingredients on low speed of mixer for one minute, scraping the bowl constantly. Increase to medium speed and beat 1 minute longer. Pour batter into pans and bake uncovered at 325° for 1 hour or until wooden pick inserted near center comes out clean. Cool 10 minutes in the pans. Cool completely before slicing. Store in the refrigerator. Makes 2 loaves.

Janet Henegar
Changing Thymes

Per ½-inch slice_____

Calories 225 Protein 2.29 g Carbohydrates 31 g Fat 10.5 g Cholesterol 26.5 mg Sodium 147 mg

Chocolate Zucchini Bread

2	cups sugar	1	teaspoon baking soda
1	cup vegetable oil	1	teaspoon salt
2	eggs	3	cups grated zucchini squash
1	teaspoon vanilla	1	cup chopped nuts
2¾	cups all-purpose flour	1	cup miniature chocolate
¼	cup cocoa		morsels
¼	teaspoon baking powder	1	cup shredded coconut

Combine sugar, oil, eggs and vanilla, blending well. Combine flour, cocoa, baking powder, baking soda and salt. Add to egg mixture, blending thoroughly. Stir in zucchini, nuts, chocolate morsels and coconut. Pour batter into 2 greased 9 × 5 × 3-inch loaf pans. Bake at 325° for 1 hour. Cool in pans for 10 minutes, then invert on wire rack to complete cooling. Makes 2 loaves.

Gwen Walden Irwin
Changing Thymes

Per ½-inch slice_____

Calories 215 Protein 2.37 Carbohydrate 25.9 g Fat 12.5 g Cholesterol 13.3 mg Sodium 98.2 mg

Super Quick Banana Bread

1	package (18.5 ounces) nut bread mix	½	teaspoon vanilla extract
		1	egg
1	cup mashed ripe bananas	⅓	cup chopped walnuts,
2	tablespoons water		optional

Grease and flour the bottom of a loaf pan. Mix all ingredients with a spoon for 40 to 50 strokes until well blended. Pour into pan. Bake at 350° for 50 to 55 minutes until a toothpick comes out clean. Cool in pan for 15 minutes. Remove from pan and cool completely before wrapping. Yields 1 loaf.

This freezes well.

Mrs. Sid Mann (Kathi)
Lone Star Legacy II

Pear Bread with Half Hour Apple Butter

½	cup margarine, softened	**Apple Butter:**	
1	cup sugar	2	cups applesauce
2	eggs	½	cup sugar
2	cups all-purpose flour	1	teaspoon cinnamon
1	teaspoon baking powder	¼	teaspoon allspice
½	teaspoon baking soda	⅛	teaspoon ginger
½	teaspoon salt	⅛	teaspoon ground cloves
½	teaspoon nutmeg		
¼	cup plain yogurt		
1	cup chopped unpeeled pears		
1	teaspoon vanilla		

Cream butter and sugar together until smooth. Add eggs, one at a time, beating after each addition. Combine flour, baking powder, baking soda, salt and nutmeg. Alternately add dry ingredients and yogurt to creamed mixture, mixing well. Stir in pears and vanilla. Pour batter into greased 9 × 5 × 3-inch loaf pan. Bake at 350° for 1 hour. Cool in pan for 10 minutes, then invert on rack wire to cool completely. Prepare apple butter by combining applesauce, sugar, cinnamon, allspice, ginger and cloves in large saucepan. Bring to a boil and cook for 30 minutes, stirring often. While still hot, spoon into a small canning jar and process according to canning directions. Makes 1 loaf and 1¼ cups apple butter.

I put these loaves in Christmas gift baskets for family and friends.

Wanda Rich

Changing Thymes

Per ½-inch slice_____

Calories 156 Protein 2.4 g Carbohydrates 23.6 g Fat 6 g Cholesterol 23.8 mg Sodium 152 mg

Per 1 tablespoon apple butter_____

Calories 30 Protein .049 g Carbohydrates 7.86 g Fat .25 mg Cholesterol 0 Sodium .624 mg

Pumpkin Date Nut Bread

4	cups sugar	1	teaspoon salt
1	cup vegetable oil	1	teaspoon cinnamon
2	eggs	1	teaspoon ground cloves
3	cups canned pumpkin	1	cup finely chopped dates
5	cups all-purpose flour	1	cup chopped pecans or
1	tablespoon plus 1 teaspoon		walnuts
	baking soda	½	cup orange juice

Combine sugar and oil. Beat several minutes until fluffy. Add eggs and beat thoroughly. Blend in pumpkin. Combine flour, baking soda, salt, cinnamon and cloves. Add dry ingredients, dates and pecans to pumpkin mixture, stirring to mix; do not overmix. Blend orange juice into batter. Pour batter into three 9 × 5 × 3-inch loaf pans, filling each ½ full. Bake at 350° for 1 hour. Cool in pans for 10 minutes. Makes 3 loaves.

Sue Kidwell
Changing Thymes

Per ½-inch slice

Calories 189 Protein 2.06 g Carbohydrates 31.3 g Fat 6.5 g Cholesterol 8.83 mg Sodium 117 mg

Apple Crunch Coffee Cake

2	cups chopped peeled apples	2	teaspoons cinnamon
2	cups all-purpose flour	2	teaspoons baking powder
2	cups sugar	½	teaspoon salt
1	cup vegetable oil	1	cup chopped nuts
2	eggs		

Combine all ingredients in order listed and stir well. Batter will be thick. Spread batter in greased and floured 13 × 9 × 2-inch baking pan. Bake at 350° for 55 minutes. Serves 16.

One of the most asked for recipes at our neighborhood coffees.

Kathy Marsh
Changing Thymes

Per serving

Calories 343 Protein 3.01g Carbohydrates 41.1 g Fat 19.5 g Cholesterol 26.5 mg Sodium 75.7 mg

Strawberry Bread with Cream Cheese Spread

3	cups flour	2	packages (10 ounces each) frozen strawberries, thawed
2	cups sugar		
1	teaspoon baking soda		
1	teaspoon cinnamon	1	cup oil
1	teaspoon salt	4	eggs, well beaten
1	cup strawberry juice, divided	8	ounces cream cheese, softened

Combine and mix well flour, sugar, baking soda, cinnamon, and salt. Make a well in center and add ½ cup strawberry juice, strawberries, oil and eggs. Mix by hand. Grease and flour two 4 × 8 inch loaf pans. Bake at 350° for 1 hour or until toothpick inserted in center comes out clean. To prepare cream cheese spread, combine cream cheese with enough strawberry juice to make a spreadable mixture. Spread on bread and refrigerate until served. Yields 2 loaves.

Loaves can be frozen; slice thinly before completely thawed.

Jan Palmer
Lone Star Legacy

Spicy Buttermilk Coffee Cake

2½	cups flour	¾	cup oil
½	teaspoon salt	1	cup chopped walnuts or pecans
2	teaspoons cinnamon, divided		
¼	teaspoon ginger	1	teaspoon baking soda
1	cup brown sugar	1	teaspoon baking powder
¾	cup sugar	1	egg, beaten
		1	cup buttermilk

Mix flour, salt, 1 teaspoon cinnamon, ginger, sugars and oil together in a bowl. Remove ¾ cup of this mixture and add it to the walnuts with 1 teaspoon cinnamon. Mix well and set aside. To the remaining batter; add baking soda, baking powder, egg and buttermilk and mix. Pour batter into a well greased 9 × 13 inch pan and sprinkle the topping mixture evenly over the surface. Bake at 350° for 35 to 40 minutes. Serves 12.

Mrs. Larry Crain (Pat)
Lone Star Legacy II

Sour Cream Coffee Cake

2	eggs	¼	teaspoon salt
1	cup butter	1	teaspoon baking powder
2	cups sugar	1	cup chopped pecans
1	cup sour cream	2	teaspoons cinnamon
1	teaspoon vanilla extract	½	cup brown sugar
2	cups flour		

Cream together eggs, butter and sugar. Add the sour cream and vanilla and mix. Slowly stir in flour, salt and baking powder. For the nut mixture, combine pecans, cinnamon and brown sugar in a separate bowl. Place half the nut mixture in the bottom of a well greased bundt pan; add half the cake batter; then the remaining nut mixture; end with cake batter. Place in a preheated 350° oven and bake for 55 minutes. Serves 12 to 16.

The cake should be very moist, but done. This is a favorite family recipe.

Mrs. Bill Pohl (Kelly)
Lone Star Legacy II

Holiday Brunch Coffee Cake

May be prepared in advance and frozen

1 cup margarine, softened	1 (8 ounce) can whole
1 cup sugar	cranberry sauce
2 eggs	½ cup slivered almonds
½ teaspoon almond extract	Glaze:
2 cups all-purpose flour	1 cup powdered sugar
1 tablespoon baking powder	2 tablespoons milk
½ teaspoon salt	½ teaspoon almond extract
1 cup low-fat sour cream	

Cream margarine and sugar together until light and fluffy. Add eggs, one at a time, beating well after each addition. Alternately add almond extract, flour, baking powder and salt with sour cream to egg mixture. Pour batter into greased 13 × 9 × 2-inch baking pan. Spoon cranberry sauce over batter. Sprinkle with almonds. Bake at 350° for 35 to 40 minutes. Prepare glaze by blending powdered sugar, milk and almond extract. Drizzle glaze over warm coffee cake. Serves 24.

This is great to serve the morning of Thanksgiving while waiting for the turkey to cook or on Christmas morning after Santa has arrived.

Cheryl Briggs Patton
Changing Thymes

Per serving_____

Calories 206 Protein 2.6 g Carbohydrates 25.5 g Fat 11 g Cholesterol 21.7 mg Sodium 148 mg

Overnight Coffee Cake

¾ cup butter, softened	½ teaspoon salt
1 cup sugar	1 teaspoon nutmeg
2 eggs	Topping:
1 cup sour cream	¾ cup firmly-packed brown
2 cups all-purpose flour	sugar
1 teaspoon baking powder	½ cup chopped pecans
1 teaspoon baking soda	1 teaspoon cinnamon

Cream butter and sugar together until fluffy. Add eggs and sour cream, mixing well. Combine flour, baking powder, baking soda, salt and nutmeg. Add to creamed mixture, blending thoroughly. Pour batter into 13 × 9 × 2-inch baking pan. Combine brown sugar, pecans and cinnamon. Sprinkle mixture on batter. Chill, covered, overnight. Bake, uncovered, at 350° for 35 to 40 minutes. Serves 12.

Ann Bommarito Armstrong
Changing Thymes

Per serving

Calories 364 Protein 4.32 g Carbohydrates 43.5 g Fat 20 g Cholesterol 74.9 mg Sodium 300 mg

Blueberry Coffee Cake

Cake:

½ cup butter	1½ teaspoons baking powder
¾ cup sugar	½ teaspoon salt
1 egg	½ cup milk
1½ cups flour	1 cup blueberry pie filling

Cream butter and sugar together; stir in egg. Mix flour, baking powder and salt together. Add to butter mixture, alternating with milk. Pour half the mixture into an 8 × 8-inch greased pan. Cover with blueberry pie filling. Pour remaining batter over pie filling.

Topping:

½ cup brown sugar	1½ teaspoons cinnamon
2 tablespoons butter, melted	½ cup chopped pecans
	1½ tablespoons flour

Mix all ingredients together and sprinkle on top of batter. Bake at 350° for 50 minutes. Serves 8.

Mrs. Thomas Schwartz (Ellana)
Lone Star Legacy II

Cinnamon Coffee Cake

1	box (18½ ounces) yellow cake mix	4	eggs
1	small box vanilla instant pudding	1	teaspoon vanilla
		1	teaspoon butter flavoring
⅔	cup oil	½	cup brown sugar
¾	cup water	¼	cup nuts, chopped

Filling:

¼	cup sugar	2	teaspoons cinnamon

Glaze:

1	cup powdered sugar	½	teaspoon butter flavoring
½	teaspoon vanilla		Milk

Mix cake mix, pudding, oil, water, eggs, vanilla, and butter flavoring and beat for 5 minutes. Grease and flour a bundt pan. Cover bottom of pan with brown sugar and sprinkle with chopped nuts. Mix sugar and cinnamon for filling. Alternate cake batter and filling in three layers of bundt pan. Bake at 350° for 40 to 50 minutes. Mix ingredients for glaze; pour ½ glaze over while it is still in pan. Cool cake for a few minutes, then remove from pan and top the cake with remaining glaze.

Mrs. Ron Garrick (Bonnie)
Lone Star Legacy

Quickie Chili Relleños

2	cans (7 ounces each) whole green chilies	4	eggs
		2	cups evaporated milk
24	ounces Monterey Jack cheese, grated	½	cup flour
		¾	teaspoon salt
8	ounces Cheddar cheese, grated	1	clove garlic, minced
		5	green onions, chopped

Lightly butter a 9 x 13 inch pan. Wash chilies, remove seeds and pat dry. Open chilies and cut into 2 inch squares. Layer bottom of casserole with chilies, then half the cheese. Repeat layers. Mix eggs, milk and seasonings with flour and pour over top. Bake at 325° for 45 minutes to 1 hour. Serves 8.

This is good even if you are not a chili lover.

Mrs. Larry Morris (Diane)
Lone Star Legacy II

153

Cheesy Broccoli Squares

⅔	cup chopped onion	1⅓	cups milk
1	tablespoon margarine	3	eggs
2	(10 ounce) packages frozen	¾	cup buttermilk baking mix
	chopped broccoli, thawed	¼	teaspoon black pepper
3	cups (12 ounces) shredded		
	Cheddar cheese, divided		

Sauté onion in margarine until tender. Rinse broccoli and drain well. Combine onion, broccoli and 2 cups cheese. Spread mixture in greased 8 × 8 × 2-inch baking dish. Beat milk, eggs, baking mix and black pepper together until smooth. Pour over broccoli mixture. Bake at 400° for 25 to 30 minutes. Sprinkle with 1 cup cheese and bake for additional 1 to 2 minutes. Let stand for 5 minutes before cutting. Serves 8.

Gayle Williamson
Changing Thymes

Per serving

Calories 351 Protein 18.3 g Carbohydrates 21.1 g Fat 22 g Cholesterol 130 mg Sodium 612 mg

Huevos Miguel

3	slices bacon	1	tablespoon picante sauce
2	eggs	⅓	cup grated Cheddar
Dash of salt			cheese
Dash of pepper			

Microwave bacon 2 to 3 minutes on HIGH or until done, but not quite crisp. Coat an individual casserole pan with nonstick vegetable cooking spray. Arrange bacon slices side by side in casserole pan. Carefully break eggs onto the bacon. Sprinkle with salt and pepper. Top eggs with picante sauce. Cover with waxed paper. Place in microwave on ROAST and cook until center of the eggs is set. Sprinkle with cheese and return to microwave until cheese is bubbly. Serves 1.

Mary Tawney
Lone Star Legacy II

Brunch Puff

16	slices bacon, cooked and crumbled, reserve drippings	8	eggs, beaten
2	onions, sliced	4	cups milk
12	slices white bread, quartered	1½	teaspoons salt
½	pound Cheddar cheese, grated	¼	teaspoon pepper
		½	teaspoon dry mustard

Saute onion in bacon drippings until soft. Place ½ of the bread in the bottom of a greased 9 × 13 inch pan. Sprinkle ½ of bacon, onions and cheese on bread; repeat these layers. Combine eggs, milk and spices; pour over top layer. Refrigerate for at least 24 hours before cooking. Remove from refrigerator one hour before serving. Bake at 350º for 45 to 50 minutes. Serves 10 to 12.

Instead of bacon, add any one of the following: 1 pound cooked bulk sausage, 1 pound crab meat, 1 pound shrimp, cooked Italian sausage, chopped spinach or chopped broccoli.

Mrs. Bob Kelly (Margaret)
Lone Star Legacy

Hot Frittata

1	large onion, chopped	1	green bell pepper, chopped
1	can (4 ounces) chopped green chilies, drained	½	cup picante sauce
1	fresh jalapeño pepper, chopped	1	tablespoon chili powder
2	large garlic cloves, minced	2	tablespoons butter
16	little smoked sausages, cut into fourths	16	eggs, slightly beaten
1	cup peeled, steamed and diced potatoes	1½	cups grated Cheddar or Monterey Jack cheese

Sauté all ingredients except eggs and cheese in a large skillet with 2 tablespoons butter until the onion is translucent. Transfer to a lightly oiled 8 × 10 inch baking dish. Add eggs and 1 handful of cheese. Bake at 350° for 20 minutes. Remove and sprinkle remaining cheese on top. Lower temperature to 300°. Bake until brown and firm in center, 5 to 10 additional minutes. Serves 12.

Mrs. Larry Lerche (Gail)
Lone Star Legacy II

Frittata

1	cup finely chopped onions	½	teaspoon salt
2	tablespoons butter	½	cup grated Parmesan cheese
	Thyme to taste		
	Dash salt	1	cup grated Swiss cheese
1	cup chopped tomatoes	2	large tomatoes, sliced ¾ inch thick
3	eggs, beaten		
1	cup milk		

Sauté onions in butter until transparent. Add thyme, salt and tomatoes; cover and simmer 5 minutes. Uncover pan; mash tomatoes and cook until mixture is dry and thick. Set aside to cool. Beat eggs with milk and salt. Stir in grated cheeses and cooled tomato mixture. Put sliced tomatoes on bottom of a 9 inch square pan, and pour mixture on top. Bake at 350° for 30 to 35 minutes. Cut into squares and serve. Serves 4 to 6.

Mrs. Jim Carney (Jean)
Lone Star Legacy

Green Chili Eggs

Freezes well for a make-ahead dish

10	eggs	2	cups small curd cottage cheese
½	cup all-purpose flour		
1	teaspoon baking powder	4	cups (16 ounces) shredded Monterey Jack cheese
½	teaspoon salt		
¼	cup butter, melted	2	(4 ounce) cans chopped green chilies, drained

Beat eggs until fluffy. Add flour, baking powder, salt, butter, and cheeses to eggs, mixing lightly but thoroughly. Fold in chilies. Pour mixture into greased 13 × 9 × 2-inch baking pan. Bake at 350° for 35 minutes. Serves 10.

If making ahead freeze before baking. When ready to serve remove from freezer and bake 45 minutes or until firm.

Gwen Walden Irwin
Changing Thymes

Per serving

Calories 356 Protein 23.5 g Carbohydrates 8.4 g Fat 25.5 g Cholesterol 271 mg Sodium 896 mg

Mexican Scrambled Eggs

6	flour tortillas	¼	teaspoon salt
8	eggs		Dash pepper
¼	cup water		Nonstick cooking spray
2	tablespoons chopped green chilies	¾	cup picante sauce, divided
2	tablespoons picante sauce	½	cup grated Cheddar cheese, divided

Wrap tortillas in foil; bake at 350° for 7 minutes. Set aside and keep warm. Combine eggs, water, green chilies, 2 tablespoons picante sauce, salt and pepper in a large bowl; mix well with a wire whisk. Pour egg mixture into a large skillet coated with nonstick cooking spray; cook over medium heat, stirring often, until eggs are firm but still moist. Spoon equal amount of egg mixture onto each tortilla. Top with 1 tablespoon picante sauce and 1 tablespoon cheese; fold opposite sides over. Garnish each tortilla with 1 tablespoon picante sauce and ½ tablespoon cheese. Serves 6.

Barbara Beall Stanley
Lone Star Legacy II

Green Enchiladas

1	package (10 ounces) frozen chopped spinach, thawed and drained	2	cans (4 ounces each) chopped green chilies
1	can (14 ounces) chicken broth	1	pint sour cream
		12 to 16 ounces Monterey Jack cheese, grated
1	can cream of mushroom soup	2	medium onions, chopped
		2	tablespoons oil
1	can cream of chicken soup	24	corn tortillas, softly fried

Combine spinach, broth, soups and chilies in a blender until smooth. Add sour cream and set aside. Sauté onion in oil and combine with cheese, reserving some cheese for topping. Place 1 heaping tablespoon of onion mixture on each tortilla and roll up. Place in a large casserole dish; cover with reserved sauce and top with cheese. Bake at 325° for 30 minutes or until cheese melts. Serves 10 to 12.

Mrs. Denman Smith (Sandra)
Lone Star Legacy

Eggs Sonora

Salsa:

1	can (28 ounces) tomatoes	1	teaspoon salt
1	can (4 ounces) chopped green chilies, drained	¼	teaspoon dried oregano, optional
1	large onion, finely chopped	1	clove garlic, minced
2	tablespoons oil	¼	teaspoon sugar

Drain tomatoes; reserving liquid. Chop tomatoes and combine with reserved liquid and remaining ingredients. Mix well. Cover and chill for at least 2 hours before using.

Filling:

6	flour tortillas	1	medium onion, finely chopped
8	eggs, scrambled		
3	cups shredded Cheddar cheese	1	cup guacamole
		¼	cup sliced ripe olives
1	pound bacon, cooked, drained and crumbled		Sour cream
			Salsa

Warm tortillas. Layer eggs, cheese, bacon, onion, guacamole and olives evenly on each tortilla. Top with sour cream and salsa. Serves 6.

Nancy Young Moritz
Lone Star Legacy

Artichoke Quiche

2	jars (6 ounces) marinated artichoke hearts	6	crackers, crushed
		½	pound sharp Cheddar cheese, grated
12	green onions, sliced with tops		Salt and pepper
1	clove garlic, minced	1	unbaked (9 inch) pie shell
4	eggs		

Drain artichokes, reserving some marinade; chop. Sauté onions, tops and garlic in reserved marinade. Beat eggs; slowly add crackers and onion mixture. Blend in artichokes, cheese, salt and pepper. Pour into pie shell and bake at 325° for 30 to 40 minutes. Cool slightly before cutting. Serves 6 to 8.

Mrs. Larry Strickland (Linda)
Lone Star Legacy

Chilies and Sausage Quiche

2	uncooked (8 inch) pie shells	2	cups half and half cream
1	can (7 ounces) whole green chilies	½	cup grated Parmesan cheese
1	pound hot bulk sausage, cooked and crumbled	½	cup grated Swiss cheese
4	eggs, lightly beaten		Salt and pepper to taste

Line bottom of pie shells with split and seeded whole green chilies. Sprinkle sausage over chilies. Combine eggs, cream, cheeses and seasonings. Pour over sausage. Bake at 350° for 30 to 40 minutes or until top is golden brown. Remove from oven and allow to set 5 minutes before serving. Serves 8.

This quiche can be made in a 9 × 13 inch casserole without the crust. Cut into squares and serve as an appetizer.

Mrs. Chris Williston (Janice)
Lone Star Legacy

Quiche Lorraine

8	ounces Swiss cheese, cut into thin strips	8	slices bacon, cooked and crumbled
2	tablespoons flour	½	teaspoon salt
1½	cups half and half cream		Dash of pepper
4	eggs, slightly beaten	1	unbaked (9 inch) pie shell

Toss cheese with flour. Add cream, eggs, bacon and seasonings; mix well. Pour into pastry shell and bake at 350º for 40 to 45 minutes or until set. Serves 8.

Try substituting ¾ cup chopped ham for the bacon. It is just as good.

Mrs. Larry Morris (Diane)
Lone Star Legacy

Sausage Bread

1	cup raisins	3	cups all-purpose flour
1	pound hot bulk pork sausage, uncooked	1	teaspoon baking powder
		1	teaspoon ginger
1½	cups sugar	1	teaspoon pumpkin pie spice
1½	cups firmly-packed brown sugar		
		1	teaspoon baking soda
2	eggs	1	cup cold coffee
1	cup chopped pecans		

Place raisins in saucepan with water to cover. Simmer for 5 minutes. Drain. Combine raisins, sausage, sugar, brown sugar, eggs and pecans, mixing well. Combine flour, baking powder, ginger and pumpkin pie spice. Dissolve baking soda in coffee. Add coffee and dry ingredients to sausage mixture, blending well. Pour batter into greased and floured 9-inch tube pan. Bake at 350° for 1½ hours. Serves 24.

Ann Bommarito Armstrong
Changing Thymes

Per serving

Calories 270 Protein 6.48 g Carbohydrates 40 g Fat 10 g Cholesterol 33.4 mg Sodium 289 mg

Quick Pancakes

⅔	cup warm water	1	egg
2	packages yeast	1	cup milk
2	cup biscuit mix		

Make the batter by mixing all ingredients together and chill in the refrigerator. When ready to serve, pour out onto a greased griddle of skillet. Brown lightly on one side until the batter is bubbly. Turn to brown on the other side. Serves 4.

This batter can be frozen. This is a great recipe to use when feeding a crowd because the portions can easily be doubled or tripled.

Mrs. James Albrecht (Donne)
Lone Star Legacy II

Stuffed French Toast

¼	cup chopped pecans (or walnuts)	2	eggs, well beaten
4	ounces cream cheese, softened and whipped	½	cup milk
		1	teaspoon vanilla
			Pinch of nutmeg
6	slices firm textured wheat or white bread, crusts trimmed	1	tablespoon margarine
			Strawberry jam, slightly warmed, optional

Combine pecans and cream cheese. Spread mixture on 3 slices of bread and cover with remaining bread to form 3 sandwiches. Combine eggs, milk, vanilla and nutmeg, mixing thoroughly. Dip sandwiches into egg mixture. Grill in melted margarine in non-stick skillet over medium heat, turning several times, until golden brown. Cut sandwiches in halves or quarters and serve with strawberry jam. Serves 4.

This recipe is inspired by a breakfast dish served at a bed and breakfast inn in Maine. It is especially good made with homemade bread or English toasting bread.

Jeanne Cassidy
Changing Thymes

Per serving_____

Calories 376 Protein 10 g Carbohydrates 30.5 g Fat 23.5 g Cholesterol 142 mg Sodium 425 mg

BEST OF

Lone Star ★ Legacy

VEGETABLES, RICE & PASTA

Asparagus in Wine

1	pound fresh asparagus	¼	teaspoon salt
1	tablespoon olive oil		Garlic powder to taste
¼	cup dry white wine		Juice of ½ lemon

Break off tough ends of asparagus and wash. Slice large stalks in half. Slowly heat olive oil over low-medium heat; add asparagus. Add wine immediately. Sprinkle with salt and garlic powder. Simmer until tender, approximately 10 minutes. Squeeze the juice of half a lemon over asparagus just before serving. Serves 4.

Mrs. Art DeFelice (Connie)
Lone Star Legacy

Asparagus Francaise

1	pound thin asparagus	2 to 3 tablespoons spicy
2	tablespoons butter	Italian salad dressing
		Lemon juice

Cook asparagus quickly in a skillet of boiling, salted water until they are a bright, rich green. Drain in a colander and refresh with cold water. Place skillet over medium heat to melt butter; add asparagus and coat with butter. Drizzle dressing over asparagus and add fresh lemon juice to taste. Toss and serve. Serves 4.

For a variation sprinkle with a scant amount of grated Parmesan cheese.

William Furman
Lone Star Legacy II

Sesame Broccoli

1½	pounds fresh broccoli, cut into spears	1	tablespoon lemon juice
1	tablespoon sesame seeds	1	tablespoon soy sauce
1	teaspoon vegetable oil	1	tablespoon sugar

Steam broccoli over boiling water for 7 minutes or until tender. Drain, place in serving bowl and keep warm. Sauté sesame seeds in oil in saucepan over medium heat, stirring constantly, until lightly browned. Add lemon juice, soy sauce and sugar. Bring to a boil. Immediately drizzle sauce over broccoli and toss lightly to coat. Serves 4.

Vicki Ashley Atkins
Changing Thymes

Per ½ cup serving

Calories 87 Protein 5.93 g Carbohydrates 12.9 g Fat 3 g Cholesterol 0 Sodium 305 mg

Broccoli California

2	packages (10 ounces each) frozen broccoli spears	¼	cup chopped almonds
1/3	cup olive oil	2/3	cup sliced ripe olives
1	clove garlic, crushed	2	teaspoons lemon juice

Cook broccoli until tender crisp. Drain well. Heat oil and garlic for 2 minutes. Add remaining ingredients and heat thoroughly. Pour over broccoli. Serves 4 to 6.

Mrs. Drue Denton (Jan)
Lone Star Legacy II

Spinach-Stuffed Zucchini

1	(10 ounce) package frozen chopped spinach	1	cup milk
4	zucchini squash	½	cup (2 ounces) shredded Swiss cheese
3	tablespoons chopped onion		Salt and black pepper to taste
3	tablespoons margarine	1	tablespoon grated Parmesan cheese
3	tablespoons all-purpose flour		

Prepare spinach according to package directions. Drain well and press to remove excess, moisture. Cook whole zucchini in boiling water for 5 minutes. Drain. Trim ends and cut in halves lengthwise. Remove and discard pulp, leaving ¼-inch thick shells. Place in13 × 9 × 2-inch baking dish. Sauté onion in margarine until tender, Add flour and cook for 1 minute. Add milk, stirring until thickened. Add spinach, Swiss cheese, salt and black pepper to mixture. Spoon mixture into zucchini shells and sprinkle with Parmesan cheese. Bake, uncovered, at 350° for 25 minutes. Serves 8.

Kathy Gordon
Changing Thymes

Per serving_____

Calories 126 Protein 5.48 g Carbohydrates 10.6 g Fat 7.5 g Cholesterol 10.9 mg Sodium 150 mg

Spinach Madeleine

2 packages (10 ounces each) frozen chopped spinach
4 tablespoons butter
1 medium onion, chopped
2 tablespoons flour
½ cup evaporated milk
½ cup vegetable liquid
½ teaspoon pepper
¾ teaspoon Beau Monde powder
½ teaspoon garlic powder
½ teaspoon salt
1 teaspoon Worcestershire sauce
Red pepper to taste
1 roll (6 ounces) Jalapeño cheese, cubed
½ to ¾ cup buttered bread crumbs

Cook spinach according to directions. Drain and reserve liquid. Melt butter in saucepan over low heat. Sauté onions until soft, then remove from pan. Stir in flour and mix until blended and smooth, but not brown. Slowly add liquid, stirring constantly; cook until smooth and thick over low heat. Blend in seasonings and onions, stirring well. Add cheese to flour mixture, stirring until melted. Add spinach; pour into casserole. Top with crumbs. Bake at 350° until bubbly around the edges, 15 to 20 minutes. Serves 5 to 6.

This dish is better prepared the day before.

Mrs. D. D. Baker, Jr. (Agnes)
Lone Star Legacy

Cream Cheese Spinach

2 packages (10 ounces each) frozen chopped spinach
3 ounces cream cheese, softened
2 tablespoons butter
½ teaspoon instant dried onion
Parmesan cheese

Cook spinach and drain well. Mix cream cheese, butter and onion together. Stir in spinach and mix well. Place in a casserole and sprinkle top with Parmesan cheese. Bake at 350° for 20 to 25 minutes. Serves 8.

Mrs. Bill Wittenbrook (Linda)
Lone Star Legacy II

Quick Spinach and Artichoke Casserole

1	can (14 ounces) artichokes, drained and cut in half	1	stick butter, softened
2	packages (10 ounces each) frozen chopped spinach, cooked and drained	1	can (8½ ounces) water chestnuts, chopped
			Salt and pepper to taste
8	ounces cream cheese, softened	½	cup seasoned Italian bread crumbs
		2	tablespoons butter

Arrange artichoke halves in 9 inch square baking dish. Mix remaining ingredients, except bread crumbs and butter. Pour over artichokes. Cover with crumbs, dot with butter. Bake uncovered at 350° about 20 minutes. Serves 6.

This is a great freeze ahead, too.

Mrs. Jim Schultz (Mary Kay)
Lone Star Legacy

Cognac Carrots

2	cups slivered raw carrots	½	cup butter
1	teaspoon sugar	⅓	cup cognac

Place all ingredients in a covered baking dish and bake at 350° until tender, about 30 minutes. Serves 4.

Mrs. Marcus Bone (Beverly)
Lone Star Legacy II

Mexican Corn

8	ounces cream cheese	2	cans (16 ounces each) whole kernel corn, drained
¼	cup milk		
2	tablespoons butter	2	cans (4 ounces each) chopped green chilies
¼	teaspoon garlic salt		

Melt cream cheese, milk, butter, and garlic salt over low heat. Add corn and chilies. Put in casserole and bake uncovered at 350° for 20 to 25 minutes. Great with enchiladas. Serves 6.

Florence Batey
Lone Star Legacy

Potatoes and Corn Mexicano

2	pounds baking potatoes, peeled and sliced	5	tablespoons butter
Salt and pepper to taste		2	cups buttermilk
4	medium ears corn, grated	2	tablespoons minced fresh chives
1	can (4 ounces) green chilies		Monterey Jack cheese, grated

Arrange half of the potato slices in a single layer on bottom of a 9 × 13 inch buttered baking dish. Season with salt and pepper. Sprinkle with ½ cup corn and half the chilies; dot with butter. Repeat layering. Pour buttermilk over and bake at 375° for 1 hour. Remove from oven and sprinkle with chives and top with cheese; return to oven until cheese melts. Serves 6 to 8.

Mrs. Steve McMillon (Mary Beth)
Lone Star Legacy II

Jalapeño Corn Rice Casserole

1	cup uncooked rice	1	jalapeño pepper, seeded and finely chopped
1	medium onion, chopped		
1	medium green bell pepper, chopped	2	cans (17 ounces each) cream style corn
1	cup chopped celery	1	cup grated mild Cheddar cheese
½	cup butter		
1	tablespoon sugar		

Cook rice according to the package directions; set aside. Sauté onion, bell pepper and celery in butter until tender. Combine with all other ingredients and pour into a greased 2 quart casserole. Bake at 325° for 30 minutes. Serves 6.

Mrs. Andrew Tewell (Judy)
Lone Star Legacy II

Corn Pudding

2	tablespoons cornstarch	1	can (17 ounces) cream style corn
2	eggs		
¾	cup sugar	2	tablespoons butter
1	can (13 ounces) evaporated milk		

In a small casserole mix together cornstarch, eggs and sugar. Add milk and corn and mix well. Melt 2 tablespoons butter and pour over top. Bake at 325° for 1 hour and 15 minutes or until firm. The top should be slightly browned, and a knife inserted in the middle will come out clean. Serves 4 to 6.

Mrs. Bill Wittenbrook (Linda)
Lone Star Legacy II

Peg Corn

¼	cup margarine	1	can (4 ounces) diced green chilies, drained
8	ounces cream cheese, softened		Salt and pepper to taste
¼	cup milk		
2	cans (12 ounces each) shoe peg corn, drained		

Melt margarine, cream cheese and milk together in a saucepan. Add corn and chilies to cheese mixture; salt and pepper to taste. Pour into a greased casserole dish and bake at 350° for 30 minutes. Serves 8 to 10.

Mrs. Jack Ford (Connie)
Lone Star Legacy II

Acorn Squash Supreme

4 small acorn squash	1 can (20 ounces) sliced
½ cup boiling water	apples, drained
Salt to taste	Ground nutmeg
¾ cup firmly packed brown	
sugar, divided	

Wash squash and cut in half lengthwise; remove seeds and membrane. Place cut side down in shallow baking pan and add boiling water. Bake at 350° for 45 minutes or until tender. Remove from oven; turn cut side up and sprinkle with salt and 1 tablespoon brown sugar. Combine apples with remaining brown sugar. Spoon into squash cavities. Sprinkle with nutmeg. Bake at 425° for 10 minutes. Serves 4.

Good on a cold night with honey baked ham.

Mrs. Jim Rado (Vicki)
Lone Star Legacy II

Calabazo Mexicano

3 to 4 medium yellow squash	1 can (4 ounces) chopped
1 small onion, chopped	green chilies, drained
½ teaspoon salt	2 medium tomatoes, diced

Slice squash into ½ inch pieces. Cook squash and onion in saucepan with salted water to cover, until soft, approximately 10 minutes. Drain off liquid and add chilies and tomatoes. Serves 4.

Mrs. Ken Moyer (Bonnie)
Lone Star Legacy

Red Cabbage

3 tablespoons butter	6 tablespoons brown sugar
2 tablespoons minced onion	3 tablespoons cider vinegar
6 cups shredded red	1 tablespoon caraway
cabbage	seeds

Melt butter and sauté onion until tender. Add the remaining ingredients; cover and cook over low heat until tender. Serves 6.

Betty M. Williams
Lone Star Legacy II

Mushrooms a la Bordelaise

2	pounds fresh mushrooms, quartered	3	cloves garlic, minced
3	tablespoons oil	8	tablespoons fine bread crumbs
6	tablespoons butter		Salt and pepper to taste
1	bunch green onions, chopped	4	tablespoons chopped fresh parsley

Sauté mushrooms very quickly in hot oil and butter until no liquid remains and mushrooms are a little browned and crisp. Add onions, garlic and bread crumbs and sauté for just a minute after each addition. Remove from heat. Add salt, pepper and parsley. Serves 12.

Excellent as a side dish with steaks, also.

Mrs. Sid Mann (Kathi)
Lone Star Legacy II

Vegetable Fettuccine Carbonara

4	eggs	¼	cup sliced green onion
¼	cup whipping cream	1	clove garlic, minced
8	slices bacon	1	package (16 ounces) fettuccine
½	cup sliced mushrooms		
½	cup sliced carrots	¼	cup butter
½	cup sliced cauliflower	1	cup grated Parmesan cheese
½	cup frozen English peas, thawed		Salt and pepper to taste
½	cup sliced zucchini		
½	red bell pepper, seeded and cut into strips		

Beat eggs with cream in a small bowl and set aside. Cook bacon in a heavy skillet until crisp. Remove with slotted spoon and set aside. Add mushrooms, carrots, cauliflower, peas, zucchini, red bell pepper, onion and garlic to skillet, and sauté until tender crisp. Meanwhile, cook fettucine according to package directions and drain well. Transfer to a large serving bowl. Add butter and toss through. Add egg mixture and toss lightly. Add vegetables, bacon and cheese and toss again. Serve immediately. Serves 6 to 8.

Mrs. Lawrence Christian (Joyce)
Lone Star Legacy II

Frijoles Borrachos (Drunk Beans)

4	cups pinto beans, two pounds	½	teaspoon sugar	
1	tablespoon baking soda	2	tablespoons chili powder, optional	
2	chopped onions	1	tablespoon cumin, optional	
2	garlic cloves, chopped	1	teaspoon oregano, optional	
4	slices bacon	1	can beer	
1	tablespoon salt			

Cover beans with water and soak overnight. Drain and discard any bad beans. In a large pot about four times as deep as beans, cover beans with an inch of water and bring to a boil. Boil for about 15 minutes; reduce heat and slowly add baking soda. Stir until mixture foams to the top of pot, about 1 minute, and then quickly drain and rinse in a colander. Return to pot; add onion, garlic, bacon and water to cover by about two inches; cover pot and cook slowly for 2 to 4 hours. Add salt and other optional spices during the last ½ hour of cooking time along with your favorite Texas beer. Serves 8 to 10.

These beans are better the second day if there are any left.

Denman Smith
Lone Star Legacy

Frijoles Refritos (Refried Beans)

2	cups black, pinto or kidney beans	2	onions, finely chopped or grated
3	quarts water	2	cloves garlic, minced
¼ to ½ cup bacon drippings		Salt to taste	

Using a colander, wash the dried beans in cold running tap water for one minute. In a 4 quart pot, bring three quarts water to a rolling boil. Drop beans slowly into the pot so that boiling does not stop. Cook, covered, at a low boil for 3 hours, checking the water level each hour. When a bean mashes easily between two fingers; only then, are they suitable for refrying. Drain beans. In a medium sized pan, using as little drippings as possible, sauté the onions and garlic. Then add some beans, mashing them well with a wooden spoon or potato masher. Continue adding beans, mashing and cooking. Salt to taste. If too dry, add a little of the bean liquid while mashing them. Serves 12.

Mrs. Dan Steakley (Susan)
Lone Star Legacy

Black Beans

1	pound black beans	1 or 2	green bell peppers, chopped
2	quarts water		
2	teaspoons salt, divided	2	tablespoons olive oil
1	teaspoon ground cumin	1	tablespoon fresh lemon juice
1	teaspoon oregano		
¼	teaspoon dry mustard	1 or 2	jalapeño peppers, chopped
2	onions, chopped		
2 cloves garlic		¼	cup pureed tomatoes

Soak beans in water in Dutch oven overnight. For quick soak method, place beans in water, bring to a boil, cook for 3 minutes, turn off heat and let stand for 2 to 3 hours. After soaking, add 1 teaspoon salt to water. Bring to a boil and cook, covered until beans are almost tender. Black beans require a longer cooking period than other varieties. Combine 1 teaspoon salt, cumin, oregano and mustard. Chop onion and garlic in food processor. Remove from bowl. Chop bell pepper in food processor. Sauté onion and garlic in olive oil in large skillet for 5 minutes. Add bell pepper and sauté until onion is tender. Add seasoning mixture and lemon juice to vegetables. Stir in ½ cup hot bean liquid. Simmer, covered, for 10 minutes. Add seasoned vegetable mixture to beans. Stir in jalapeño peppers and tomatoes. Cook for about 1 hour or until beans are tender . To thicken, remove 1 cup beans with liquid, pour into food processor and pulse to liquefy. Return puree to beans in Dutch oven. Makes approximately 6 cups.

Serve in bowls with mound of ½ cup hot cooked rice in center, garnished with sliced green onion, lemon slice, cilantro and dollop of sour cream. Beans also make a great soup; omit preparation of 1 cup bean puree.

LaNyce Whittemore
Changing Thymes

Per ½ cup serving

Calories 87 Protein 3.92 g Carbohydrates 12.9 g Fat 2.5 g Cholesterol 0 Sodium 403 mg

Black Bean-Tortilla Casserole

2	tablespoons vegetable oil	2	cloves garlic, minced
1½	cups chopped onion	1	teaspoon ground cumin
½	cup chopped green bell pepper	2½	cups cooked black beans, drained and rinsed
1	(14½ ounce) can tomatoes, chopped, with juice	10	(6 inch) corn tortillas
¾	cup mild or medium hot picanté sauce	2½	cups (10 ounces) shredded Cheddar or Monterey Jack cheese

Sauté onion and bell pepper in oil for several minutes. Add undrained tomatoes, picanté sauce, garlic and cumin. Simmer for 10 minutes and add beans. In 13 × 9 × 2-inch casserole dish, spread ⅓ of the bean mixture over the bottom. Top with half of the tortillas, then half the cheese. Add another layer of beans, the remainder of the tortillas and cover with the rest of the bean mixture. Cover and bake for 30 minutes at 350°. Remove and sprinkle with remaining cheese and let stand for 5 minutes. Cut into squares and serve with sliced olives, green onions, sour cream and jalapeño slices. Serves 10.

Jeanne Cassidy
Changing Thymes

Per serving

Calories 281 Protein 13.4 g Carbohydrates 30.4 g Fat 12.5 g Cholesterol 25.5 mg Sodium 367 mg

Creamy Hominy Casserole

2	cans (29 ounces each) hominy, drained	½	pint whipping cream
			Salt and pepper to taste
2	cans (4 ounces each) chopped green chilies, drained	¼	cup margarine
		1	cup grated Jack or Gruyere cheese
1	carton (8 ounces) sour cream		

In a bowl, mix hominy, green chilies, sour cream, whipping cream, salt and pepper. Pour into deep casserole dish. Dot with margarine and sprinkle with cheese. Cover and bake at 350° for 30 minutes. Serves 8.

Mrs. Larry Wisian (Kay)
Lone Star Legacy

Texas Hominy

4	slices bacon	1	teaspoon Worcestershire
2	large onions, chopped		sauce
1	green pepper, chopped	1	can (10 ounces) Ro-Tel
1	can (4 ounces) mushrooms,		tomatoes and green chilies
	drained	1	teaspoon salt
1	can (29 ounces) hominy,	¼	teaspoon pepper
	drained	1	cup grated cheese

Fry bacon until crisp; drain and crumble. Add onion and green pepper to drippings; sauté until tender. Stir in mushrooms, hominy, Worcestershire, tomatoes, and seasonings. Cook 20 to 30 minutes. Stir in bacon. Alternate layers of hominy mixture and cheese in greased 2 quart casserole, ending with cheese. Bake, uncovered, at 350° for 20 minutes. Serves 6 to 8.

Mrs. Don Panter (Carolyn)
Lone Star Legacy

Herbed Green Beans

1½	pounds fresh slender	1	(4 ounce) jar diced
	green beans		pimiento, drained
½	cup sliced green onion	¼	teaspoon black pepper
½	cup sliced mushrooms	½	teaspoon dried basil
¼	cup lightly-salted margarine	½	teaspoon dried marjoram

Cook beans in small amount of boiling water for 10 to 15 minutes or until tender. Drain well. Sauté green onion and mushrooms in margarine until tender. Add green beans, pimiento, black pepper, basil and marjoram to onion and mushrooms. Cook over medium heat, stirring constantly, until thoroughly heated. Serve immediately. Serves 16.

Pamela Jones
Changing Thymes

Per ½ cup serving

Calories 44 Protein 1.03 g Carbohydrates 4.13 g Fat 3 g Cholesterol 0 Sodium 27 mg

Caliente Green Beans

1	green pepper, chopped	1	can (16 ounces) whole
1	large onion, chopped		tomatoes
1	can (4 ounces) green chilies,	1	can (4¾ ounces) tomato
	minced		purée
2	tablespoons bacon		Salt and cayenne to taste
	drippings	1	cup grated Cheddar
1	can (16 ounces) cut green		cheese
	beans, drained		

Sauté green pepper, onion and green chilies in bacon drippings until tender. Add green beans, tomatoes, tomato puree, salt and cayenne. Cook slowly for 1 hour until almost dry. Pour into a buttered 1½ quart casserole and top with cheese. Bake, uncovered, at 350° for 15 minutes, or until cheese melts. Serves 8.

Mrs. Bill Hayes (Ginger)
Lone Star Legacy

Green Beans Italiano

3	cloves garlic	2	tablespoons chopped
2 to 4 tablespoons olive oil			parsley
1	can (28 ounces) tomatoes	½	cup water
1	tablespoon oregano	2	packages (10 ounces each)
Salt and pepper to taste			frozen cut green beans

Brown garlic in olive oil. Discard the garlic. Crush the tomatoes and add to pan along with the oregano, salt, pepper, parsley and water. Boil uncovered for 15 minutes, stirring occasionally. If mixture becomes too dry, add ¼ cup water. Lower heat and add beans. Cover and simmer long enough to thaw and cook beans, about 10 minutes. Serves 6.

You may also use fresh parboiled green beans.

Mrs. Jim Rado (Vicki)
Lone Star Legacy II

Mixed Bean Casserole

1	clove garlic, minced	1	can (15 ounces) lima beans
1	medium onion, chopped	½	cup catsup
3	tablespoons bacon drippings	3	tablespoons vinegar
1	can (15 ounces) baked beans	1	tablespoon brown sugar
1	can (15 ounces) kidney beans	1	teaspoon dry mustard
		1	teaspoon salt
		¼	teaspoon pepper

Cook garlic and onions in bacon drippings until onion is limp. Pour all ingredients into a 2 quart casserole and mix. Bake at 350° for 45 minutes. Serves 6.

A great dish to serve with barbecue.

Mrs. Porter Young (Chris)
Lone Star Legacy

Vegetable Quesadillas

¼	cup seeded, diced tomato	1	teaspoon chopped cilantro
¼	cup diced yellow or red bell pepper	2	(6 inch) flour tortillas
2	tablespoons chopped green onion	½	cup (2 ounces) shredded Monterey Jack cheese
1	teaspoon seeded, chopped hot chili pepper	1	teaspoon vegetable oil or margarine

Combine tomato, bell pepper, green onion, chili pepper and cilantro. Set aside. In 10-inch non-stick skillet over medium heat, cook each tortilla about 1 minute on each side or until flexible. Place on plate. Sprinkle ¼ cup cheese on ½ of each tortilla. Top with ½ of vegetable mixture. Fold tortilla over to cover filling. Repeat with second tortilla. Heat oil in skillet and cook folded tortillas for 1 to 2 minutes on each side or until cheese is melted. Cut tortillas in halves to serve. Serves 2.

Barbara Bittner
Changing Thymes

Per serving

Calories 220 Protein 9.73 g Carbohydrates 17.4 g Fat 12.5 g Cholesterol 25.3 mg Sodium 298 mg

Vegetable Medley Casserole

1	(11 ounce) can white corn, drained
1	(16 ounce) can French-style green beans, drained
½	cup chopped celery
½	cup chopped green bell pepper
½	cup chopped onion
½	cup (2 ounces) grated Cheddar cheese
½	cup sour cream
1	(10¾ ounce) can cream of celery soup, undiluted
	Salt and black pepper to taste
½	cup margarine, melted
1½	cups crushed round buttery crackers

Combine corn, beans, celery, bell pepper, onion, cheese, sour cream and soup. Season with salt and black pepper. Pour mixture into 13 × 9 × 2-inch baking dish or 2-quart casserole. Combine melted margarine and cracker crumbs. Sprinkle on vegetable mixture. Bake, uncovered, at 350° for 45 minutes. Makes approximately 6 cups.

Linda Moore
Changing Thymes

Per ½ cup serving

Calories 178 protein 3.44 g Carbohydrates 12.2 g Fat 13.5 g Cholesterol 12 mg Sodium 553 mg

Fried Okra

1	quart young okra
2	quarts boiling water
2	teaspoons salt
	Salt and pepper
2	cups yellow cornmeal
2	cups cooking oil

Wash okra, discard stems, cut into ¼ inch pieces. Parboil in 2 quarts salted boiling water for 5 to 7 minutes. Drain in colander. Sprinkle with salt and pepper and roll in cornmeal. Let rest for 20 to 30 minutes so the cornmeal will stick to the okra when ready to fry. Fry in deep oil just a few minutes until golden. Drain on paper towels, and season with salt and pepper. Serves 4.

S. D. Jackman
Lone Star Legacy II

Mushrooms Florentine

1	pound fresh mushrooms	¼	cup chopped onion
1	tablespoon margarine	¼	cup margarine, melted
2	(10 ounce) packages frozen	1	cup (4 ounces) grated
	chopped spinach, thawed		Cheddar cheese
1	teaspoon salt	⅛	teaspoon garlic salt

Cut stems from mushrooms. Sauté stems and caps in 1 tablespoon margarine until browned. Drain and set aside. Remove excess liquid from spinach by pressing between paper towels. Combine spinach, salt, onion and melted margarine. Spread mixture in 13 × 9 × 2-inch baking dish. Sprinkle ½ cup cheese on spinach, layer mushrooms on cheese, season with garlic salt and top with remaining cheese. Bake at 350° for 20 minutes or until cheese is melted. Serves 12.

Pamela Jones
Changing Thymes

Per ½ cup serving

Calories 104 Protein 4.7g Carbohydrates 4.73 g Fat 8 g Cholesterol 9.92 mg Sodium 341 mg

Fried Onion Rings

1½ cups flour	3 very large yellow onions
1½ cups beer, active or flat,	3 to 4 cups shortening or
cold or at room temperature	vegetable oil

Make a batter by combining flour and beer in a large bowl; blend thoroughly. Cover the bowl and allow the batter to sit at room temperature for no less than 3 hours. Preheat oven to 200°. Carefully peel the onions and cut into ¼ inch thick slices. Separate the slices into rings and set aside. Melt enough shortening in a 10 inch skillet to come to a two inch depth. Heat the shortening to 375°. Dip onion rings into the batter and place in hot fat. Fry rings, turning once or twice, until they are a golden color. Drain on paper towels. To keep warm, place on middle shelf of preheated oven. To freeze, arrange on a cookie sheet. When frozen, pack in plastic bags. To reheat, arrange on cookie sheets and place in a preheated 400° oven for 4 to 6 minutes. Serves 6.

Mrs. Larry Hall (Jane)
Lone Star Legacy

Artichoke Casserole

1	(14 ounce) can artichoke hearts, drained and quartered	1	(10¾ ounce) can cream of mushroom soup, undiluted
3	hard-cooked eggs, sliced	¼	cup milk
½	cup pimiento-stuffed green olives, sliced	½	cup buttered breadcrumbs
¼	cup water chestnuts, sliced	½	cup (2 ounces) grated Cheddar cheese

Layer artichoke hearts, eggs, olives and water chestnuts in greased 9 × 9 × 2-inch baking dish. Blend soup and milk together. Pour over ingredients in casserole dish. Top with breadcrumbs and cheese. Bake, uncovered, at 350° for 25 to 30 minutes or until bubbly and browned. Serves 8.

This dish is a tradition in our family with all holiday meals. The only disagreement is who gets to bring it! We rarely have leftovers and, when we do, they don't last long.

Betty M. Williams
Changing Thymes

Per ½ cup serving

Calories 144 Protein 6.55 g Carbohydrates 10.8 g Fat 9 g Cholesterol 88.4 mg Sodium 646 mg

Potatoes Romanoff

5	green onions, chopped	5	large potatoes, cooked and cubed
1	carton (12 ounces) cottage cheese		Salt and pepper to taste
1	carton (8 ounces) sour cream	1	cup grated Cheddar cheese

Combine onions, cottage cheese, sour cream, potatoes, salt, and pepper in a 1½ quart casserole. Top with grated cheese. Bake at 350° for 40 minutes. Serves 6.

Mrs. Larry Strickland (Linda)
Lone Star Legacy

Twice Baked Potatoes

6	medium potatoes, baked	½	cup chopped green onions
½	cup butter	1	cup grated Cheddar
½	cup half and half cream		cheese
½	cup sour cream	1	cup finely chopped
12	slices bacon, cooked, crumbled and divided		spinach, frozen or fresh, optional

Slice the top off the potatoes when they are cool enough to handle. Scoop potatoes from skins and put skins aside to refill. Whip potatoes, butter, cream and sour cream until fluffy. Stir in most of bacon and green onions. Stuff potato skins; top with remaining bacon and cheese. Bake at 350° until heated through, about 20 to 30 minutes. If spinach is used, it should be squeezed as dry as possible and should be added with the bacon and green onions. Serves 6.

Cookbook Committee
Lone Star Legacy II

Oven Potato Fans

2	large potatoes, peeled	⅛	teaspoon seasoned salt
¼	cup butter, melted		

Cut potatoes in half lengthwise. Place outside down in baking dish. Score diagonally about ½ through with knife. Pour melted butter and salt over. Bake at 325° for 1 hour, until golden brown. Spoon butter over occasionally. Serves 4 (or 2 if you're skinny).

Mrs. Jim Schultz (Mary Kay)
Lone Star Legacy

Grilled Cajun Potatoes

4	large potatoes, cut in ½ inch slices	¼	teaspoon red pepper
½	teaspoon minced garlic	¼	teaspoon oregano
⅓	cup margarine, melted	¼	teaspoon paprika
½	teaspoon salt	2	tablespoons chopped parsley
¼	teaspoon black pepper		

Combine potatoes, garlic, margarine, salt, black pepper, red pepper, oregano and paprika, tossing to mix. Pour into 13 × 9 × 2-inch microwave-safe dish. Cover with plastic wrap, vented slightly. Microwave on high (100 percent) setting for 6 to 8 minutes, stirring halfway through cooking time. Let stand for 3 minutes. Place potato slices on hot grill, reserving butter mixture. Grill potatoes for 5 minutes on each side. Place potatoes in serving bowl. Add reserved butter mixture and parsley, tossing to mix. Serve immediately. Serves 8.

Sally Guyton Joyner
Changing Thymes

Per serving

Calories 169 Protein 2.26 g Carbohydrates 23.5 g Fat 7.5 g Cholesterol 0 Sodium 210 mg

Potato Casserole

6	medium potatoes, peeled	1	teaspoon salt
1	(12 ounce) carton small-curd cottage cheese	1	tablespoon butter, melted
⅓	cup sour cream	¼	cup toasted slivered almonds
2	tablespoons minced onion		

Cook potatoes in water until tender. Drain. Mash until smooth. Combine potatoes, cottage cheese, sour cream, onion and salt. Spread mixture in lightly greased 2-quart casserole. Drizzle with butter and sprinkle with almonds. Bake, uncovered, at 350° for 30 minutes or until thoroughly heated. Makes approximately 8 cups.

Linda Moore
Changing Thymes

Per ½ cup serving

Calories 97 Protein 4.25 g Carbohydrates 13 g Fat 3.5 g Cholesterol 5.92 mg Sodium 228 mg

Chantilly Potatoes

12 large potatoes	1 cup whipping cream,
4 tablespoons butter	whipped
½ cup milk	8 tablespoons grated
Salt and pepper	Cheddar cheese

Peel and wash potatoes and cook in boiling salted water until done. Drain and mash with the butter and milk and beat until light and fluffy. Season with salt and pepper. Pour into a buttered casserole. Cover with whipped cream and sprinkle with cheese. Bake at 350° until browned on top. Serves 12.

Mrs. Stephen Scheffe (Betsy)
Lone Star Legacy II

Praline Sweet Potatoes

5 cups mashed cooked sweet potatoes	1 cup firmly-packed brown sugar
1 cup sugar	⅓ cup all-purpose flour
2 eggs	1 cup finely chopped
1 teaspoon vanilla	pecans
⅓ cup milk	
½ cup plus ⅓ cup butter or margarine, divided	

Combine sweet potatoes, sugar, eggs, vanilla, milk and ½ cup butter. Using electric mixer, beat until smooth. Spread mixture in greased 13 × 9 × 2-inch baking dish. Combine brown sugar, flour, ⅓ cup butter and pecans, mixing to crumb consistency. Sprinkle on sweet potato mixture. Bake at 350° for 30 minutes. Serves 12.

This is a Thanksgiving and Christmas tradition in our family. I have never found anyone who didn't like this dish—even those who don't like sweet potatoes love it!

Barbara Hoover McEachern
Changing Thymes

Per ½ cup serving

Calories 405 Protein 3.77 g Carbohydrates 53.5 g Fat 20.5 g Cholesterol 66.5 mg Sodium 158 mg

Sweet Potato Supreme

Sweet Potato Layer:

4 to 5 sweet potatoes	1 cup brown sugar
½ cup butter	Salt to taste
1 teaspoon cinnamon	Milk
½ teaspoon nutmeg	

Peel and cube potatoes and boil until tender. Mash potatoes with butter, cinnamon, nutmeg, brown sugar and salt. Add enough milk to make mashed potato consistency. Pour into a 10 inch baking dish.

Topping:

4 tablespoons butter	¼ teaspoon salt
½ cup sugar	1 teaspoon vanilla extract
2 tablespoons milk	½ cup chopped pecans

Combine butter, sugar, milk and salt in a saucepan and cook over low heat, stirring until thick and bubbly. When cool, add vanilla. Sprinkle chopped pecans over sweet potatoes, then pour the topping over the pecans. Bake at 400° for 15 to 20 minutes. Serves 6.

Mrs. Bryan Wooten (Sherri)
Lone Star Legacy II

Mom's Cornbread Dressing

1	recipe of cornbread	1½	cups water
1	package (8 ounces) herb seasoned stuffing	2½	cups turkey stock
		3	eggs, well beaten
2 to 3 slices dry white bread, crumbled		1	teaspoon salt
		½	teaspoon pepper
1	teaspoon sage	½	cup chopped onion
½	teaspoon onion salt	2	teaspoons margarine

Crumble cooled cornbread into a large bowl. Add seasoned stuffing, bread, sage, onion salt and water. Mix well and refrigerate overnight. The next day, add turkey stock, eggs, salt and pepper to mixture; sauté onions in margarine and add. Mix thoroughly, adding water as needed, to make moist dressing. Do not use milk to thin. Pour into a greased oblong baking dish and bake at 325° for 1 hour or until lightly browned. Serves 8 to 10.

I make cornbread from a mix, adding 1 tablespoon sugar per recipe. The dressing can be made ahead and frozen either before or after baking. This was a requested Christmas present from my mother, Ruth Buckellew in 1971.

Mrs. Ken Moyer (Bonnie)
Lone Star Legacy II

Jalapeño Dressing

1 bunch green onions,	3½ cups chicken broth
½ stalk celery with leaves, chopped	1 cup jalapeño pepper juice
½ cup bacon drippings	½ teaspoon salt
1 cup water	⅛ teaspoon black pepper
8 cups crumbled cornbread	1 to 3 jalapeño peppers, chopped
4 cups crumbled day-old bread	

Sauté onion and celery in bacon drippings. Add water and cook, covered, for about 7 minutes or until tender. Combine vegetables and liquid, breads, broth and jalapeño juice. Season with salt and pepper. Add jalapeño peppers to taste. Add water to bread mixture as needed to achieve a very moist consistency. Spoon dressing into cavity of 20 pound turkey, placing extra dressing in greased casserole. Bake casserole at 350° for 30 minutes. Makes approximately 12 cups.

Family tradition at Thanksgiving—only in Texas! Mom always makes one pan of regular dressing for the weak at heart and one pan of jalapeño dressing.

Nancille Sewell Willis
Changing Thymes

Per ½ cup serving

Calories 357 Protein 9.13 g Carbohydrates 52.8 g Fat 12 g Cholesterol 38.4 mg Sodium 926 mg

Curried Orange Rice

¼ cup butter	1 cup chicken broth
1 medium onion, thinly sliced	1 teaspoon salt
2 teaspoons curry powder	½ cup seedless raisins
1 cup uncooked rice	1 bay leaf
1 cup orange juice	

Melt butter in heavy saucepan. Sauté onion until soft and golden but not brown. Stir in curry and rice. Cook two minutes longer, stirring constantly. Add remaining ingredients; stir with fork. Bring to boiling; lower heat; cover and simmer 15 to 20 minutes, or until rice is tender and liquid has been absorbed. Remove bay leaf before serving. Serves 6.

Mrs. B.L. Turlington (Jill)
Lone Star Legacy

Arroz Con Salsa Verde

1 carton (8 ounces) sour cream	2 cups cooked rice
1 can (4 ounces) Herdez Salsa Verde or green chilies, chopped	6 ounces Monterey Jack cheese, grated
	2 ounces American cheese, grated

Combine sour cream and salsa (or green chilies). Place thin layer of rice in bottom of buttered 1½ quart casserole. Add a layer of Monterey Jack cheese, topped by the sour cream mixture. Repeat layers, ending with rice. Bake at 350° for 10 to 15 minutes. Put reserved American cheese on top. Return to oven until cheese melts, approximately 5 minutes. Mixture should be heated through and cheese melted. Serves 6.

Mrs. Dudley D. Baker (Kathy)
Lone Star Legacy

Lemon Cilantro Rice

4 cups chicken broth	1 tablespoon vegetable oil
2 cups uncooked regular rice	Zest of 1 lemon
2 teaspoons salt or to taste	Juice of 1 lemon
1 teaspoon cracked black pepper	3 to 4 tablespoons chopped cilantro
2 medium-sized onions, minced	

Pour broth into large saucepan. Bring to a boil. Stir in rice, salt and black pepper. Reduce heat and simmer for 18 to 20 minutes. Sauté onion in oil until translucent. Stir in lemon zest. Add onion mixture, lemon juice and cilantro to cooked rice, fluffing with fork. Let stand for 4 to 5 minutes to blend flavors before serving. Makes approximately 8 cups.

Instant rice can be used. Follow package directions, substituting broth for water.

Barbara Pate Bannister
Changing Thymes

Per ½ cup serving

Calories 105 Protein 2.99 g Carbohydrates 19.4 g Fat 1.5 g Cholesterol 0 Sodium 462 mg

Pecan Rice

1 cup uncooked brown rice	1 cup toasted pecans
2¼ cups chicken broth	1 teaspoon Worcestershire
½ cup diced green onion	sauce
1 cup diced celery	1 teaspoon salt or to taste
2 tablespoons margarine	Black pepper to taste

Combine rice and broth in sauce pan. Bring to a boil, reduce heat and simmer, covered, for 35 minutes. Let stand for 10 minutes after heat has been turned off. Sauté onion and celery in margarine until vegetables are tender. Add pecans and Worcestershire sauce, tossing to mix. Combine rice and vegetable mixture. Season with salt and black pepper. Makes 5½ cups.

Jeanne Cassidy
Changing Thymes

Per ½ cup serving_____

Calories 158 Protein 3.29 g Carbohydrates 15.7 g Fat 9.5 g Cholesterol 0 Sodium 248 mg

Pecan Wild Rice Casserole

1 box (6 ounces) wild and	1 cup chopped green onions
long grain rice	½ cup minced fresh parsley
½ cup butter	1 cup pecan halves
½ pound fresh mushrooms	

Prepare rice according to package directions. Sauté mushrooms and onions in butter until tender. Mix rice, vegetables, parsley and pecans together in a 1 quart casserole dish. This may be refrigerated or held until ready to bake uncovered at 350° for 30 minutes. Serves 4 to 6.

If refrigerated, allow extra time for baking.

Mrs. Chris John (Anne)
Lone Star Legacy II

Mushroom and Brown Rice Pilaf

1	tablespoon all-purpose flour	½	teaspoon salt
1	tablespoon vegetable oil	¾	teaspoon dried whole thyme
2½	cups sliced fresh mushrooms	½	teaspoon garlic powder
½	cup chopped onion	¼	teaspoon ground red pepper
¼	cup chopped red bell pepper	1	(14 ounce) package instant brown rice
2¼	cups chicken broth		
1½	cups water		

Combine flour and oil in large saucepan prepared with vegetable cooking spray. Cook over medium heat, stirring constantly, until lightly browned. Add mushrooms, onion and bell pepper to flour paste. Cook, stirring constantly, until vegetables are tender. Stir broth, water, salt, thyme, garlic powder and red pepper into vegetable mixture. Bring to a boil. Add rice to vegetables and liquid. Simmer, covered, for 10 minutes or until liquid is absorbed and rice is tender. Remove from heat and let stand for 5 minutes. Makes approximately 8 cups.

Vicki Ashley Atkins
Changing Thymes

Per ½ cup serving _____

Calories 115 Protein 3.26 g Carbohydrates 21.2 g Fat 2 g Cholesterol 0 Sodium 179 mg

Arroz Con Tomaté

2	tablespoons olive oil	1	cup long grain rice
½	cup chopped green bell pepper	1	cup peeled and chopped tomato
¼	cup finely chopped onion	1	teaspoon salt
1	clove garlic, minced	⅛	teaspoon pepper
½	teaspoon dried basil	2	cups water
½	teaspoon dried rosemary		Jalapeño peppers, optional

In a skillet cook the bell pepper, onion, garlic, basil and rosemary in hot oil until tender. Stir in rice, chopped tomatoes, salt, pepper and water. Cover and cook over low heat for about 20 minutes or until rice is done. Serves 6.

Cyndee McBee
Lone Star Legacy II

Mexican Rice

1½ cups long grain white rice
Hot water to cover
⅓ cup peanut oil
½ pound tomatoes, chopped
¾ cup chopped onion

½ tablespoon minced garlic
3½ cups chicken broth
½ teaspoon salt
⅛ teaspoon pepper

Wash rice in cold water 3 times. Pour hot water over rice in pot and let sit for 20 minutes. Drain rice and rinse well in cold water. Shake colander well and let drain for 10 minutes. Heat oil in skillet until it smokes. Give rice a final shake to remove moisture. Stir into hot oil until grains are well covered with oil; fry until light golden color, stirring and turning rice over to cook evenly and not stick to bottom of skillet, about 10 minutes. Be sure flame is high or rice will be mushy. Tip pan to one side and pour off any excess oil. Blend tomato, onion and garlic until smooth and add to fried rice. Cook over high heat, stirring and scraping pan until mixture is dry. Add broth, salt and pepper and stir well. Cook over medium heat uncovered, without stirring until liquid is absorbed and small air holes appear. Remove from heat; cover tightly with lid or aluminum foil for 30 minutes. Before serving, stir well from bottom of the pan. Serves 10.

S. D. Jackman
Lone Star Legacy II

Shelley's Barley Pilaf

1 cup pearl barley
⅓ cup pine nuts, cashews
   or pecans
¼ cup butter
1 cup chopped green onion

½ cup chopped parsley
¼ teaspoon salt
¼ teaspoon black pepper
3½ cups boiling chicken broth

Rinse barley in cold water and drain. Sauté nuts in butter until lightly browned. Remove nuts with slotted spoon and set aside. Sauté onion and barley in butter until lightly toasted. Remove from heat. Add parsley, salt, black pepper, nuts and broth to barley mixture. Pour into buttered 2-quart casserole. Bake at 350° for 1 hour and 10 minutes. Makes approximately 4 cups.

Martha Rife
Changing Thymes

Per ½ cup serving

Calories 211 Protein 5.96 g Carbohydrates 22.7 g Fat 12 g Cholesterol 15.5 mg Sodium 461 mg

Jalapeño Grits

¾ cup uncooked regular grits
3½ cups water
Dash of salt
2   eggs or ½ cup egg substitute

½ cup margarine
1½ cups (6 ounces) shredded
    jalapeño cheese

Combine grits and salted water in saucepan. Bring to a boil and cook for 5 minutes. Remove from heat. Stir eggs, margarine and jalapeño cheese into grits mixture. Pour into 1½-quart casserole prepared with vegetable cooking spray. Bake at 325° for 45 minutes. Makes approximately 4 cups.

Pamela Jones
Changing Thymes

Per ½ cup serving

Calories 260 Protein 8.26 g Carbohydrates 12.2 g Fat 20 g Cholesterol 75.4 mg
Sodium 318 mg

Sausage Cheese Grits

1 package (1 pound) bulk
   hot saugage
1 cup instant grits
1 teaspoon salt
4 cups boiling water

1 stick margarine
1 roll (6 ounces) garlic
   cheese
2 eggs, slightly beaten
½ cup milk, approximately

Cook hot sausage in skillet until brown; drain and set aside. Add salt to boiling water and stir in grits. Cook according to package directions. Add 1 stick margarine and the roll of garlic cheese to hot grits. Put beaten eggs into a measuring cup and fill with enough milk to make one cup. Add to grits mixture. Crumble cooked sausage into grits mixture and place in a buttered 2 quart casserole. Bake at 350° for one hour. Serves 6 to 8.

Mrs. Ken Moyer (Bonnie)
Lone Star Legacy

Pasta Ricotta

²/₃ cup ricotta or cottage cheese
½ cup grated Parmesan cheese

Dash of nutmeg
1 package (8 ounces) pasta
2 tablespoons butter
Salt and pepper to taste

Mash cheeses together and add seasoning. Cook pasta in salted, boiling water and place into a hot buttered casserole. Stir in cheese mixture, add butter, and bake at 350° for 5 to 7 minutes. Serves 4.

This pasta goes well with anything or can be eaten alone with a glass of good red wine.

Mrs. Joe Bowles (Mary)
Lone Star Legacy II

Pasta with Texas Pecan Sauce

1 pound fettucine or linguine
1 clove garlic, minced
2 tablespoons olive oil
½ cup butter, melted

1½ to 2 cups Texas pecans
¼ cup chopped parsley or spinach
Salt and white pepper to taste

Cook pasta al dente. While pasta is cooking, sauté garlic in olive oil and mix with melted butter. Finely chop pecans and parsley or spinach in food processor. Drain cooked pasta and immediately toss with butter and garlic mixture. Add pecans and parsley or spinach and season to taste with salt and white pepper. Serves 4 to 6.

Mrs. Denman Smith (Sandra)
Lone Star Legacy II

Calabrian Style Pasta with Broccoli

1 bunch broccoli, broken into pieces
2 teaspoons olive oil
2 cloves garlic, minced
2 pounds ripe tomatoes, coarsely chopped
3 tablespoons raisins
2 to 3 tablespoons sunflower seeds

Salt and pepper
¼ teaspoon oregano
¼ teaspoon sweet basil
1 pound tortellini pasta
3 tablespoons minced parsley for garnish

Steam broccoli until it is a tender, bright green, about 7 minutes. Rinse under cold water and set aside. Heat oil in a heavy saucepan and sauté the garlic until it is golden brown. Add tomatoes and simmer 15 minutes, uncovered. Add raisins and sunflower seeds and simmer 5 minutes. Season with salt, pepper, oregano and sweet basil. While sauce is simmering, heat the water for pasta and cook about 6 to 8 minutes at full boil. Spoon cooked pasta into a large, warmed serving dish. Spoon on the sauce, add broccoli and toss. Garnish with parsley. Serves 6 to 8.

Mrs. Don Bradford (Melinda)
Lone Star Legacy II

Fettuccine Supreme

1 package (8 ounces) fettuccine
¼ cup whipping cream
½ cup butter, melted
½ teaspoon dried basil

¼ cup minced fresh parsley
Dash of pepper
1 cup freshly grated Parmesan cheese

Cook fettuccine according to package directions; drain. Add whipping cream, butter, basil, parsley and pepper. Toss until noodles are well-coated. Add Parmesan cheese and toss gently. Serve immediately. Serves 6.

Mrs. Marcus Bone (Beverly)
Lone Star Legacy II

Fettucine Alla Carbonara

¼ pound thick sliced bacon	½ cup grated Parmesan cheese
¾ pound fettucine	
1 tablespoon olive oil	½ teaspoon black pepper
6 cloves garlic, minced	½ teaspoon red pepper
¼ cup dry white wine	¼ cup chopped parsley
2 eggs, room temperature	
½ cup heavy cream, room temperature	

Slice bacon into ¼ to ½ inch pieces and blanch in boiling water for 2 minutes. Drain well. Cook fettucine according to package directions. Heat olive oil and sauté bacon until it starts to brown. Add the garlic and sauté for 1 to 2 minutes. Add the wine and simmer until wine evaporates. Mix eggs, cream and cheese in a small bowl. Drain cooked pasta well and add to skillet with bacon mixture. Toss and add the egg mixture; toss again, adding the peppers and parsley. Serve immediately. Serves 4.

You can easily change this recipe by sautéing any fresh vegetables you have on hand, such as carrots, peas, or cauliflower. This makes a good light supper with a tossed salad.

Mrs. Jim Rado (Vicki)
Lone Star Legacy II

Light Pasta Primavera

1	(8 ounce) package angel hair pasta	2	cups sliced fresh mushrooms
2	cups chopped broccoli	½	teaspoon salt
1	cup thinly sliced carrots	½	teaspoon black pepper
½	cup sliced green onion	½	cup red wine
2	cloves garlic	2	tablespoons freshly grated Parmesan cheese
1	tablespoon dried basil		
3	tablespoons low-fat margarine		

Prepare pasta according to package directions. While pasta cooks, prepare sauce. Sauté broccoli, carrots, onion, garlic and basil in margarine for 5 minutes or until vegetables are crisp tender. Add mushrooms, salt, black pepper and wine. Simmer for 2 minutes or until mushrooms are tender. Drain pasta. Serve vegetables and sauce over warm pasta, sprinkling each serving with Parmesan cheese. Serves 4.

Dayna Beikirch
Changing Thymes

Per serving

Calories 379 Protein 12.7 g Carbohydrates 61 g Fat 8 g Cholesterol 2.46 mg Sodium 416 mg

Garden Fresh Pasta Marinara

Capellini or linguini works best

1	(8 ounce) package pasta
1	tablespoon olive oil
2	cloves garlic, minced
¼	large onion, chopped
½	pound fresh mushrooms, sliced
2	large vine ripened tomatoes, peeled and coarsely chopped
½	cup tomato sauce
⅛	teaspoon Italian seasoning

1	tablespoon chopped fresh basil or ⅛ teaspoon dried basil
¼	cup dry white wine (optional)
	Salt and black pepper to taste
	Freshly grated Parmesan cheese (optional)

Prepare pasta according to package directions while chopping vegetables for sauce. Heat a sauté pan at medium temperature. Add olive oil. Sauté garlic and onion in oil just until onions begin to soften. Add mushrooms and continue sautéing until onions are translucent. Add tomatoes and sauté 2 minutes more. Stir in the remaining ingredients (excluding Parmesan cheese) and simmer for 5 to 8 minutes; covered. (Be careful not to overcook the tomatoes! They should be soft but not mushy.) Ladle sauce over warm pasta. Sprinkle with freshly grated Parmesan cheese, if desired. Serves 4.

For variety, add ½ pound peeled and deveined fresh shrimp and simmer until opaque, or add 2 grilled and sliced chicken breasts and simmer until chicken is thoroughly heated.

Vicki Ashley Atkins
Changing Thymes

Per serving

Calories 281 Protein 9.54 g Carbohydrates 51.2 g Fat 5 g Cholesterol 0 Sodium 264 mg

Shells and Cheddar Florentine

2	cups uncooked shell pasta	1	(10 ounce) package
1	cup low-fat cottage cheese		frozen chopped spinach,
1	tablespoon Dijon mustard		thawed and well drained
²/₃	cup low-fat sour cream	3	tablespoons chopped
½	teaspoon black pepper		chives
2	cups (8 ounces) shredded low-fat Cheddar cheese, divided		

Prepare pasta according to package directions. While pasta cooks, prepare sauce. Combine cottage cheese and mustard in food processor. Process until smooth. Place in large bowl. Stir in sour cream and black pepper. Drain pasta well. Add to cottage cheese mixture. Blend 1½ cups Cheddar cheese, spinach and chives into pasta mixture. Pour into 13 × 9 × 2-inch baking dish prepared with butter-flavored cooking spray. Sprinkle with ½ cup Cheddar cheese. Bake at 350° for 25 minutes or until lightly browned. Serves 12.

Chopped frozen broccoli or frozen peas can be substituted for spinach. Non-fat sour cream can be substituted for low-fat sour cream.

Vicki Ashley Atkins
Changing Thymes

Per serving

Calorie 136 Protein 10.3 g Carbohydrates 15.6 g Fat 3.5 g Cholesterol 9.92 mg Sodium 121 mg

Cajun Chicken with Pasta

½ (8 ounce) package fettuccine or linguine
2 (4 ounce) skinless, boneless chicken breast halves
1/3 medium-sized red bell pepper
1/3 medium-sized green bell pepper

1 teaspoon chopped shallots
2 tablespoons butter
½ teaspoon Cajun spice
½ cup whipping cream
Salt and black pepper to taste

Prepare pasta according to package directions. While pasta is cooking, prepare sauce. Slice chicken and peppers into strips. Sauté chicken, red and green bell pepper and shallots in butter in large skillet over medium heat for 5 to 10 minutes or until chicken is just done. Sprinkle Cajun spice on chicken mixture. Stir in cream. Season with salt and black pepper. Keep warm. Drain pasta and rinse to prevent sticking. Add in chicken sauce and toss to mix thoroughly. Serve immediately. Serves 4.

Red and green bell peppers make this spicy and very colorful. Serve with salad, French bread and wine.

Patsy Eppright
Changing Thymes

Per serving_____

Calories 371 Protein 16.7 g Carbohydrates 26.8 g Fat 22 g Cholesterol 90.7 mg Sodium 109 mg

Aunt Adeline's Asparagus Pasta

½	pound lean ground beef	2	tablespoons olive oil
1	tablespoon parsley	3	cups sliced fresh
2	slices white bread,		asparagus
	soaked in water	1	tomato, chopped
1	egg	2	cups water
1	clove garlic, pressed	1	(8 ounce) package
⅓	cup (1⅓ ounces) grated		fettuccine, linguine or
	Romano cheese		other pasta, broken
Salt and black pepper to taste			in 1½ inch pieces
1	medium-sized onion,		
	chopped		

Combine beef, parsley, bread, egg, garlic, Romano cheese, salt and black pepper. Shape into ½-inch meatballs. Sauté onion in oil until tender. Add asparagus and sauté until lightly brown. Seasoned with salt and pepper. Add tomato and water to vegetables. Bring to a boil. Drop meatballs into a sauce. Reduce heat and simmer for 20 to 25 minutes or until thoroughly cooked. While meatballs are cooking, prepare pasta according to package directions. Drain well and place in serving bowl. Add sauce to pasta, toss to mix and serve immediately. Serves 8.

This recipe has been in my family since time begun. My great grandfather came to America from Sicily in the early 1900's and was convinced that unless you ate pasta at least once a day, you had not eaten!

Ann Bommarito Armstrong
Changing Thymes

Per serving_____

Calories 299 Protein 16.7 g Carbohydrates 32.7 g Fat 11.5 g Cholesterol 59.1 mg Sodium 152 mg

BEST OF

Lone Star ★ Legacy

MAIN DISHES

200

Monterey Chicken

4	chicken breasts, skinned, boned and halved	2	tablespoons flour
Salt and pepper		1	teaspoon salt
½	cup flour	½	teaspoon white pepper
½	cup butter, divided	½	cup chicken stock
½	cup chopped onion	½	cup white wine
1	clove garlic, minced	1	avocado, mashed
8	ounces mushrooms, chopped	1½	cups grated Monterey Jack cheese, divided
		¼	cup chopped green chilies, optional

Place chicken between 2 sheets of waxed paper and pound until about ¼ to ½ inch thick. Sprinkle with salt, pepper and flour. Quickly sauté in ¼ cup butter until golden. Remove to plate and add remaining ¼ cup butter to pan and sauté onion, garlic and mushrooms slowly until cooked but not browned. Stir in flour, salt, pepper, chicken stock and wine. Cook until thickened, about 5 minutes. Stir in mashed avocados and ½ cup cheese. Arrange chicken breasts in glass baking dish. Top with sauce, remaining cheese and green chilies if desired. Bake at 350° for 10 minutes. Serves 8.

Best of the Best 1999.

Mrs. Denman Smith (Sandra)
Lone Star Legacy II

Lemon-Herb Chicken Breast

6	chicken breasts	1	teaspoon rosemary
3	large cloves garlic	1½	teaspoons pepper
Juice of 3 lemons		1½	teaspoons salt
½	cup olive oil		

Rinse chicken breasts with skins on, pat dry and set aside. Combine remaining ingredients and mix well. Using a large freezer bag, combine chicken with liquid mixture and marinate for 12 hours. Turn bag occasionally. Remove chicken from bag and drain. Grill over mesquite chips, or bake uncovered at 350° for 1 hour. Serves 6.

This recipe takes only a few minutes in the morning to prepare, making the supper hour more relaxed and enjoyable.

Mrs. Dan S. Steakley (Susan)
Lone Star Legacy II

Party Stuffed Chicken Breasts

4	whole chicken breasts, halved and boned	1	package (3 ounces) chicken coating mix
6	ounces Gruyere or Swiss cheese, grated	¼	cup butter or margarine
¼	pound salami, diced	¼	cup flour
½	cup chopped green onions	2	cups milk
1	egg, beaten		Parsley or watercress

Preheat oven to 400°. Put each piece of chicken between 2 sheets of waxed paper. Pound with mallet until ¼ inch thick; set aside. Toss 1 cup cheese, salami and green onion. Put ¼ cup cheese mixture in center of each breast. Roll up and fasten with toothpick. Dip chicken in beaten egg; then roll in coating mix. Place in 9 × 13 inch greased casserole. Bake for 40 minutes until brown. Meanwhile, make sauce. Melt butter in small saucepan. Stir in flour until bubbly and smooth. Gradually beat in milk. Cook and stir until thick. Add remaining cheese; remove from heat and stir until melted. Pour over baked chicken. Garnish with parsley or watercress. Serves 8.

Each serving contains about 360 calories.

Mrs. Larry Lerche (Gail)
Lone Star Legacy II

Chicken Capers

2	tablespoons oil	½	teaspoon rosemary
1	onion, coarsely chopped	½	cup vermouth
2	teaspoons Hungarian sweet paprika	1	tablespoon capers
1	pound boneless chicken breasts	2	tablespoons tomato paste
			Salt and pepper to taste
1	tomato, cubed	½	cup plain yogurt

Sauté onion and paprika in hot oil until onion is translucent. Add chicken breasts and cook quickly until they lose their pink color. Add tomato, rosemary, vermouth and capers. Cook over moderate heat for about 30 minutes. Stir in tomato paste. Season with salt and pepper. Stir in yogurt. Serves 2.

Mrs. Cecil Smith (Diana)
Lone Star Legacy II

Chicken Stew

2	chickens	5	ribs celery, chopped
4	cups sliced okra	1	medium onion, chopped
4	medium green bell	3	teaspoons salt
	peppers, chopped	2	teaspoons pepper
2	jalapeño peppers, seeded	2	teaspoons basil
	and chopped	1	teaspoon garlic powder
5	carrots, chopped		Cooked rice

Boil chicken and save broth. Remove from broth and debone, cutting chicken into bite sized pieces. Place okra, bell pepper, jalapeños, carrots, celery and onions in chicken broth. Cover and cook until tender. Add seasonings and chicken and cook until heated. Serves 8 to 10.

If desired, add one can of cream of mushroom, chicken or celery soup. Serve over rice.

Mrs. Charlie Tupa (Sidney)
Lone Star Legacy II

Island Chicken

1	can (8 ounces) pineapple chunks	1	tablespoon soy sauce
2	pounds chicken pieces	1	clove garlic, minced
2	tablespoons shortening	1	green bell pepper, seeds
1	can (10 ¾ ounces) chicken broth		removed and cut in squares
¼	cup white vinegar	4	tablespoons cornstarch
2	tablespoons brown sugar	¼	cup water

Drain pineapple chunks, saving syrup. Brown chicken slowly in shortening; pour off fat. Add reserved syrup, broth, vinegar, sugar, soy sauce and garlic. Cover; cook over low heat 40 minutes. Add bell pepper and pineapple chunks; cook 5 minutes more or until chicken is tender, stirring occasionally. Combine cornstarch and water; gradually stir into sauce. Cook, stirring, until thickened. Serve with cooked parsley rice. Serves 4.

Mrs. Ron Bruney (Carol)
Lone Star Legacy II

Artichoke Chicken Casserole

4	pounds chicken pieces	2	cloves garlic, minced
1	cup butter	½	tablespoon red pepper
½	cup flour	1	can (6 ounces)
3½	cups milk		mushrooms, drained
3	ounces Swiss cheese, cubed	2	cans (14 ounces each) artichoke hearts, drained
2	ounces Cheddar cheese, cubed	1	package (12 ounces) noodles

Cook and debone chicken, saving broth. Cut chicken into bite sized pieces. In a saucepan make a cream sauce of the butter, flour and milk. Add cheeses, spices, mushrooms, artichokes and chicken. Cook noodles in chicken broth. Drain noodles and put into a 9 × 13 baking dish. Pour the chicken mixture over the noodles and bake at 350º for 30 minutes. Serves 8.

Mrs. Terry Jackson (Joyce)
Lone Star Legacy II

Jalapeño Chicken

2	cups chopped onions	4	green onions, tops only
2	tablespoons butter	½	teaspoon salt
1	package (10 ounces) frozen chopped spinach, cooked and drained	1	large package (12 ounces) Doritos
6	jalapeño peppers	4 to 6	cups chopped, cooked chicken
1	pint sour cream		
2	cans cream of chicken soup	2	cups grated Monterey Jack cheese

Sauté onions in butter; blend in spinach, jalapeños, sour cream, soup, onion tops and salt. In a large Pyrex pan alternate layers of Doritos, chicken, spinach mixture and cheese. Layer again ending with cheese: Bake at 350° for 30 to 40 minutes. Serves 10 to 12.

Mrs. Jim Schultz (Mary Kay)
Lone Star Legacy

Chicken Enchiladas

12 corn tortillas	**¼** cup butter
½ cup oil	**¼** cup flour
2 packages (8 ounces each) Monterey Jack cheese	**2** cups chicken broth
	1 cup sour cream
1 chicken, cooked and diced	**1** can (4 ounces) jalapeños or
¾ cup chopped onion	green chilies, sliced

Spicy Sauce:

1 finely chopped tomato	**¼** cup tomato juice
½ cup chopped onion	**½** teaspoon salt
2 jalapeños, chopped	

Dip tortillas in hot oil until soft. Place 2 tablespoons cheese, 1½ tablespoons chicken, and 1 tablespoon onion in each tortilla; roll up. Place seam side down in a 9 × 13 inch casserole. Melt butter in saucepan; blend flour. Add broth; cook, stirring constantly until mixture thickens and bubbles. Stir in sour cream and peppers. Cook until heated through, but do not boil. Pour over tortillas. Bake at 350° for 30 minutes. Sprinkle remaining cheese on top and cook 5 more minutes or until cheese melts. Mix spicy sauce ingredients and serve on top of the enchiladas. Serves 6.

Mrs. Don Panter (Carolyn)
Lone Star Legacy

Sour Cream Chicken Enchiladas

3½ cups sour cream, divided
2 cups cooked chicken
1 can (4 ounces) green chilies, drained
⅓ cup diced onion
1 teaspoon chili powder
½ teaspoon salt

½ teaspoon garlic powder
¼ teaspoon pepper
Salad oil
12 corn tortillas
⅓ pound Cheddar cheese, grated

About 1 hour before serving, in a 13 × 9 inch pan, spread 1 cup sour cream; set aside. In a 2 quart saucepan, flake chicken; add ½ cup sour cream, green chilies, onion, chili powder, salt, garlic powder and pepper. Cook over low heat, stirring occasionally, just until heated. Preheat oven to 450°. In an 8 inch skillet with ½ inch salad oil, fry each tortilla a few seconds on each side or until soft. Spread ¼ cup chicken mixture along center of each tortilla. Fold sides over filling and place seam side down in sour cream. Spread enchiladas with remaining sour cream, then sprinkle with cheese. Bake 8 minutes or until cheese is melted. Serves 6.

Joyce Dailey
Lone Star Legacy II

Tamales Vera Cruz

12	chicken, port or beef tamales, cut in 2-inch pieces	3	slices bacon, cooked and crumbled
4	cups chopped cooked chicken	1	cup chicken broth
		1	tablespoon chili powder
2	cups fresh, frozen or canned corn, drained	½	teaspoon salt
		1	tablespoon Worcestershire sauce
2	cups canned tomatoes	1	cup (4 ounces) grated sharp Cheddar cheese
½	cup raisins		
½	cup sliced green olives		

Combine tamales, chicken, corn, tomatoes, raisins, olives and bacon. Blend broth, chili powder, salt and Worcestershire sauce together. Add to tamale mixture, mixing lightly. Pour into greased 4-quart casserole. Bake at 350° for 40 to 45 minutes. Sprinkle cheese on tamale mixture and continue baking until cheese is melted and lightly browned. Serve with black beans. Serves 12.

Jeanne Cassidy
Changing Thymes

Per serving

Calories 488 Protein 36.6 g Carbohydrates 29 g Fat 25.5 g Cholesterol 103 mg Sodium 1156 mg

Salsa Chicken

1	small bunch broccoli	2	large or 3 medium tomatoes, diced
1½	cups chopped onion		
3	large cloves garlic, minced	1	(16 ounce) can kidney beans
1	tablespoon olive oil		
1	cup chopped red bell pepper	1	cup medium hot salsa
1	pound skinless, boneless chicken breast, cut in bite-sized chunks	¼	cup chopped cilantro (optional)
			Salt and black pepper to taste

Cut broccoli in bite-sized pieces and steam for 2 to 3 minutes, drain and set aside. Sauté onion and garlic in oil in large non-stick skillet or Dutch oven for 3 minutes or until softened. Add bell pepper and sauté for 2 minutes. Add chicken, tomatoes, broccoli, beans, salsa and cilantro to onion mixture. Over medium heat, bring to a boil, stir lightly, reduce heat and simmer, covered, just until chicken is cooked. Season with salt and black pepper. Serves 6.

Serve over rice or angel hair pasta.

Terre Churchill
Changing Thymes

Per serving_____

Calories 217 Protein 23.9 g Carbohydrates 22.9 g Fat 4 g Cholesterol 43.8 mg
Sodium 656 mg

Spanish Style Chicken

5 pounds chicken pieces
Flour
Salt and pepper
4 tablespoons oil
½ cup minced onion
1 can (10¾ ounces) tomato soup

1 jar (6 ounces) stuffed olives, sliced
Dash of hot pepper sauce
1 can (10 ounces) green peas
1 jar (6 ounces) mushroom pieces

Salt and pepper chicken pieces and coat with flour. Heat oil in skillet and brown chicken. Remove chicken to warm platter. Remove all but 2 tablespoons of oil from skillet. Sauté onion, then add soup and olives and simmer for 10 minutes. Add chicken, hot pepper sauce, liquid from peas and mushrooms. Simmer until chicken is tender, about 30 minutes. Add peas and mushrooms. Thicken, if desired, with flour and cold water paste. Serve with rice. Serves 8 to 10.

S. D. Jackman
Lone Star Legacy II

Pollo de Rado

½ cup butter, softened
1 clove garlic, minced
1 fryer, cut into pieces
3 cups chicken broth, divided

Salt and pepper
Paprika
8 ounces fresh mushrooms
Chopped parsley for garnish

Combine butter and minced garlic and spread on chicken pieces. In a metal pan place chicken pieces skin side up. Add 1 cup chicken broth and broil until brown. Turn over and lightly broil the other side. Remove pan from the broiler and turn chicken skin side up. Add 2 cups of broth and season with salt, pepper and paprika. Lower oven temperature to 350° and bake chicken for 25 minutes. Add mushrooms, making certain mushrooms are covered with broth. Return pan to oven and bake until mushrooms are cooked to your taste. Serve chicken on a platter surrounded by mushrooms. Sprinkle a little chopped parsley on top. Serves 4 to 6.

Mrs. Jim Rado (Vicki)
Lone Star Legacy II

Chicken Marsala

1	teaspoon salt	4	tablespoons butter,
½	teaspoon pepper		divided
½	cup flour	1	cup sliced fresh
4	chicken breast halves,		mushrooms
	skinned and boned	½	cup Marsala wine
2	tablespoons olive oil	½	cup chicken broth, divided

Combine salt, pepper and flour. Dredge chicken lightly on both sides. Shake off excess flour. Heat oil and 2 tablespoons butter in a skillet over medium heat. Brown chicken pieces for 3 minutes on each side; remove from skillet and keep warm. Sauté mushrooms in pan drippings. Add wine and ¼ cup broth. Boil for 2 minutes, stirring constantly. Return chicken to pan and simmer covered for 15 minutes. Remove chicken again to warm platter; add remaining broth and boil pan drippings until thickened. Remove from heat and stir in remaining 2 tablespoons butter. Pour over chicken and serve. Serves 4.

Serve with wild rice, fresh buttered carrots and a crisp green salad.

David Bradberry
Lone Star Legacy II

Savory Chicken Casserole

6	chicken breasts	1	can (6 ounces)
1	cup chopped green pepper		mushrooms, sliced
1	cup chopped onion	1	jar (7½ ounces) stuffed
1	cup chopped celery		olives, sliced
½	cup butter	1	package (12 ounces) green
½	pound Velveeta cheese		noodles
1	can cream of mushroom soup		

Boil chicken in salted water; drain and reserve chicken stock. Bone and dice chicken. Sauté green pepper, onion, and celery in butter. Add Velveeta and melt. Blend in soup, mushrooms and olives. Add chicken and 1 cup of reserved stock. Boil noodles in remaining stock until done; add to chicken mixture. Bake at 350º for 30 minutes in a large casserole dish. Serves 8 to 10.

Mrs. Wayne Davison (Cindi)
Lone Star Legacy

Easy Chicken Divan

2	packages (10 ounces each) frozen broccoli stalks	½	teaspoon curry powder,
2	cups sliced cooked chicken	½	cup shredded sharp cheese or ⅓ cup grated Parmesan cheese
1	cup mayonnaise		
2	cans cream of chicken soup	½	cup bread crumbs
1	teaspoon lemon juice	1	tablespoon butter, melted

Cook broccoli as directed until tender; drain. Arrange stalks in a greased oblong baking dish. Place chicken over broccoli. Combine mayonnaise, soup, lemon juice and curry powder. Pour over chicken. Sprinkle with cheese. Combine crumbs and butter and sprinkle over all. Bake at 350° for 25 to 30 minutes. Serves 6.

Mrs. Ed Cornet (Kathi)
Lone Star Legacy

Parmesan Chicken

1	fryer, skinned and cut in pieces	½	cup grated Parmesan cheese
1	stick melted butter	¼	cup chopped parsley
2	cups cracker crumbs	1	teaspoon garlic salt
⅓	cup grated Romano cheese		Salt and pepper to taste

Dip chicken pieces in butter, then in a mixture of remaining ingredients. Place chicken in a large baking pan and bake uncovered at 350° for 1 hour. Serves 4 to 6.

Mrs. Norman Snider (Natalie)
Lone Star Legacy

211

Lemon Honey Chicken

1	fryer (3 pounds), cut in pieces	1	egg yolk, slightly beaten
Salt and pepper		2	tablespoons lemon juice
¼	cup oil	2	tablespoons soy sauce
¼	cup honey	¼	teaspoon nutmeg
		1	teaspoon paprika

Season chicken with salt and pepper; place in a baking dish. Combine remaining ingredients and mix until well blended. Pour over chicken and bake uncovered at 350° for 1 hour or until tender. Turn and baste chicken while baking. Serves 4 to 6.

Mrs. David Armour (Betsy)
Lone Star Legacy

Chicken Breasts Supreme

2	tablespoons butter, divided	1	tablespoon cornstarch
Salt and pepper		⅓ to ½ cup white wine or sherry	
4	chicken breasts, skinned		
½	pint whipping cream	1	cup grated Swiss cheese

Melt 1 tablespoon butter in a large skillet with salt and pepper. Add chicken breasts and brown lightly. Remove to a casserole. In same skillet add another tablespoon of butter, whipping cream, and cornstarch. Cook slowly and stir; add white wine. When sauce thickens, pour over the chicken. Cover generously with grated cheese. Bake covered at 350° for 1 hour. Remove top the last few minutes so the cheese will brown. Serves 4.

Mrs. Joe Bowles (Mary)
Lone Star Legacy

Chinese Chicken

8 boned chicken breasts
¾ cup white wine or dry sherry
2 tablespoons soy sauce
½ cup flour
¼ cup oil
1 teaspoon ginger
½ teaspoon salt
1 large green pepper, chopped

¼ cup chopped green onion
¼ pound fresh mushrooms, sliced
¼ cup sliced almonds
1 can (8 ounces) sliced water chestnuts
Hot rice or fried rice

Cut breasts into bite size pieces. Marinate in wine and soy sauce for 1½ hours. Lightly coat chicken in flour and brown. Set aside. Place oil, ginger and salt in skillet or wok; stir fry green pepper, onions and mushrooms. When just tender, add chicken, almonds and water chestnuts. Stir fry until well mixed. Serve with rice or fried rice. Serves 6 to 8.

Mrs. Sam White (Jane)
Lone Star Legacy

Light Italian Chicken with Basil

4	skinless, boneless chicken breast halves	2	medium plum tomatoes, diced
2	tablespoons all-purpose flour	2	teaspoons fresh lemon juice
½	teaspoon salt		Grated peel of 1 lemon
½	teaspoon dried oregano	1½	teaspoons chicken bouillon granules
3	tablespoons low-fat margarine, divided	½	cup water
1	medium-sized onion, diced	¼	cup sliced basil leaves or ½ teaspoon dried basil
2	medium zucchini, cut in bite-sized pieces		Basil leaves or parsley sprigs for garnish

Cut each piece of chicken in half and pound to ¼-inch thickness. Combine flour, salt and oregano. Dredge chicken pieces in seasoned flour to coat. Sauté chicken in 2 tablespoons margarine in non-stick 12-inch skillet, turning to brown on both sides. Remove and keep warm. Add 1 tablespoon margarine to skillet. Add onions and sauté until golden. Add zucchini and cook, stirring occasionally, until golden and tender-crisp. Add tomatoes, lemon juice, lemon peel, bouillon and water to vegetables. Over high heat, bring to a boil and cook for 1 minute, scraping skillet to dislodge browned bits. Stir in sliced basil. Arrange chicken on platter. Spoon sauce over chicken and garnish with basil leaves or parsley. Serves 4.

Sally Guyton Joyner
Changing Thymes

Per serving————————————————————————————

Calories 202 Protein 29.2 g Carbohydrates 10.5 g Fat 5 g Cholesterol 68.6 mg Sodium 651 mg

214

Chicken and Chestnuts

2	tablespoons all-purpose flour	1	(8 ounce) can water chestnuts, drained and sliced
Salt and black pepper to taste			
8	skinless, boneless chicken breast halves	1	(4 ounce) can sliced mushrooms, drained
¼	cup vegetable oil	2	tablespoons chopped green bell pepper
¾	cup sautérne or white wine		
1	(10¾ ounce) can cream of chicken soup, undiluted	¼	teaspoon thyme

Combine flour, salt and black pepper. Dredge chicken pieces in seasoned flour. Sauté chicken in oil, turning to lightly brown on all sides. Place chicken in 3-quart casserole. Add wine to pan drippings. Stir in soup, water chestnuts, mushrooms, bell pepper and thyme. Simmer for 2 minutes. Pour sauce over chicken. Bake, covered, at 350° for 45 minutes. Remove cover and bake for 15 to 20 minutes or until tender. Serves 8.

Pam Posey Brown
Changing Thymes

Per serving _____

Calories 181 Protein 14.9 g Carbohydrates 7.15 g Fat 8.5 g Cholesterol 35.6 mg Sodium 319 mg

Chicken Dressed for Dinner

8	skinless, boneless chicken breast halves	½	cup white wine or water
8	slices Monterey Jack cheese	1	cup herb-seasoned stuffing mix, crushed
1	(10¾ ounce) can cream of chicken soup, undiluted	¼	cup butter or margarine, melted

Place chicken in greased 13 × 9 × 2-inch baking dish. Arrange cheese slices on chicken. Combine soup and wine, blending well. Spoon over chicken. Sprinkle with stuffing mix and drizzle with butter. Bake at 350° for 45 to 55 minutes. Serves 8.

Kathy Marsh
Changing Thymes

Per serving _____

Calories 279 Protein 21.7g Carbohydrates 5.5 g Fat 17.5 g Cholesterol 60.9 mg Sodium 496 mg

Orange Chicken Italiano

4	skinless chicken breast halves	1	small onion, chopped
1	cup orange juice	1	large tomato, chopped
½	cup white wine	¼	pound fresh mushrooms, sliced
	Paprika to taste	1	teaspoon peanut, canola or olive oil
½	tablespoon Italian seasoning		

Place chicken in shallow baking dish. Combine juice and wine and pour over chicken. Sprinkle with paprika and Italian seasoning. Bake, uncovered, at 350° for 30 minutes. While chicken bakes, sauté onion, tomatoes and mushrooms in oil until onion is translucent. Spoon vegetables over chicken and bake uncovered for 1 hour more. Serves 4.

Serve over brown rice with a fresh steamed vegetable and crusty Italian bread.

Vicki Ashley Atkins
Changing Thymes

Per serving

Calories 207 Protein 28.9 g Carbohydrates 10.9 g Fat 3 g Cholesterol 68.4 mg Sodium 83.1 mg

Stir Fry Chicken

1/3	cup sherry	1	cup broccoli flowerets
2 to 3 tablespoons soy sauce		2	cups bean sprouts
1/2	teaspoon sugar	2	cups pea pods
Dash of ground ginger		1	(8 ounce) can sliced water
Dash of mustard			chestnuts, drained
4	skinless, boneless chicken	1/2	pound fresh mushrooms,
	breast halves, cut in 2-inch		sliced
	strips	1	cup chicken broth
3	tablespoons vegetable oil	1	tablespoon cornstarch
4	small carrots, thinly sliced		

Combine sherry, soy sauce, sugar, ginger and mustard, mixing well. Add chicken strips and chill for 1 hour. Drain chicken, reserving marinade. Heat oil to 350° in skillet. Add chicken and stir fry for 2 to 3 minutes. Remove chicken from skillet. Add cut vegetables and stir fry for 2 minutes. Remove vegetables from skillet and drain. Combine broth, reserved marinade and cornstarch, blending well. Pour into skillet. Add vegetables and cook, stirring often, until slightly thickened. Add chicken to vegetables and sauce and heat through. Serves 4.

Serve over rice or Chinese noodles.

Julie Clark
Changing Thymes

Per serving

Calories 240 Protein 20.7 g Carbohydrates 26.4 g Fat 5 g Cholesterol 34.2 mg Sodium 1055 mg

217

Chinese Chicken Rolls

1	cup shredded cabbage	2	skinless, boneless chicken
1	green onion, minced		breast halves
¼	cup thinly sliced celery		Salt and black pepper to taste
1	teaspoon soy sauce	1	chicken bouillon cube
⅛	teaspoon ground ginger	½	cup boiling water

About 1 hour before serving, combine cabbage, onion celery, soy sauce and ginger in a small bowl. Set aside. Cut chicken breasts in halves lengthwise. Pound to ¼-inch thickness. Season with salt and black pepper. Place ¼ of cabbage mixture on each chicken piece. Roll up, jelly roll fashion, and secure with wooden picks. Place in baking dish. Dissolve bouillon in boiling water. Pour over chicken rolls. Bake, covered with aluminum foil, at 350° for 30 minutes. Remove foil and bake for additional 15 minutes. Serves 2.

Mary Francis
Changing Thymes

Per serving———————————————————

Calories 155 Protein 28. 9 g Carbohydrates 4.45 g Fat 2 g Cholesterol 68.8 mg Sodium 1363 mg

Crunchy Pecan Chicken

½	cup all-purpose flour	2	eggs
½	cup cornmeal	¼	cup water
¾	cup finely chopped pecans	8	skinless, boneless chicken
1 to 2 tablespoons Creole			breast halves
	seasoning	½	cup vegetable oil

Combine flour, cornmeal, pecans and Creole seasoning, mixing well. In separate bowl, blend eggs and water. Dip chicken in egg mixture, then into pecan mixture, coating each piece completely. Cook chicken in oil in heavy skillet over medium high heat for about 10 minutes on each side. Remove from skillet and drain. Serves 8.

Kathy Gordon
Changing Thymes

Per serving———————————————————

Calories 402 Protein 31.3 g Carbohydrates 14.9 g Fat 24.5 g Cholesterol 121 mg Sodium 96.3 mg

Chicken Poppicotti

4	**(6 ounce) skinless boneless whole chicken breasts**	**¼**	**cup grated Parmesan cheese**
12	**ounces cream cheese, softened**	**2**	**tablespoons ricotta cheese**
¼	**cup plus 2 tablespoons cottage cheese**	**½**	**teaspoon granulated garlic**
		2	**pinches of white pepper**
		4	**ounces fresh spinach, torn**

Pound rough side of chicken breasts until flattened. Thoroughly blend all remaining ingredients, except for spinach. Add spinach but do not overmix. Stuff each breast with mixture and fold over. Sauté stuffed chicken pieces in non-stick skillet prepared with vegetable cooking spray for 2 minutes on each side, turning carefully. Place in baking dish. Bake at 350° for 8 to 10 minutes or until chicken is done. Serves 4.

The Old Pecan St. Café
Changing Thymes

Per serving_____

Calories 661 Protein 49.1 g Carbohydrates 4.81 g Fat 49 g Cholesterol 213 mg Sodium 607 mg

Chicken Florentine with Mushroom Sauce

Best of the Best Recipes 1999

½   cup minced onion
1   tablespoon margarine
2   (10 ounce) packages
    frozen chopped spinach,
    thawed and drained

1   cup (4 ounces) shredded
    Swiss cheese
½   teaspoon ground nutmeg
4   skinless, boneless chicken
    breast halves, pounded flat

Mushroom Sauce:
2   cups sliced fresh
    mushrooms
1   tablespoon margarine
2   teaspoons lemon juice

1   cup chicken broth
1   cup milk
½   cup dry white wine
White pepper to taste

Sauté onion in margarine. Remove from heat and add spinach, cheese and nutmeg. Spoon spinach mixture into 4 mounds in lightly-greased 13 × 9 × 2-inch baking dish. Place chicken piece over each mound. Bake at 350° for 20 to 30 minutes or until chicken is done. Sauté mushrooms in margarine until liquid evaporates. Add lemon juice, broth, milk, wine and white pepper to mushrooms. Bring to a boil and cook until liquid is reduced by ⅔ and sauce slightly thickened. Spoon ¼ of sauce over each serving. Serves 4.

Ginny Ashley
Changing Thymes

Per serving⎯⎯⎯⎯⎯⎯⎯⎯⎯⎯⎯⎯⎯⎯⎯⎯⎯⎯⎯⎯⎯⎯⎯⎯⎯⎯⎯⎯⎯

Calories 540 Protein 47.6 g Carbohydrates 19.2 g Fat 29.5 g Cholesterol 124 mg Sodium 578 mg

Chicken in Bow Ties

1 (12 ounce) package bow tie pasta
2 tablespoons pine nuts
3 skinless, boneless chicken breast halves, thinly sliced
1 tablespoon olive oil, divided
Salt and black pepper to taste
2 small red bell peppers, thinly sliced
2 shallots, minced
2 cloves garlic, minced
1 cup low-salt chicken broth
¼ cup balsamic vinegar
2 teaspoons chopped rosemary or 1 teaspoon dried rosemary
1 (9 ounce) package frozen artichoke hearts, thawed

Prepare pasta according to package directions, cooking until tender but firm. Drain and rinse with cold water. Set aside. Toast pine nuts in small skillet over medium heat for 3 to 4 minutes or until golden brown and fragrant, stirring almost constantly. Set aside. Sauté chicken in 2 teaspoons oil in non-stick skillet over high heat for 2 to 3 minutes or until just cooked through. Season with salt and black pepper. Using slotted spoon, remove from skillet and set aside. Sauté bell pepper, shallots and garlic in 1 teaspoon oil in skillet for 2 minutes or until bell pepper is tender. Using slotted spoon, remove from skillet and set aside. Pour broth and vinegar into skillet. Add rosemary. Bring to a boil. Add artichokes and cooked pasta to hot liquid. Cook for 2 minutes or until thoroughly heated. Add chicken and vegetables to pasta and toss to mix. Pour into serving dish and sprinkle with pine nuts. Serve warm. Serves 6

Pamela Jones
Changing Thymes

Per serving _____

Calories 379 Protein 25.6 g Carbohydrates 50.5 g Fat 9 g Cholesterol 34.2 mg Sodium 187 mg

Chicken Bombers

6	tablespoons cream cheese with chives	6	skinless, boneless chicken breast halves, pounded flat
6	tablespoons butter	6	slices bacon

Place 1 tablespoon cream cheese and 1 tablespoon butter in center of each chicken breast. Roll tightly. Wrap 1 bacon slice around each chicken roll. Place in greased 13 × 9 × 2-inch baking dish. Bake, uncovered, at 350° for 45 minutes. Serves 6.

Kids love these, especially because of their silly name!

Vicki Stafford Bohls
Changing Thymes

Per serving_____

Calories 353 Protein 33.2 g Carbohydrates .424 g Fat 23.5 g Cholesterol 119 mg Sodium 255 mg

Sweet and Sour Barbecued Chicken

1	jar (8 ounces) apricot preserves	1	bottle (8 ounces) Russian dressing
1	envelope dry onion soup mix	2	broiler chickens, quartered

Mix together sauce ingredients. Place chicken in large baking pan. Spoon sauce over chicken and bake at 350° for 1½ hours. Serves 8.

Serve with rice. Also good with Catalina French dressing and jelled cranberry sauce.

Mrs. Jerry Hunt (Gail)
Lone Star Legacy

Citrus Ginger Grilled Chicken

½   cup fresh lime juice
2   tablespoons orange or
     lime marmalade
2   teaspoons minced ginger
1   large clove garlic, minced
¼   cup dry white wine
¼   cup safflower oil

⅛   teaspoon freshly ground
     black pepper
6   skinless, boneless chicken
     breast halves
3   tablespoons butter,
     softened
Lime wedges for garnish

Combine lime juice, marmalade, ginger, garlic, wine, oil and black pepper in jar with tight-fitting lid. Shake to blend well. Reserve 1 tablespoon. Place chicken in shallow glass dish or plastic bag and add marinade. Marinate for 2 to 6 hours. Blend reserved marinade and butter, mixing with wooden spoon. Place on waxed paper or plastic wrap and roll to cylinder shape. Chill until firm. Grill chicken over medium heat for 7 to 10 minutes, turn and grill for additional 7 to 10 minutes, basting occasionally with marinade. As chicken completes cooking, bring remaining marinade to a boil and cook for 45 seconds. Place chicken on individual serving plates. Cut chilled butter mixture into ¼-inch slices and place on chicken. Garnish with lime wedges and serve immediately with heated marinade as sauce. Serves 6.

Serve chicken with steamed fresh vegetables and rice pilaf.

La Nyce Whittemore
Changing Thymes

Per serving_____

Calories 295 Protein 23.7 g Carbohydrates 2.61 g Fat 19.5 g Cholesterol 88.1 mg Sodium 131.75 mg

Picnic Cornish Hens

Cornish hens	Minced shallots
Salt and pepper	Butter
Dijon mustard	White wine
White bread crumbs	

Rub each bird with salt and pepper and one tablespoon mustard. Sprinkle with bread crumbs. Place in a square of foil and fold up sides. Add 1 teaspoon minced shallots, 1 tablespoon butter and 3 tablespoons wine to each package. Seal foil over tightly. Bake at 400° for 45 minutes. Open foil; baste hen, and bake 15 minutes more until browned. Reseal foil and carry to picnic. Good served cold. If serving at home, stuff cavity with fresh parsley and serve juices separately. Servings equal number of hens prepared.

Mrs. Leo Mueller (Nancy)
Lone Star Legacy

Mrs. Lyndon B. Johnson's Recipe for Barbecued Chicken

1	chicken, quartered	¼	cup lemon juice
Salt and pepper to taste		¼	cup vinegar
¼	cup butter	¼	cup catsup
Garlic, to taste		¼	cup Worcestershire sauce
Chopped onion, to taste			

Wash and drain chicken. Season with salt and pepper and place in pan large enough that pieces do not overlap. Melt butter in saucepan, add garlic and onion, if desired, and sauté until transparent. Add remaining ingredients and bring to a boil. Broil chicken until golden brown on both sides. Add sauce and cook uncovered in oven for about 1 hour or until nice and tender. Baste often.

LBJ Ranch
Lone Star Legacy

Barbecued Lemon Chicken

Must be marinated at least 6 hours

2	(2 to 3 pound) broiler-fryers, halved or quartered, or 4 to 6 pounds chicken pieces	2	teaspoons basil
		2	teaspoons onion powder
		1	teaspoon paprika
1	cup vegetable oil	½	teaspoon dried thyme
½	cup fresh lemon juice	1	clove garlic, chopped
1½	teaspoons salt		

Place chicken in large heavy plastic zipper-lock bag or baking dish. Combine oil, lemon juice, salt, basil, onion powder, paprika, thyme and garlic in a jar and shake well. Pour marinade over chicken. Marinate, covered, in refrigerator overnight or for at least 6 hours. Remove from refrigerator 1 hour before cooking. Drain and reserve marinade. Grill chicken over low heat, skin side up, for 20 to 25 minutes, brushing with marinade. Turn chicken and grill, skin side down, for 20 minutes or until done. Serves 10.

La Nyce Whittemore
Changing Thymes

Per serving_____

Calories 479 Protein 34.28 g Carbohydrates .775 g Fat 37 g Cholesterol 138 mg Sodium 533 mg

225

Old Fashioned Chicken and Dumplings

4	chicken breasts or 1 whole chicken	1	tablespoon dried parsley
6	cups water	2	tablespoons margarine
1	teaspoon salt	¼	teaspoon celery seed
1	tablespoon minced onion	1	teaspoon pepper
1	tablespoon instant chicken bouillon	1	cup milk

Dumplings:

2	cups flour	2	eggs
1	teaspoon salt	½	cup milk

In a large pot combine chicken, water, salt and onion, and boil until done. Remove chicken, cool and debone. Cut into bite size pieces. Save broth for cooking.

Mix dumpling ingredients to form a very stiff dough and drop by teaspoons into boiling chicken broth. Add deboned chicken, and remaining ingredients; boil 20 minutes, stirring occasionally. Keep warm until serving. If broth is not thick enough, add flour and water. If broth is too thick, add more milk. Serves 6.

Mrs. Larry Wisian (Kay)
Lone Star Legacy

Mexican Lasagna

1½ pounds ground turkey or ground beef
1 (17 ounce) can whole kernel corn, drained
1 cup picanté sauce
1 (15 ounce) can tomato sauce or Italian style tomatoes
1 envelope taco seasoning
1 (16 ounce) carton cottage cheese
2 eggs
1 teaspoon oregano
10 corn tortillas
1½ cups (6 ounces) shredded Cheddar or Monterey Jack cheese

In a 12-inch skillet, brown meat, stirring to crumble. Drain excess grease. Add corn, picanté sauce, tomato sauce and taco seasoning. Simmer for 5 minutes. Combine cottage cheese, eggs and oregano, mixing thoroughly. Place 5 tortillas in bottom of lightly greased 13 × 9 × 2-inch baking dish, overlapping to fit. Layer, in order listed, ½ of meat mixture, cheese mixture, 5 tortillas and remaining meat mixture. Sprinkle with cheese. Bake, uncovered, at 375° for 30 minutes. Let stand 10 minutes before serving. Serves 12.

Gwen Walden Irwin
Changing Thymes

Per serving_____

Calories 386 Protein 29.4 g Carbohydrates 25.7 g Fat 19 g Cholesterol 112 mg Sodium 783 mg

Cornish Hens Rosé

For more intense herb flavor, cover and refrigerate 2 to 3 hours before baking.

4	Cornish game hens, split lengthwise	½	teaspoon onion powder
2	cups light rosé wine, divided	½	teaspoon celery seeds
½	teaspoon black pepper	½	teaspoon poultry seasoning
½	teaspoon garlic powder	½	teaspoon paprika
		½	teaspoon dried basil

Place hen halves, cavity side up, in 9 × 9 × 1½-inch baking dish. Pour 1½ cups wine over hens. Combine seasonings and sprinkle ½ of mixture over hens. Bake, uncovered, at 350° for 1 hour. Turn hens over. Pour ½ cup wine over hens and sprinkle with remaining seasoning mixture. Bake for additional 30 minutes, basting every 10 minutes with pan juices.

Combine 1 tablespoon of each seasoning in a tightly-covered spice jar for future use.

Vicki Ashley Atkins
Changing Thymes

Per serving

Calories 157 Protein 36 g Carbohydrates 0 g Fat 9 g Cholesterol 110 mg Sodium 394 mg

Mary Ann's Light
Chicken Enchiladas

4	chicken thighs	1	(4 ounce) can chopped
1	sprig celery leaves		green chilies, undrained
¾	cup (3 ounces) grated	1	(16 ounce) can chopped
	Monterey Jack cheese, divided		tomatoes, undrained
¼ to ⅓	cup sour cream		Salt and black pepper to taste
1	clove garlic, minced	10	corn tortillas
3	green onions, chopped	⅛	teaspoon ground cumin
2	tablespoons vegetable oil	¼	teaspoon dried oregano

In a 10-inch covered skillet, cook chicken and celery leaves in ½-inch water until chicken is tender. Skin and bone chicken and shred meat. Reserve broth. Combine chicken, ½ cup cheese and sour cream. Sauté garlic and onion in oil until soft but not browned. Add chilies, tomatoes and ¼ cup reserved broth to onion. Season with salt and black pepper. Simmer for 5 to 10 minutes. Dip each tortilla in sauce to soften. Spoon portion of chicken mixture on each tortilla, roll up and place in shallow 1½-quart casserole. Pour remaining sauce over rolled tortillas. Sprinkle with cumin, oregano and ¼ cup cheese. Bake, uncovered, at 350° for 15 minutes or until thoroughly heated. Serves 5.

Barbara Stromberg Boyd
Changing Thymes

Per serving _____

Calories 457 Protein 21.9 g Carbohydrates 33.4 g Fat 27 g Cholesterol 85 mg Sodium 830 mg

Herb Roasted Turkey and Potatoes

1½ pounds boneless turkey breast	2 tablespoons margarine, melted
1 clove garlic, thinly sliced	¾ teaspoon onion salt
4 red potatoes, quartered	¾ teaspoon dried oregano
	Paprika

Cut slits in surface of turkey and insert garlic slices. Place turkey, skin side up in 13 × 9 × 2-inch baking pan. Place potatoes around turkey. Drizzle potatoes with margarine. Combine onion salt and oregano. Sprinkle over turkey and potatoes. Season potatoes with paprika. Bake at 350° for 1½ hours or until internal temperature of turkey is 170°. Let stand 5 minutes before slicing. Serves 6.

Nanci Norin Jordt
Changing Thymes

Per serving_____

Calories 297 Protein 34.2 g Carbohydrates 9.32 g Fat 13 g Cholesterol 81.7 mg
Sodium 412 mg

Quail in Orange Sauce

1 teaspoon seasoned salt	1 carrot, peeled and thinly sliced
½ cup flour	
¼ teaspoon pepper	1 cup chicken broth
8 quail	1 cup dry white wine
½ cup oil	1 tablespoon grated orange peel
½ cup chopped onion	
½ green bell pepper, chopped	1 teaspoon Worcestershire sauce
2 cloves garlic, minced	Sour cream for garnish

Combine salt, flour and pepper in a paper bag. Shake quail, 1 at a time in the bag, until lightly coated. Brown quail in hot oil. Remove to an oven proof casserole dish. Sauté the onion, bell pepper and garlic in the remaining oil. Add the carrot, broth and wine. Cover and simmer 15 minutes. Strain sauce over birds and sprinkle with orange rind and Worcestershire sauce. Cover and bake 45 minutes. Turn off heat and leave in oven 30 minutes. Serve with a dollop of sour cream. Serves 8.

Mrs. Jim Rado (Vicki)
Lone Star Legacy II

Lobster Stuffed Tenderloin

2 lobster tails, 4 ounces each
3 to 4 pounds whole beef tenderloin
1 tablespoon butter, melted
1½ teaspoons lemon juice
6 slices bacon, partially cooked

½ cup chopped green onion
½ cup butter
½ pound fresh mushrooms
½ cup dry white wine
⅛ teaspoon garlic salt

Place lobster tails in boiling salted water to cover. Return to boiling, reduce heat, and simmer for 5 to 7 minutes. Cut beef tenderloin lengthwise to within ½ inch of bottom to butterfly. Carefully remove lobster from shells. Cut in half lengthwise. Place lobster end to end, inside beef. Combine 1 tablespoon melted butter with lemon juice and drizzle on lobster. Close meat around lobster and tie roast with string at 1 inch intervals. Place on rack in a shallow roasting pan. Roast at 425° for 25 minutes for rare. Lay partially cooked bacon slices on top and roast 5 minutes more. Meanwhile, in a saucepan cook green onions in remaining butter; add mushrooms and sauté until tender. Add wine and garlic salt and heat through, stirring frequently. To serve, slice roast and spoon on wine sauce. Serves 8.

Mrs. John Wilbur (Nancy)
Lone Star Legacy II

Beef Tenderloin with Bearnaise Sauce

Beef Tenderloin:

2 beef tenderloins, 3½ pounds each Worcestershire sauce Soy sauce	Garlic salt Salt and pepper 12 bacon strips

Tie two beef tenderloin strips together. Sprinkle generously with Worcestershire sauce, soy sauce, garlic salt, salt and pepper. Criss-cross bacon strips on top, securing with toothpicks. Let stand at room temperature 3 hours. Bake at 475° for 45 minutes or at 500° for 30 minutes.

Bearnaise Sauce:

½ cup sour cream
½ cup mayonnaise
½ teaspoon salt
2 tablespoons white
    vinegar
	1 teaspoon tarragon leaves
	½ teaspoon dried shredded
	    green onions

Combine sour cream, mayonnaise, salt, vinegar, tarragon leaves and onions. Cover and refrigerate. Warm gently before serving. Serves 12 to 14.

This dish can be served warm or cold with the sauce. If served cold, do not heat sauce, serve cold.

Mrs. David Sandberg (Bonnie)
Lone Star Legacy II

White House Swiss Steak

1 onion, sliced	1 cup vegetable cocktail juice
2 tablespoons oil, divided	1 cup beef bouillon
¼ teaspoon thyme	1 cup julienne sliced carrots
Seasoned salt	1 cup julienne sliced celery
6 top round steaks, 8 ounces each	1 teaspoon chopped parsley
Flour	Cooked rice

Simmer onion in 1 tablespoon oil until golden. Remove pan from heat and add thyme. Season and sprinkle steaks on both sides with flour. Brown steaks in 1 tablespoon oil on both sides in an iron skillet. Transfer steaks to pan with the onions. Pour vegetable juice and bouillon over steaks. Cover pan and simmer very slowly for 1 hour in the oven or on top of the stove. After 1 hour of cooking time, turn steaks over and cover the steaks with the vegetables and continue cooking for 30 minutes. Sprinkle with parsley and serve over rice. Serves 6.

This recipe came as a framed print from my husband's grandmother. It was served during President Johnson's administration.

Mrs. William Steigelman (Kathleen)
Lone Star Legacy II

Fajitas Borrachos Olé

3 cans (12 ounces each) beer	10 pounds tenderized skirt steak
1 jar (15.5 ounces) jalapeño slices, undrained	Flour tortillas
1 bottle (16 ounces) Italian salad dressing	

Mix first 3 ingredients together and pour over steak. Marinate for 24 to 48 hours. Cook over hot coals, turning often. Slice thinly across the grain and serve with flour tortillas. Top with your favorite condiments, such as guacamole grated cheese, sautéed onions, sour cream, picanté sauce, pico de gallo, etc. Serves 20 to 24.

Rusty Batey
Lone Star Legacy II

Green Chili Enchiladas

1	pound ground beef	1	can (10 ounces) tomatoes with green chilies
1	onion, finely chopped		
8	ounces American cheese, grated	1	teaspoon ground cumin
		½	cup shortening
8	ounces sharp Cheddar cheese, grated	12	corn tortillas
		1	can (10½ ounces) cream of chicken soup
1	can (4 ounces) chopped green chilies		
		1	can (6 ounces) evaporated milk
1	jar (4 ounces) chopped pimiento		

Brown beef and onions; drain. Add both cheeses, green chilies, pimiento, tomatoes with chilies and cumin. Heat on low until cheeses melt, stirring to mix well. Heat shortening in another skillet and dip tortillas in hot shortening to soften. Place a portion of beef mixture in each tortilla and wrap securely. Arrange in a 9 × 13 inch baking dish. Combine soup and milk and pour over tortillas. Bake at 350° for 30 minutes. Serves 6.

Be sure to heat the tortillas until they are soft or they will split when you roll them. You can also top the enchiladas with additional grated cheese after baking and return to oven to melt cheese.

Mrs. Marcus Bone (Beverly)
Lone Star Legacy II

Stacked Enchiladas

1	pound extra lean ground beef	1	(8 ounce) can green chili sauce
2	(8 ounce) cans tomato sauce	16	corn tortillas
2	tablespoons chili powder	1	pound grated cheese
2	freshly roasted green chilies, seeded and chopped	1	medium-sized onion, chopped
		½	head lettuce, chopped
		2	tomatoes, chopped
			Fried eggs (optional)

Brown beef in skillet, stirring to crumble. Place in large saucepan. Discard skillet drippings. Combine tomato sauce, chili powder and green chilies in skillet. Simmer for 20 minutes. Prepare separate skillet with non-stick vegetable cooking spray. Heat each tortilla for 2 to 3 seconds on each side. Keep warm. For each serving, place 1 tortilla on plate, top with sauce, cheese, onions and beef. Repeat layer. Top each stack with lettuce, tomatoes and fried egg, if desired. Serves 8.

Millie Skidmore
Changing Thymes

Per serving _____

Calories 591 Protein 36.7 g Carbohydrates 40.5 g Fat 32.5 g Cholesterol 120 mg Sodium 900 mg

Layered Enchiladas

Filling:

2	pounds ground sirloin
1	onion, chopped
½	green bell pepper chopped
¼	teaspoon coriander
½	teaspoon chopped garlic
1	can (10 ounces) chili without beans
⅛	teaspoon hot pepper sauce

¼	cup picanté sauce
1	teaspoon Worcestershire sauce
1	tablespoon chili powder
½	cup chopped ripe olives
12 to 15 tortillas, quartered
2	cups grated Cheddar cheese

Sauté ground sirloin, onion and bell pepper. Drain, then add remaining ingredients except tortillas and cheese.

Sauce:

½	cup butter, melted
2	tablespoons flour

1½ cups milk
2	cups sour cream

In a small saucepan combine butter and flour and mix well. Slowly add milk and cook until thickened and smooth. Cool, then add sour cream.

Spread a little of the sauce in the bottom of a 9 × 13 inch baking dish. Place one half of the tortilla quarters over sauce and follow with one half of meat mixture, one half of white sauce, and one half of cheese. Repeat layers, and bake at 375° for 20 minutes. Serves 6 to 8.

Mrs. John Biggar (Phyllis)
Lone Star Legacy II

Fajitas

½	cup oil	1	teaspoon whole oregano
3	tablespoons lemon juice	2	tablespoons minced dried
1	tablespoon wine vinegar		onion
½	teaspoon garlic salt	½	cup water
½	teaspoon whole thyme	2	pounds skirt steak
½	teaspoon chili powder		Flour tortillas

Combine all ingredients in a bowl. Pour or spoon over 2 pounds of skirt steak in a shallow container. Place in refrigerator, covered, for about 6 to 8 hours, turning every few hours. Grill over hot coals about 10 minutes. Serve with flour tortillas and condiments. Serves 4 to 5.

Mrs. Jette Campbell (Sally)
Lone Star Legacy II

Tacos

1	pound lean ground beef	8	crispy taco shells
1	medium onion, chopped	2	tomatoes, diced
1	can (8 ounces) tomato sauce	½	head lettuce, shredded
1½	teaspoons chili powder	2	cups grated Cheddar cheese
	Salt and pepper to taste		Picanté sauce
	Garlic powder to taste		

Brown ground beef and onion in skillet. Drain and add tomato sauce, chili powder, salt, pepper and garlic powder. Simmer 10 minutes. Warm taco shells. To prepare tacos, put meat in shell and top with tomatoes, lettuce, and cheese. Add picanté sauce for extra zing. Serves 4 to 6.

For soft tacos, substitute warm flour tortillas and wrap around filling.

Mrs. Jim Schultz (Mary Kay)
Lone Star Legacy

Tacos de Fajitas al Carbon

Marinade:

4	ounces lime juice	2	tablespoons cumin
2	ounces Mexican beer	2	tablespoons brown sugar
1	ounce Worcestershire sauce	1	large onion, peeled and
4	ounces olive oil		sliced into thin rings
10	peppercorns	1	large garlic clove, minced
2	whole cloves	2	dry chili peppers,
1	bay leaf		crumbled
1	teaspoon marjoram	1	cup chopped cilantro
1	tablespoon celery powder	2½	pounds skirt steak
2	tablespoons paprika		Salt and pepper

To make marinade, combine lime juice, beer and Worcestershire sauce in a glass bowl. With a whisk beat in olive oil a few drops at a time. Add peppercorns, cloves, bay leaf, marjoram, celery powder, paprika, cumin, brown sugar, onion, garlic, chili peppers and cilantro. Stir vigorously. Trim fat from meat and sprinkle uniformly with salt and pepper. Poke vigorously all over with a fork, piercing meat completely. Turn over and repeat on the other side. Put meat into marinade. Cover and refrigerate for 48 hours stirring occasionally.

Cumin Mixture:

1	tablespoon cumin	Butter
1	tablespoon paprika	Lime juice
1	teaspoon salt	Flour tortillas
1	teaspoon brown sugar	Mexican condiments
1	tablespoon pepper	

Combine cumin, paprika, salt, brown sugar, and pepper and set aside. Prepare very hot fire on charcoal grill, adding chunks of moist mesquite wood. You should not be able to hold your hand five inches from grill. Remove meat from marinade and cook for 1½ minutes. Turn over and brush with marinade; cook for 1½ minutes. Turn and brush again. Cook for 4 minutes and sprinkle with cumin mixture. Turn and sprinkle with seasoning. Top with several thin pats of butter and a few drops of lime juice. Cook for 4 minutes more. Remove from grill and let sit 5 minutes. Slice crosswise on bias. Serve on flour tortillas topped with your choice of picanté salsa, guacamole, grated cheese, sour cream or sautéed onions. Serves 8.

Thomas Schwartz
Lone Star Legacy II

Lasagne

2	pounds ground beef	1	can (6 ounces) tomato paste
2	cloves garlic, minced		
2	cans (28 ounces each) whole tomatoes	1	box (8 ounces) lasagna noodles
1¾	teaspoons salt	12	ounces Mozzarella cheese
¾	teaspoon pepper	1	carton (16 ounces) cottage cheese or Ricotta cheese
2	teaspoons oregano		

Brown ground beef and garlic. Add tomatoes and the juice from one can, salt, pepper, oregano and tomato paste. Simmer for 20 minutes. Boil noodles according to package directions and drain. In a 9 × 13 inch pan, layer noodles, strips of Mozzarella cheese, cottage cheese and meat sauce. Repeat layers. Bake at 400° for 40 minutes. Serves 8 to 10.

Mrs. Fred Markham (Marilyn)
Lone Star Legacy II

Italian Casserole

2	pounds ground beef	½	teaspoon salt
½	cup chopped onion	¼	teaspoon pepper
1	red or green bell pepper, diced, optional	1	package (10 ounces) medium egg noodles
1	tablespoon chopped garlic	8	ounces cream cheese
1	bottle (32 ounces) spaghetti sauce	1	carton (16 ounces) sour cream
2	cans (8 ounces each) mushroom stems and pieces	1	cup grated Parmesan cheese
½	teaspoon oregano	1	pound Mozzarella cheese, grated

Brown ground beef, onion, bell pepper and garlic. Drain; add spaghetti sauce, mushrooms and seasonings, and simmer 10 to 15 minutes. Cook egg noodles according to package directions; drain. Mix cream cheese, sour cream and other cheeses. Layer noodles, meat mixture and cheeses in 2 layers in a deep 9 × 13 pan. Bake at 350° for 30 minutes. Serves 8 to 12.

Mrs. Denman Smith (Sandra)
Lone Star Legacy II

Steak San Marco

2	pounds round steak, cut into serving pieces	1	teaspoon oregano
1	envelope (1.25 ounces) onion soup mix		Pepper
			Garlic powder to taste
1	can (16 ounces) peeled tomatoes	2	tablespoons oil
		2	tablespoons wine vinegar

Arrange meat in a large skillet or electric frying pan. Sprinkle soup mix evenly over meat. Add tomatoes and sprinkle with oregano, pepper and garlic powder. Then sprinkle oil and vinegar over top. Simmer, covered, for about 1½ hours or until meat is fork tender. Serves 4 to 6.

Serve over rice with a green salad for an easy, tasty meal.

Mrs. Greg Gordon (Kathy)
Lone Star Legacy II

Texas Goulash

2	teaspoons butter	1	can (16 ounces) whole tomatoes, reserve liquid
1	cup chopped onion		
1	cup chopped green bell pepper	2	cups liquid (tomato juice and water)
1	pound ground beef	1	tablespoon chili powder
1	cup cooked rice		Salt and pepper to taste

Saute onion and bell pepper in butter until soft. Add ground beef and stir until brown. Add rice, tomatoes, tomato liquid, chili powder, salt and pepper. Bake at 350° for 1 hour. Serves 4 to 6.

This freezes well.

Mrs. James Albrecht (Donne)
Lone Star Legacy II

Stuffed Bell Peppers

6	green bell peppers	2	tablespoons
1	pound ground beef		Worcestershire sauce
1/3	cup chopped onion		Salt and pepper to taste
1	can (16 ounces) stewed	1½	cups grated Cheddar
	tomatoes		cheese, divided
¾	cup rice		

Cut off tops of bell peppers, remove seeds and membranes and cook in boiling, salted water until tender-crisp; set aside. Brown ground beef with onion; drain, then add tomatoes, rice, Worcestershire sauce, salt and pepper and simmer about 5 minutes. Remove from heat and add 1 cup cheese. Stuff the peppers with the mixture and set upright in a baking dish; pour the rest of filling around peppers. Bake uncovered at 350° for 25 minutes. Sprinkle remaining cheese on top and return to oven for 5 minutes. Serves 6.

Mrs. Sid Mann (Kathi)
Lone Star Legacy II

Party Beef Tenderloin

1 whole beef tenderloin	Teriyaki sauce
Salt	Worcestershire sauce
Black peppercorns, ground	Garlic powder
Soy sauce	

Allow ½ pound serving per person. Sprinkle meat generously with all the seasonings and bake at 425° for 15 to 20 minutes per pound. The ends will be well done and the center will be medium rare. Let stand 15 minutes before carving. Yields ½ pound per person.

You can season ahead of time and pop in the oven after guests arrive and are having cocktails.

Mrs. Steve McMillon (Mary Beth)
Lone Star Legacy II

Estopado

1	pound lean beef, cut into 1 inch cubes	1½	teaspoons salt
1	tablespoon oil	⅛	teaspoon pepper
1	cup dry red wine	1	teaspoon dried basil
1	can (8 ounces) tomatoes	1	teaspoon dried thyme
1	large onion, sliced	1	teaspoon dried tarragon
1	green bell pepper, cut in strips	1	bay leaf
¼	cup raisins	½	cup sliced fresh mushrooms
¼	cup dried apricots, halved	¼	cup sliced ripe olives
1	clove garlic, minced	1	tablespoon flour
		¾	to 1 cup cold water

In a large skillet, brown meat in hot oil. Add red wine, tomatoes, onion, bell pepper, raisins, apricots, garlic, salt and pepper. In a cheese cloth tie the basil, thyme, tarragon and bay leaf together and add to skillet. Simmer, covered 1 hour. Add mushrooms and olives; simmer 30 minutes more. Discard cheese cloth with spices. Combine flour and cold water; stir into stew. Cook, stirring constantly, until mixture thickens and bubbles. Serve over hot cooked rice or risotto. Serves 6 to 8.

Betty M. Williams
Lone Star Legacy II

Best Ever Brisket

Preheat gas grill to low. Wash a 6 to 8 pound brisket. Trim loose fat and dry. Rub both sides liberally with coarse salt. Place on grill for 30 minutes, turning every 15 minutes. Turn grill to low and place meat off fire. Cook for 1 hour turning every 30 minutes. Heat oven to 250°. Place 1 tablespoon flour in cooking bag and shake to coat. Put brisket in bag, make 2 or 3 small slits and bake for 2½ hours. Slice and serve. Serves 12 to 16.

This method assures the meat will be tender and good without a sauce.

Mrs. Bob Bluntzer (Jo)
Lone Star Legacy II

Best Ever Brisket II

Beef brisket, about 10 to 11
  pounds
Salt and pepper

2 large onions, sliced
¼ to ½ cup flour
1 cup water

Place meat fat side up in a large deep pan. Add water to ½ inch depth in pan bottom. Salt and pepper meat freely. Arrange onion slices on top; cover with foil and bake at 300° for 8 to 9 hours. When done, remove brisket to warm platter. Skim off fat from pan drippings and add a mixture of flour and water. Boil, stirring constantly for 3 to 5 minutes. Remove from heat and serve on top of meat.

Mrs. Larry Wisian (Kay)
Lone Star Legacy

Empress Beef

3 tablespoons vegetable oil
¼ teaspoon salt
½ pound boneless sirloin steak cut into shoestring strips
1 large onion, thinly sliced
3 ribs celery, coarsely chopped
¼ pound fresh or frozen snow peas, each cut in half

4 ounces fresh whole mushrooms, thinly sliced
½ cup coarsely chopped water chestnuts
1 tablespoon cornstarch
½ tablespoon sugar
5 tablespoons soy sauce
½ cup water
Cooked rice

Heat oil in large skillet; add salt, then beef. Cook over high heat about 5 minutes, stirring often to brown meat. Add onion, celery, snow peas, mushrooms and water chestnuts. Continue cooking over high heat, stirring constantly, 2 to 3 minutes. Combine cornstarch, sugar, soy sauce and water in a small dish; mix well. Add to skillet; cook, stirring constantly, until mixture thickens and bubbles, about 1 minute. Serve immediately over fluffy steamed rice. Serves 2 to 3.

Mrs. Larry Lerche (Gail)
Lone Star Legacy II

243

Classic Beef Stroganoff

1	small onion, diced	¼	teaspoon garlic powder
4	ounces mushrooms, sliced	1	teaspoon minced parsley
4	tablespoons butter	1	teaspoon paprika
1	pound sirloin steak, cut	1	cup sour cream
	into thin strips		Cooked noodles
½	teaspoon salt		
⅛	teaspoon coarsely ground		
	pepper		

Sauté onion and mushrooms in butter. Add steak strips and simmer gently about 5 minutes. Do not brown the meat. Add seasonings and simmer, stirring, an additional 3 to 4 minutes. Stir in sour cream and continue cooking until sour cream is hot. Do not boil. Serve immediately over noodles. Serves 3 to 4.

This recipe is very quick, but the finished product gives the impression you worked long and hard!

Mrs. J. P. Greve (Fran)
Lone Star Legacy II

Beef Stroganoff

4	tablespoons flour, divided	½	cup chopped onion
½	teaspoon salt	1	clove garlic, chopped
1	pound sirloin steak, cut into	1	tablespoon tomato paste
	strips	1¼	cups beef bouillon
4	tablespoons butter, divided	1	cup sour cream
1	cup mushrooms, thinly	2	tablespoons sherry
	sliced		Hot cooked rice or noodles

Dust meat with 1 tablespoon flour and salt. Brown quickly in 2 tablespoons butter. Add mushrooms, onion and garlic, and cook until onions are barely tender. Remove meat; add 3 tablespoons flour, 2 tablespoons butter, and tomato paste. Slowly stir in beef bouillon. Cook until thickened; add meat, sour cream, and sherry. Heat but do not boil. Serve over rice or noodles. Serves 4 to 6.

Mrs. Jack Dempsey (Estelle)
Lone Star Legacy

Peppered Rib Eye Steak

1 rib eye (6 to 8 pounds), fat removed	1 onion, chopped
2 tablespoons oil	1 carrot, sliced
Salt	1 rib celery, chopped
¼ to ½ can cracked or fresh ground pepper	½ cup red burgundy wine
	1 can beef consommé

Rub meat with oil, salt, and pepper. The amount depends on taste. Spread onion, carrot and celery in a shallow pan. Place meat on top and roast uncovered at 350° for 15 minutes for each pound. Baste frequently with a mixture of wine and consommé. Serves 12 to 14.

Mrs. Randy Hagan (Robin)
Lone Star Legacy

Beef and Chilies Enchiladas

1 small onion, chopped	½ pound Velveeta cheese
1 pound lean ground beef	1 can (4 ounces) chopped green chilies
½ pound Cheddar cheese, grated	1 jar (2 ounces) diced pimientos
1 can cream of chicken soup	1 dozen corn tortillas
1 can (5.33 ounces) evaporated milk	

Brown onion and meat in a large skillet; drain fat. Add grated Cheddar cheese. Heat soup, milk and Velveeta cheese until cheese melts. Add chilies and pimientos. Set aside. Steam tortillas a few at a time in a colander over boiling water. Fill tortillas with meat mixture; roll and place in an oblong casserole. Pour cheese mixture on top. Cover and bake at 350° for 30 minutes. Serves 4 to 6.

Jean Rogers Carney
Lone Star Legacy

Beef Wine Stew

2	pounds chuck, cut in bite-size chunks	8	slices bacon
½	cup sliced onions	1½	cups tomatoes, peeled, quartered and seeded
½	cup sliced carrots	¼	cup sliced mushrooms
1¼	cups robust red wine		8 or more black olives, pitted
2	tablespoons olive oil		Bouquet of thyme, bay leaf
	Ground black pepper		and parsley, tied in
	1 to 2 cloves garlic, crushed		cheesecloth

Place chuck, onion, carrots, wine, oil and seasonings in glass bowl. Stir well; cover and refrigerate 4 hours or overnight. Next day, place ½ of the bacon in the bottom of a 1½ quart casserole. Put meat, vegetables and marinade on top. Add tomatoes and cover with remaining bacon. Cover tightly and cook at 300° for 4 hours or longer. Add mushrooms and olives for the last 30 minutes. Skim off fat if necessary. Serves 6.

Mrs. Clark E. Rector (Sue)
Lone Star Legacy

Green Onion Casserole

2	pounds ground chuck	1	package (10 ounces) thin egg noodles
3	teaspoons salt		
4	teaspoons sugar	8	ounces cream cheese
½	teaspoon pepper	2	cups sour cream
2	cans (16 ounces each) tomatoes	12	green onions, chopped with tops
2	cans (8 ounces each) tomato sauce	2	cups grated sharp Cheddar cheese
4	cloves garlic, chopped		

Combine meat, salt, sugar, pepper, tomatoes, sauce, and garlic; simmer 10 minutes. Cook egg noodles; drain. Combine hot noodles with cream cheese. Add sour cream and green onions. In a 4 quart casserole, layer noodles, meat mixture and top with grated cheese. Bake at 325° for 30 minutes. Serves 8 to 10.

This casserole can be made ahead of time and frozen. Great for drop-in company.

Mrs. B. L. Turlington (Jill)
Lone Star Legacy

Meatballs and Wagon Wheels

1	pound lean ground beef	1	(16 ounce) package wagon wheel pasta
1/3	cup milk		
1/3	cup breadcrumbs	1	(10 ounce) can cream of mushroom soup, undiluted
1	egg		
2	tablespoons chopped onion	1	(8 ounce) package cream cheese, cubed
1/2	teaspoon Worcestershire sauce		
1/2	teaspoon salt	1/2	cup water
Dash of black pepper			

Combine beef, milk, breadcrumbs, egg, onion, Worcestershire sauce, salt and black pepper. Shape into meatballs. Sauté meatballs in skillet until browned. Reduce heat to low and cook, covered, for 15 minutes. Remove meatballs from skillet discard drippings. While meatballs are cooking, prepare pasta according to package directions.

Combine soup, cream cheese and water in skillet and heat thoroughly, mixing to blend, until cheese is melted and sauce is smooth. Add meatballs to sauce and heat thoroughly. Serve over warm pasta. Serves 8.

Mary Lou Cindrich
Changing Thymes

Per serving

Calories 568 Protein 28.4 g Carbohydrates 55.8 g Fat 25 g Cholesterol 114 mg Sodium 629 mg

Peppered Tenderloin with Port-Ginger Sauce

2	tablespoons black peppercorns	4	(6 ounce) beef tenderloins
2	teaspoons green peppercorns in brine, drained	1	teaspoon olive oil
			Salt to taste

Port-Ginger Sauce:

1	cup ruby port wine	1½ tablespoons butter
¼	cup minced shallots	Salt to taste
1½	tablespoons minced fresh ginger	

Crush peppercorns and rub on tenderloins. Season with salt. Sauté tenderloins in oil in heavy skillet over high heat, cooking to desired doneness (4 to 5 minutes per side for medium). Place on platter and tent with foil to keep warm. Add port, shallots and ginger to same skillet. Bring to a boil and cook, stirring frequently, for about 5 minutes or until reduced to thin syrup consistency. Strain sauce, pressing solids with back of spoon to release flavors. Discard solids and return liquid to skillet; boil until thickened (should measure about ½ cup). Whisk in butter and season with salt to taste. Spoon small amount of sauce on each tenderloin and serve remaining sauce on the side. Serves 4.

Vicki Ashley Atkins
Changing Thymes

Per serving with 1 tablespoon sauce_____

Calories 326 Protein 50.19 g Carbohydrates 1.57 g Fat 11.5 g Cholesterol 119.03 mg Sodium 114.2 mg

Tex-Mex Roast

8	pounds rolled rump beef roast or brisket	1	(8 ounce) can tomato sauce
1	(16 ounce) package pinto beans	1	(6 ounce) can green chilies
2	(10 ounce) cans tomatoes with green chilies	1	cup sliced mushrooms
		1	onion, coarsely chopped
			Salt and black pepper to taste

Place roast in large roasting pan. Sort and rinse beans and place around roast. Add all remaining ingredients. Bake at 250° for 8 hours. Serves 16.

Dayna Beikirch
Changing Thymes

Per serving_____

Calories 448 Protein 74.8 g Carbohydrates 11.3 g Fat 16 g Cholesterol 217.5 mg Sodium 503 mg

Fool Proof Roast Beef

This roast, no matter what size, will be brown on the outside and rare on the inside. If less rare roast is preferred, increase final baking time slightly.

1	(5 pound) standing rib beef roast	1	tablespoon garlic power
		1	tablespoon black pepper

Rub roast with garlic powder and black pepper. Let stand until room temperature. Place in roasting pan, rib side down. Bake at 375° for 1 hour. Turn oven off but do not open oven door; let roast stand in oven for 1 hour. Reset oven temperature to 375° and bake for 50 to 60 minutes. Serves 10.

Wonderful served with Hot Mustard Sauce.

Nanci Norin Jordt
Changing Thymes

Per serving_____

Calories 557 Protein 62.4 g Carbohydrates 1.54 g Fat 32 g Cholesterol 181 mg Sodium 164 mg

Italian Pot Roast

2	pounds boneless beef rump roast	1	tablespoon Italian seasoning
4	cloves garlic, minced		Salt and black pepper to taste
2	medium-sized onions, sliced	1	tablespoon low-sodium soy sauce
1	green bell pepper, sliced	1	tablespoon Worcestershire sauce
4	stalks celery, cut in 2-inch pieces	1	(28 ounce) can tomatoes, undrained
6	large carrots, cut in 2-inch pieces	1	(15 ounce) can tomato sauce
12	new potatoes	½	cup hearty red wine
1	bay leaf		

Place meat in large roasting pan. Cover with minced garlic and slices of onion and bell pepper. Arrange remaining vegetables around roast. Add bay leaf, Italian seasoning, salt and black pepper. Combine soy sauce, Worcestershire sauce, tomatoes, tomato sauce and wine. Pour over vegetables and roast. Bake at 250° for 4 to 5 hours. Serves 8.

Featured in American Cowboy Magazine.

Vicki Ashley Atkins
Changing Thymes

Per serving

Calories 367 Protein 40.1 g Carbohydrates 31.5 g Fat 8.5 g Cholesterol 109 mg Sodium 810 mg

Not Your Everyday Meatloaf

1	pound ground turkey	1	small onion, chopped
3	carrots, shredded	1	teaspoon salt
1	cup low-fat cottage cheese	¼	teaspoon black pepper
1	egg white	½	teaspoon basil

Combine all ingredients and mix thoroughly. Place in a 9 × 5 × 3-inch loaf pan. Bake at 300° for 50 minutes.

Remove from pan, let stand for a few minutes and cut into slices to serve. Serves 4.

Kari J. Tobias
Changing Thymes

Per serving

Calories 291 Protein 41.1 Carbohydrates 9 g Fat 9 g Cholesterol 87.5 mg Sodium 872 mg

Stroganoff Casserole

¼	cup chopped onion	3	tablespoons Burgundy wine
1	clove garlic, minced		
2	(3 ounce) cans mushrooms, drained	3	tablespoons lemon juice
¼	cup margarine	1	(6 to 8 ounce) package noodles
1	pound ground beef		
	Salt to taste	1	cup sour cream
1	(14½ ounce) can beef broth		

Saute onion, garlic and mushrooms in margarine until lightly browned. Add beef, season with salt and cook until beef is no longer pink. Add broth, wine and lemon juice to beef mixture. Simmer, uncovered, for 15 minutes. Stir in noodles and simmer, covered, just until noodles are tender. Add sour cream, stirring to blend, just before serving.

Serves 8.

Barbara Stromberg Boyd
Changing Thymes

Per serving

Calories 277 Protein 20.1 g Carbohydrates 10.8 g Fat 16.5 g Cholesterol 109 mg Sodium 721 mg

No Peep Stew

2	pounds good lean beef		Salt and pepper
2	large potatoes		Seasoned salt
1	cup chopped celery	2	tablespoons tapioca
1	large onion, chopped	2	cans (10 ounces each)
1	cup sliced carrots		Snap-E-Tom juice

Cube and mix together the meat and vegetables. Season to taste with salt, pepper and seasoned salt. Place in a Dutch oven. Dissolve tapioca in the tomato juice and pour over the mixture. Bake at 250° for 5 hours. Do not peep. Serves 6 to 8.

Mrs Ron Garrick (Bonnie)
Lone Star Legacy

Easy Marinade for Beef

1	cup vegetable oil	2	cloves garlic, pressed or
¾	cup soy sauce		minced
½	cup lemon juice	2	teaspoons coarsely ground
¼	cup Worcestershire sauce		black pepper
3	tablespoons prepared mustard		

Combine all ingredients, mixing well. Let stand for several hours. To use, pour marinade over beef. Marinate in refrigerator overnight. Makes approximately 2¾ cups.

Nancy Norin Jordt
Changing Thymes

Per tablespoon_____

Calories 49 Protein .495 g Carbohydrates .893 g Fat 5 g Cholesterol 0 Sodium 249 mg

Cecil's Chili Verde

2	large onions, finely chopped
5	cloves garlic, minced
2	jalapeño peppers, stemmed, seeded and finely chopped
5	serrano peppers, stemmed, seeded and finely chopped
1	large red pepper, chopped
3	tablespoons bacon drippings, divided
¼	cup jalapeño juice
1	can (14 ounces) beef broth
1	can (12 ounces) Mexican beer

2	pounds venison, cubed
1½	pounds chili meat
½	pound hot pork sausage
6	tablespoons ground red chili pepper, divided
4	teaspoons cumin, divided
¼	teaspoon oregano
1½	teaspoons cayenne pepper
½	teaspoon white pepper
¼	teaspoon cascabel pepper
4	teaspoons paprika
1	cup tomato sauce
4	tablespoons masa flour
	Grated cheese and onion for garnish

Saute onion, garlic, jalapeños, serranos and red pepper in 1 tablespoon bacon drippings. Add jalapeño juice, broth and beer and bring to a simmer. Meanwhile, divide meat in half and brown half at a time in 1 tablespoon bacon drippings. Sprinkle 1 tablespoon chili pepper over each half. When brown, place meat into pot with liquid. Add 1 tablespoon chili pepper and 1 teaspoon cumin. Bring meat to a boil, cover and simmer 1½ hours. Mix remaining spices together and add with tomato sauce. Simmer 1 hour covered. Serves 6 to 8.

Top with grated cheese and grated onion. Serve accompanied by a cold beer.

Cecil E. Smith
Lone Star Legacy II

Venison

3	pounds venison	2	sprigs thyme, crushed
Salt and pepper		1	tablespoon flour
2	tablespoons butter	2	cups warm water
1	onion, chopped	4	cups consommé
1	slice ham, minced	½	pound fresh mushrooms,
1	clove garlic, minced		sliced
2	bay leaves		Grated rind of 1 lemon

Cut venison into 2 inch square pieces. Salt and pepper generously. Heat butter in skillet and brown venison slowly. When almost brown, add onion; brown slightly. Stir in ham, garlic, bay leaves and thyme. Simmer, stirring for 2 minutes. Add the flour and cook a few minutes longer. Add warm water and simmer. Add consommé and cook slowly for 1 hour. Season again according to taste; then add mushrooms and grated lemon rind. Let cook for 30 minutes longer. Serve on a very hot plate. Serves 6 to 8.

Marcus R. Bone
Lone Star Legacy II

Bar-B-Q Venison Roast

1	hindquarter venison roast	1	tablespoon pepper
2	cups white vinegar	1	teaspoon garlic powder
1	cup oil	4	cloves garlic, quartered
½	cup dry onion soup mix	6	slices bacon
1	can (12 ounces) beer		Barbecue sauce
1	tablespoon salt		

Combine vinegar, oil, soup mix, beer, salt, pepper and garlic powder for marinade. Marinate roast for 24 hours, turning frequently. Pierce the surface of the roast with a sharp knife every 2 inches; insert ¼ clove garlic in each hole. Cover thickest side of roast with 6 slices of bacon, securing with toothpicks. Smoke the roast for 8 to 10 hours. Baste with your favorite barbecue sauce the last 2 to 3 hours of smoking. Serves 6 to 8.

Don Bradford
Lone Star Legacy II

Herbed Pork Roast

1 teaspoon rosemary	1 pork loin roast
1 teaspoon thyme	1 cup water
½ clove garlic	½ cup dry white wine
Salt and freshly ground pepper	

Combine spices and rub over roast. Place in a baking dish with water and wine; bake at 350° for 2½ hours or until 185° on a meat thermometer.

Serve with rice seasoned with green pepper, onion, and tomatoes.

Mrs. Ernest Butler (Sarah)

Lone Star Legacy

Spare Ribs José

1 cup water	1 tablespoon sugar
½ cup sherry	2 pounds spareribs, cut
2 tablespoons soy sauce	apart

In a large saucepan, combine water, sherry, soy sauce and sugar. Bring to a boil. Reduce heat; add ribs and simmer 1 to 2 hours. Serves 4.

Mrs. Bob Edgecomb (Mary)

Lone Star Legacy II

Lone Star Ribs
and Barbecue Sauce

3	pounds small pork ribs	1	part paprika
1	part black pepper	3	parts salt

Season the slab of pork ribs lightly on both sides with the above mixture. Place ribs on the grill in any type of covered smoker or barbecue pit, keeping away from direct heat so that the smoke does the cooking. Cook very slowly for 1½ to 2 hours, or until meat comes away from the bone easily. During the final 15 minutes of cooking, baste both sides of the meat with barbecue sauce. Cut ribs to serve.

Sauce:

1	pint catsup	1½	teaspoons black pepper
1½	pints water	1½	teaspoons chili powder
⅓	cup flour	1	tablespoon prepared
1	tablespoon salt		mustard
4	teaspoons sugar	1½	teaspoons Liquid Smoke
2½	teaspoons paprika	1	cup Worcestershire sauce

To make sauce, combine catsup and water in large pot. Bring to a boil. Mix dry ingredients together. Add mustard, Liquid Smoke, and half of the Worcestershire sauce. Stir into a paste; then add remainder of Worcestershire. Pour this into heated mixture and boil slowly for 20 minutes. Refrigerate any unused portion. Keeps for several weeks. Sauce makes approximately one quart. Ribs serve 4.

Mrs. Ken Moyer (Bonnie)
Lone Star Legacy

Pork Tenderloin with Mustard Sauce

¼	cup soy sauce	2	tablespoons brown sugar
¼	cup bourbon	3	pounds pork tenderloin

Mustard Sauce:

⅔	cup sour cream	2	tablespoons dry mustard
⅔	cup mayonnaise		3 or 4 green onions, chopped

Combine soy sauce, bourbon and brown sugar in 11 × 7 × 1½-inch baking dish. Add tenderloin. Marinate in refrigerator for at least 2 hours, turning tenderloin occasionally. Prepare sauce by combining sour cream, mayonnaise, mustard and onion. Chill for at least 1 hour. Remove tenderloin from marinade and place on rack in shallow roasting pan. Bake at 325° for 45 minutes or until internal temperature of tenderloin is 160°. Serve with Mustard Sauce. Serves 8.

Linda Cook Uhl
Changing Thymes

Per serving of pork_____

Calories 477 Protein 56.1 g Carbohydrates 1.29 g Fat 25 g Cholesterol 179 mg Sodium 256 mg

Per tablespoon sauce_____

Calories 62 Protein .527 g Carbohydrates .865 g Fat 6.5 g Cholesterol 6.45 mg Sodium 38.5 mg

Pork Medallions
with Burgundy

½	cup dried cranberries	1	tablespoon plus
¾	cup boiling water		1 teaspoon honey
1	pound pork tenderloin	¼	cup balsamic vinegar
	Salt and black pepper to taste	1	cup beef consommé
2	teaspoons vegetable oil	½	teaspoon dried thyme
1	shallot, minced	1	teaspoon cornstarch
¾	cup Burgundy wine	1	tablespoon water

Soak cranberries in boiling water. Set aside. Trim tenderloin and cut into 12 medallions. Season medallions with salt and black pepper. Sauté medallions in oil in large non-stick skillet over medium heat, cooking for 3 to 4 minutes on each side. Place on serving platter and keep warm. In same skillet, cook shallot, stirring constantly, for 1 minute. Add burgundy, honey and vinegar. Bring to a boil and cook for 3 to 5 minutes or until volume is reduced by ½. Drain cranberries, reserving liquid. Add liquid, consommé and thyme to sauce. Bring to a boil and cook for 5 minutes.

Blend cornstarch and water until smooth. Whisk into sauce. Cook, stirring frequently, until slightly thickened. Add cranberries and cook for 1 minute. Ladle sauce over medallions and serve. Serves 4.

Jeanne Cassidy
Changing Thymes

Per serving_____

Calories 427 Protein 41.3 g Carbohydrates 14.4 g Fat 19 g Cholesterol 119 mg Sodium 744 mg

Pork Roast

1	(4 pound) boneless pork roast	1	tablespoon celery salt
½	cup browning sauce	1	tablespoon garlic salt
			Salt and black pepper to taste

Coat all sides of roast with browning sauce. Sprinkle celery salt, garlic salt, salt and black pepper on all surfaces of roast. Place roast on rack in baking pan. Bake at 350° for 30 minutes per pound or to desired doneness. Let stand for a few minutes before slicing. Serves 10.

Shermette Naumann
Changing Thymes

Per serving_____

Calories 513 Protein 60.9 g Carbohydrates 3.35 g Fat 26.5 g Cholesterol 191 mg Sodium 1328 mg

Simply the Best Pork Tenderloin

Marinate 8 hours or overnight

1	cup teriyaki sauce	2	pork tenderloins, trimmed
2	large cloves garlic, pressed		

Combine teriyaki sauce and garlic in large plastic zipper bag. Add tenderloins. Marinate overnight in refrigerator or for at least 8 hours, turning bag occasionally. Remove tenderloins. Grill over hot coals or over medium high heat on gas grill for 8 to 10 minutes on each side or to desired doneness. Tenderloins may be baked at 400° for 30 to 40 minutes. Serves 6.

For added zip, add 1 teaspoon freshly grated ginger to marinade.

Vicki Ashley Atkins
Changing Thymes

Per serving_____

Calories 202 Protein 33.8 g Carbohydrates 2.98 g Fat 5.5 g Cholesterol 89.6 mg Sodium 752 mg

Pecan Glazed Ham

1	whole boneless, fully cooked ham	½	cup fine soft white bread crumbs
Whole cloves		1½	teaspoons dry mustard
Honey		½	cup coarsely chopped
1	cup firmly packed brown sugar		pecans

Place ham in roasting pan. Add water to a depth of approximately 2 inches; bring to a boil. Reduce heat and simmer, covered for 2 hours. Remove ham from pan; score with diagonal cuts and stud each corner of diamonds with whole cloves. Coat with honey. Mix brown sugar, bread crumbs, mustard and pecans and pat onto ham. Bake at 325° for 30 minutes. Serves 12.

This ham is a favorite of my mother's for Christmas gift giving.

Mrs. Marvin Sentell (Julie)
Lone Star Legacy II

Company Casserole

1	package (6 ounces) wild rice	1	can cream of celery soup
1	package (10 ounces) frozen chopped broccoli	1	cup mayonnaise
2	cups chopped cooked ham	2	teaspoons prepared mustard
1	can (4 ounces) mushrooms, drained	1	teaspoon curry powder
1	cup diced Cheddar cheese	¼	cup grated Parmesan cheese

Cook rice according to package directions. Spread on bottom of a buttered 9 × 13 inch pan. Top with broccoli, ham, mushrooms and cheese. Blend soup with mayonnaise, mustard and curry. Pour soup mixture over all. Sprinkle with Parmesan cheese; bake at 350° for 45 minutes. Serves 6 to 8.

Mrs. Larry Strickland (Linda)
Lone Star Legacy

Portuguese Roughy Fillets

¼	cup chopped onion	2	tablespoons white wine
1	clove garlic, crushed	2	tablespoons sliced
1	tablespoon olive oil,		black olives
	divided	10	ounces orange roughy
½	cup chopped green		Salt and black pepper to taste
	bell pepper	½	teaspoon Creole seasoning
¾	cup chopped canned	1	tablespoon capers, rinsed
	tomatoes		

In a saucepan, sauté onion and garlic in 1 teaspoon oil until softened. Add bell pepper and sauté for 3 minutes. Stir in tomatoes, wine and olives. Simmer, covered, for 10 minutes, stirring occasionally. Season fish on both sides with salt, black pepper and Creole seasoning. Heat remaining 2 teaspoons oil in 9-inch skillet. Add fish and cook for 3 minutes. Turn fish over and top with vegetable mixture. Add capers. Simmer, covered, for 5 minutes or until fish flakes easily; do not overcook. Serve over brown rice.

Vicki Ashley Atkins
Changing Thymes

Per serving

Calories 240 Protein 28.2g Carbohydrates 8.4 g Fat 9 g Cholesterol 36.8 mg Sodium 851 mg

Trout Amandine

2	pounds Gulf trout fillets	½	cup sliced almonds
¼	cup flour	2	tablespoons lemon juice
1	teaspoon seasoned salt	4 to 5 drops hot pepper sauce	
1	teaspoon paprika	1	tablespoon chopped
¼	cup melted butter, divided		parsley

Cut fillets into 6 portions. Combine flour, seasoned salt and paprika and sprinkle over fillets. Roll fillets and place in a single layer, skin down, in a well-greased baking dish. Drizzle 2 tablespoons melted butter over portions. Broil about 4 inches from source of heat for 10 to 15 minutes, or until fish flakes easily when tested with a fork. While fish is broiling, sauté almonds in remaining butter until golden brown, stirring constantly. Remove from heat and mix in lemon juice, hot pepper sauce and parsley. Pour over fillets and serve at once. Serves 4 to 6.

Vicki Stafford Bohls
Changing Thymes

Flounder in Spinach

2	(10 ounce) packages frozen chopped spinach	2	tablespoons lemon juice
1	cup sour cream	1	teaspoon salt
1	medium-sized onion, chopped	1½	pounds flounder fillets
		¼	pound fresh mushrooms, sliced
1½ tablespoons all-purpose flour		Paprika	

Prepare spinach according to package directions and drain well. Combine sour cream, onion, flour, lemon juice and salt. Add ½ of mixture to spinach, mixing well. Place spinach mixture in 13 × 9 × 2-inch baking dish. Arrange fish on spinach. Place mushrooms around fish. Top with remaining sour cream mixture and sprinkle with paprika. Bake at 375° for 20 minutes. Serves 6.

Patti Shields
Changing Thymes

Per serving————————————————————————

Calories 235 Protein 26.4 g Carbohydrates 11.8 g Fat 10 g Cholesterol 71.4 mg Sodium 1261 mg

Stuffed Texas Redfish

1	medium onion, chopped	3	cups herb stuffing mix
2	cups chopped celery	1	cup cooked rice
1	cup butter, divided	1	can (12 ounces) crab meat
2	teaspoons parsley	1	redfish, 3 to 5 pounds
1	teaspoon dill weed	1 to 2 limes	
1 to 2 teaspoons basil		Salt and pepper	
½	cup white wine	Paprika	
½	cup chicken broth		

Sauté onion and celery in ½ cup butter until crisp tender. Add remaining butter, parsley, dill weed, basil, wine and chicken broth, simmering for 5 minutes. In a large bowl toss stuffing mix, rice and crab; add to broth mixture. This stuffing mix may be made a day ahead to allow the flavors to blend. Using a pan large enough to hold the fish, spoon half the dressing mixture into pan and top with fish. Fill cavity of the fish with remaining stuffing. Generously squeeze lime juice over fish and sprinkle with salt, pepper and paprika. Bake at 350° for approximately 1 hour. Serves 8 to 10.

Mrs. Denman Smith (Sandra)
Lone Star Legacy II

Fried Crab Cakes

1	pound crab meat	1	tablespoon prepared
¾	cup cracker crumbs		mustard
1	egg, slightly beaten	¾	teaspoon hot pepper sauce
2	tablespoons minced onion	1	teaspoon salt
2	tablespoons mayonnaise	½	teaspoon pepper
1	tablespoon Worcestershire sauce	Saltine cracker crumbs	
		Oil	

Flake crab meat with fork and mix with cracker crumbs, egg, onion, mayonnaise, Worcestershire, mustard, hot pepper sauce, salt and pepper. Form into six 3-inch patties and roll in cracker crumbs. Heat oil in an electric skillet to 375° and fry cakes until golden brown, about 3 minutes per side. Serve immediately. Serves 6.

Mrs. Marcus Bone (Beverly)
Lone Star Legacy II

Stuffed Flounder

¼	cup chopped onions	¾	teaspoon salt, divided
¼	cup butter		Pepper to taste
1	can (3 ounces) mushrooms, drained, reserve liquid	8	flounder filets
		3	tablespoons butter
1	can (6½ ounces) crab meat, drained	3	tablespoons flour
			Milk
½	cup cracker crumbs	⅓	cup dry white wine
2	tablespoons chopped parsley	1	cup grated Swiss cheese
		½	teaspoon paprika

Cook onion in ¼ cup butter until tender not brown. Stir in mushrooms, crab, cracker crumbs, parsley, ½ teaspoon salt, and pepper. Mix well; spread over filets. Roll filets and place seam side down in baking dish. In a saucepan, melt 3 tablespoons butter. Blend in flour and ¼ teaspoon salt. Add enough milk to mushroom liquid to equal 1½ cups. Combine with wine and gradually pour into saucepan. Cook and stir until mixture thickens and bubbles. Pour over filets. Bake at 400° for 25 minutes. Sprinkle with cheese and paprika. Return to oven and bake 10 minutes longer or until fish flakes easily with a fork. Serves 8.

Mrs. Jim Rado (Vicki)
Lone Star Legacy

Shellfish Supreme

1	pound crab meat, shredded	2	(10 ounce) packages frozen peas
1	pound shrimp, peeled and deveined		
		1½	cups mayonnaise
2	cups cooked rice		Salt
½	green bell pepper, chopped		Black pepper
⅓	cup chopped parsley		Cayenne pepper

Combine crab, shrimp, rice, bell pepper, parsley, peas and mayonnaise, mixing well. Season to taste with salt, black pepper and cayenne pepper. Pour into a greased 13 × 9 × 2-inch baking dish. Bake, covered, at 350° for 1 hour. Serves 8.

Kathy Marsh
Changing Thymes

Per serving_____

Calories 539 Protein 28.6 g Carbohydrates 26.8 g Fat 35.5 g Cholesterol 167 mg Sodium 674 mg

Shrimp and Artichoke Casserole

2   packages (10 ounces each) frozen artichoke hearts
1½ pounds cooked shrimp
¼ pound fresh mushrooms, sliced
2   tablespoons butter
2   tablespoons Worcestershire sauce
¼ cup dry white wine

1½ cups basic white sauce
½ cup grated Parmesan cheese
Lemon juice to taste
Onion flakes to taste
Salt and pepper to taste
Paprika to taste
Hot cooked rice to serve

Arrange artichokes in a buttered 9 × 13 inch baking dish; spread shrimp over artichokes. Sauté mushrooms in butter for 6 minutes; add to baking dish. Mix Worcestershire sauce with wine and cream sauce, and pour into the dish. Sprinkle with cheese and the remaining ingredients to taste. Bake at 375° for 30 to 40 minutes. Serve over rice. Serves 4 to 6.

Mrs. Robert Henderson (Dale)
Lone Star Legacy

Barbecued Shrimp

1   teaspoon salt
1   teaspoon oregano
½ teaspoon pepper
2   cloves garlic, minced
¼ cup white wine

¼ cup wine vinegar
¼ cup catsup
4   dashes Tabasco
3   pounds large shrimp unpeeled

Mix marinade ingredients and pour over shrimp. Refrigerate at least 12 hours, stirring occasionally. Bake at 375° for 20 to 30 minutes, stirring occasionally. Broil for the last 5 minutes to brown. Serves 4 to 6.

Mrs. Don Panter (Carolyn)
Lone Star Legacy II

Shrimp Creole

½	cup oil	1	teaspoon salt
2	cups chopped onion	3	cups water
1	cup chopped green pepper	1	bay leaf
1	cup chopped celery	3	pounds raw shrimp, peeled
2	teaspoons minced garlic		and deveined
2	cups whole tomatoes	2	tablespoons cornstarch,
1	tablespoon paprika		optional
¼	teaspoon cayenne pepper		Hot cooked rice

Sauté in hot oil, onion, green pepper, celery and garlic until tender. Stir in tomatoes and brown. Add paprika, cayenne, salt, water and bay leaf. Simmer for 15 minutes. Add shrimp and continue simmering for 10 to 12 minutes more. If desired, thicken sauce with 2 tablespoons cornstarch. Serve with hot rice. Serves 4 to 6.

Mrs. Larry Hall (Jane)
Lone Star Legacy

Shrimp Scampi

7	tablespoons butter	¼	teaspoon salt
2	teaspoons crushed garlic	½	cup dry white wine
3	tablespoons chopped parsley	½	teaspoon dry mustard
2	tablespoons lemon juice	2	pounds large shrimp, shelled and deveined

Melt butter in a 9 × 13 inch baking pan. Add remaining ingredients except shrimp and mix well. Add shrimp and toss in mixture until coated. Broil shrimp approximately 5 minutes on each side or until done and lightly browned. Serves 6 to 8.

Mrs. Art DeFelice (Connie)
Lone Star Legacy

Shrimp Kabobs

½	cup soy sauce	Mushrooms
¼	cup oil	Small onions
¼	cup Saki (Japanese wine)	Cherry tomatoes
1	teaspoon ground ginger	Rice pilaf
1½	pounds large shrimp, shelled	

Combine soy sauce, oil, Saki and ginger; marinate shrimp about 2 hours. Skewer shrimp with a combination of mushrooms, onions, and tomatoes to taste. Broil 10 to 12 minutes, turning frequently. Serve with rice pilaf.

Mrs. Larry Keith (Virginia)
Lone Star Legacy

Shrimp Jambalaya

3	tablespoons butter	¼	cup chopped parsley
½	cup chopped onion	½	teaspoon salt
½	cup chopped green bell	⅛	teaspoon pepper
½	cup chopped green onion	1	bay leaf
½	cup chopped celery	1	cup uncooked white rice
¼	pound diced cooked ham	1½	pounds shrimp, cooked, peeled and deveined
2	cloves garlic, crushed		
1	can (10¾ ounces) chicken broth	¼	cup green bell pepper for garnish
3 to 4 medium tomatoes, chopped			

Saute onion, bell pepper, green onion, celery, ham and garlic in butter. Stir in the chicken broth, tomatoes, parsley, salt, peppers, bay leaf and rice and bring to a boil. Simmer 20 minutes until rice is tender. Mix in shrimp and bell pepper and serve when shrimp is hot. Serves 6.

Mrs. Gary McKenzie (Clare)
Lone Star Legacy II

Shrimp Cerveza

1	pound shrimp in shell		Salt to taste
1	lemon, sliced	2	dashes of allspice
15 to 20	peppercorns	1	(12 ounce) can beer
1	bay leaf		

Place all ingredients in large saucepan. Add enough water to cover shrimp. Bring to a boil, turn off heat, and let stand until cool. Drain shrimp and serve. Serves 2.

Mary Francis
Changing Thymes

Per serving

Calories 322 Protein 47 g Carbohydrates 12.1 g Fat 4 g Cholesterol 345 mg Sodium 878 mg

Grilled Red Pepper Shrimp

Marinate several hours before grilling

2	tablespoons fresh lemon or lime juice	1	teaspoon cayenne pepper
3	tablespoons olive oil	1/8	teaspoon crushed red pepper flakes
2	large cloves garlic, minced	1	teaspoon paprika
1/2	teaspoon salt	1	pound peeled large shrimp

Combine all ingredients except shrimp in a sealable container. Add shrimp to marinade. Marinate for several hours in refrigerator, stirring several times. Place shrimp on 8-inch skewers. Grill over medium heat for 5 to 10 minutes or until shrimp are curled and firm. Serve hot or cold. Serves 4.

Jeanne Cassidy
Changing Thymes

Per serving

Calories 183 Protein 23.11 g Carbohydrates 1.86 g Fat 9 g Cholesterol 173 mg Sodium 346 mg

Shrimp in Champagne Sauce with Pasta

1	cup sliced fresh mushrooms	2	plum tomatoes, diced
1	tablespoon olive oil	1	cup whipping cream,
1	pound shelled and deveined		divided
	medium shrimp	1	(8 ounce) package angel
1½	cups champagne		hair pasta
¼	teaspoon salt	3	tablespoons chopped
2	tablespoons minced		parsley
	shallots		

Sauté mushrooms in oil in medium saucepan over medium-high heat until tender. Remove mushrooms from pan and set aside. In same saucepan, combine shrimp, champagne and salt. Over high heat, bring to a boil; when liquid boils, shrimp will be done. Remove with slotted spoon and set aside. Add shallots, and tomatoes to cooking liquid. Boil for about 8 minutes or until liquid is reduced to ½ cup. Stir in ¾ cup cream and boil for 2 minutes until slightly thickened and reduced. Add shrimp and mushrooms to sauce and heat thoroughly. Prepare pasta according to package directions. Drain well. Toss pasta with ¼ cup cream and parsley. To serve, spoon shrimp and sauce over individual servings of pasta. Serves 4.

Ginny Ashley
Changing Thymes

Per serving_____

Calories 659 Protein 33.3 g Carbohydrates 52 g Fat 28.5 g Cholesterol 254 mg Sodium 340 mg

Fettuccine Al Frutti De Mare
(With Seafood Sauce)

½	pound medium shrimp, peeled and deveined	²/₃	cup dry white wine
½	pound scallops	1	pound fettuccine
1	cup mushrooms, quartered	2½	cups freshly grated Parmesan cheese
8	tablespoons butter, divided	1	cup whipping cream

In a heavy saucepan, sauté shrimp, scallops and mushrooms in 4 tablespoons butter just until seafood is cooked. Add wine and cook until liquids have reduced to a sauce consistency. Set aside. Cook fettuccine in boiling, salted water until al dente. Drain, and return to cooking pan. Add remaining 4 tablespoons butter, in pieces; then add cheese and cream. Toss together until cream sauce coats pasta. Serve immediately on a platter with seafood sauce on top. Serves 4 to 6.

Mrs. Bryan Healer (Georganne)
Lone Star Legacy

Marinated Grilled Lamb

6	pound leg of lamb, deboned and butterflied by butcher	2¼	teaspoons salt
		1	tablespoon ground pepper
¼	cup olive oil	¼	cup red wine vinegar
¾	cup soy sauce	½	teaspoon dried parsley flakes
¼	cup Worcestershire sauce		
2	tablespoons dry mustard	⅓	cup fresh lemon juice
		2	garlic cloves, crushed

Mix all ingredients together and marinate the leg of lamb overnight. Remove from marinade and reserve for basting. Cook on grill for 45 minutes to 1 hour, basting occasionally. Serves 10 to 12.

Mrs. Bill Wittenbrook (Linda)
Lone Star Legacy II

BEST OF

Lone Star Legacy

DESSERTS

Chocolate Pound Cake

1	cup butter	4 to 5 tablespoons cocoa
1	cup shortening	¾	teaspoon salt
3	cups sugar	1	cup milk
5	eggs	1	teaspoon vanilla extract
3	cups flour	Powdered sugar, optional
¾	teaspoon baking powder		

Cream butter, shortening and sugar. Add eggs, one at a time, beating well after each. Sift together dry ingredients and add to creamed mixture alternately with milk. Add vanilla and mix. Pour into a greased 10 inch tube pan and bake at 350° for 1¼ to 1½ hours. Cool in pan. Serves 15 to 20.

This cake is even better if dusted with powdered sugar or topped with an orange or mint glaze.

Mrs. Edward Sternen (Suzanne)
Lone Star Legacy II

My Favorite Chocolate Cake

1	box (18.5 ounces) devil's food cake mix	¼	cup mayonnaise
1	box (3½ ounces) instant chocolate pudding mix	4	eggs
		3	tablespoons Amaretto
¾	cup sour cream	1	teaspoon almond extract
½	cup oil	1	cup semisweet chocolate chips
½	cup water	Cocoa
½	cup toasted chopped almonds		

In a large bowl add all ingredients except chocolate chips. Mix on low speed until moistened, then beat 2 minutes at medium speed. Batter is quite thick. Stir in chips by hand. Pour batter into a bundt pan that has been greased and dusted with cocoa and bake 50 to 55 minutes at 350°. Serves 12 to 16.

This is a family favorite and is always requested for birthdays. This cake freezes well.

Mrs. Bob McGoldrick (Fran)
Lone Star Legacy II

Seduction Cake

1	package (6 ounces) semisweet chocolate chips	¼	cup water
¾	cup chopped pecans	1	teaspoon vanilla extract
1	box (18.5 ounces) chocolate butter cake mix	1	box (3½ ounces) instant chocolate pudding
4	eggs	1	carton (8 ounces) sour cream
½	cup oil		

Coat chocolate chips and pecans in a spoon or two of dry cake mix. Mix remaining ingredients together and fold in chocolate chips and pecans. Pour into a greased and floured bundt or tube pan. Bake at 350° for 50 minutes. Serves 16.

Best of the Best Dessert Recipes 1999
Mrs. Ted M. Linder (Michelle Just)
Lone Star Legacy II

Chocolate Kahlua Cake

1	box chocolate cake mix	4	eggs
½	cup oil	¾	cup strong coffee
1	small box instant chocolate pudding	¾	cup Kahlua and creme de cacao mixed

Glaze:

1	cup powdered sugar	2	tablespoons Kahlua
2	tablespoons strong coffee	2	tablespoons creme de cacao

Combine all cake ingredients at medium speed until well blended. Pour into greased and floured 9 × 13 inch pan; bake at 350° for 40 to 45 minutes. Cool in pan. Mix glaze ingredients together. Poke holes in cooled cake and glaze.

For a different cake, substitute white or yellow cake mix with instant vanilla pudding. Bake in three 8 or 9 inch layers at 350° for 30 to 40 minutes. Frost with whipped cream topping.

Mrs. Clark Rector (Sue)
Lone Star Legacy

Kahlua Cake

¾ cup butter, softened
2 cups sugar
¾ cup cocoa
4 eggs, separated
1 teaspoon baking soda

2 tablespoons cold water
½ cup cold coffee
½ cup Kahlua
1¾ cups cake flour
1 tablespoon vanilla extract

Glaze:
1 cup Kahlua
½ cup powdered sugar

Whipped cream to garnish
Strawberries to garnish

Cream butter and sugar well; add cocoa and one egg yolk at a time, beating well. Dissolve soda in water; combine soda, coffee and Kahlua. Add liquids to creamed mixture alternately with flour. Stir in vanilla. Fold in stiffly beaten egg whites. Pour into a greased and floured 10 inch bundt pan. Bake at 325° for 45 minutes or until done. Remove cake from pan while warm; pierce cake with fork.

For glaze, combine Kahlua and powdered sugar until smooth and pour over cake. Cover and store in refrigerator. Garnish with whipped cream and strawberries, if desired.

Nancy Young Moritz
Lone Star Legacy

Hershey Bar Cake

2	sticks margarine	½	teaspoon baking soda
2	cups sugar	¼	teaspoon salt
4	eggs, well beaten	1	cup buttermilk
2	cans (5½ ounce each)	2	teaspoons vanilla
	Hershey's syrup	7	small Hershey bars,
2½	cups flour		melted

Cream margarine and sugar. Add eggs and chocolate syrup. In separate bowl, sift together flour, soda, and salt. Add flour mixture alternately with buttermilk to chocolate mixture. Add vanilla and melted candy bars. Pour into a large greased and floured bundt pan and bake at 350° for 1 hour.

Will stay moist for at least 7 days if you can keep it that long!
Mrs. Larry Lerche (Gail)
Lone Star Legacy

Old Fashioned Chocolate Fudge Cake

2	cups flour	1	cup oil
2	cup sugar	1	cup buttermilk
1½	teaspoons baking soda	2	eggs, beaten
¼	teaspoon salt	3	teaspoons vanilla
½	cup cocoa	¾	cup hot water

Icing:

4	tablespoons cocoa	1	tablespoon vanilla
6	tablespoons milk	1	cup chopped pecans,
4	oz. butter		optional
1	box (1 pound) powdered		
	sugar		

Sift together flour, sugar, soda, salt and cocoa. Add oil, buttermilk, eggs, vanilla and hot water; mix well. Bake in greased 9 × 13 inch pan at 350° for 30 to 40 minutes. For icing, make a paste of the cocoa and milk in a saucepan. Add butter and bring to a boil, stirring constantly. Remove from heat, and add powdered sugar and vanilla. Beat well; add pecans. Pour over still hot cake in baking pan.

Mrs. Don Bradford (Melinda)
Lone Star Legacy

Bûche de Noël

5 eggs, separated	3 plus tablespoons cocoa
1 cup powdered sugar, divided	

Mocha Filling:

1 cup whipping cream	¼ cup cocoa
¼ cup powdered sugar	1 tablespoon instant coffee

Chocolate Butter Cream:

2 cups powdered sugar	1 teaspoon vanilla
4 tablespoons butter, softened	1 egg yolk
2 tablespoons milk	1 square unsweetened chocolate, melted

Grease 10½ × 15½ inch cookie sheet. Line bottom with well greased wax paper. In large bowl, beat egg whites until soft peaks form. Gradually add ½ cup powdered sugar and beat until stiff peaks form. In small bowl, beat egg yolks until thick. At low speed add ½ cup powdered sugar and 3 tablespoons cocoa. Scrape bowl often. Fold yolks into whites. Spread in pan and bake at 400° for 15 minutes or until top springs back when touched. Sprinkle clean kitchen towel with cocoa. Invert cake on towel and peel off paper. Roll cake like jelly roll. Put seam side down to cool.

For filling, combine cream, powdered sugar, cocoa, and instant coffee and beat at medium speed until stiff peaks form.

Make butter cream by mixing powdered sugar, butter, milk, vanilla, egg yolk, and melted chocolate to a spreading consistency.

Unroll cake. Spread with filling. Roll up. Put seam side down on platter and frost with butter cream. Mark frosting with knife to resemble tree bark. Refrigerate. Serves 8 to 10.

This is not as difficult as it looks! It can be made the day before and is beautiful for Christmas.

To make the perfect Bûche, sprinkle cocoa evenly on the towel, using a fine meshed strainer. Be sure to roll the cake while it is still warm, otherwise it may crack. Roll tightly, but gently, to keep cake's light texture. Spread filling nearly to the edges so it won't ooze out when cake is rerolled. To keep platter clean while frosting, gently lift Bûche and insert two strips of waxed paper under roll. After icing carefully remove wazed paper. Bûche is best made one day ahead.

Mrs. Jim Schultz (Marry Kay)
Lone Star Legacy

Earthquake Cake

1	cup chopped pecans	½	cup margarine
1	cup flaked coconut	1	(8 ounce) package cream
1	(18¼ ounce) package		cheese
	German chocolate	1	(16 ounce) package
	cake mix		powdered sugar

Sprinkle pecans in greased 13 × 9 × 2-inch baking pan. Sprinkle coconut over pecans. Prepare cake mix according to package directions. Pour batter over coconut. Melt margarine, cream cheese and powdered sugar together, stirring until smooth. Pour evenly over cake batter. Bake at 350° for 45 minutes. Serves 24.

Patsy Eppright
Changing Thymes

Per serving

Calories 280 Protein 2.51 g Carbohydrates 37.2 g Fat 15 g Cholesterol 10.4 mg Sodium 258 mg

Rum Cake

Cake:

1	cup margarine	2	cups flour
1¾ cups sugar		1	teaspoon rum extract
5	eggs	1	teaspoon vanilla extract

Cream margarine, sugar and eggs. Add flour and flavorings and blend well. Pour into a greased, floured tube pan and bake at 375° for 1 hour.

Icing:

1	cup sugar	1	teaspoon rum extract
½	cup water		

Bring all icing ingredients to a boil, stirring to dissolve sugar. While cake is still hot, pour icing on top. Serves 16 to 18.

Mrs. Jim Smith (Jare)
Lone Star Legacy II

Harvey Wallbanger Cake

1	box yellow cake mix	¼	cup vodka
1	small box vanilla instant pudding	¼	cup Galliano liqueur
½	cup oil	¾	cup orange juice
4	eggs		Powdered sugar, optional

Glaze:

1	cup sifted powdered sugar	1	tablespoon vodka
1	tablespoon orange juice	1	tablespoon Galliano

Mix cake mix, pudding, oil, eggs, vodka, Galliano, orange juice and beat for 4 minutes. Pour batter into greased and floured tube pan. Bake at 350° for 45 to 50 minutes or until tests done. If desired, dust with powdered sugar or frost with glaze made from powdered sugar, orange juice, vodka, and Galliano.

Mrs. Tony Hall (Jane)
Lone Star Legacy

Orange Cranberry Cake

1	cup sugar	2	orange rinds, grated
1	teaspoon baking powder	¾	cup oil
2¼	cups flour	2	eggs
1	teaspoon baking soda	1	cup buttermilk
¼	teaspoon salt	1	cup orange juice
1	cup chopped nuts	⅔	cup sugar
1	cup cranberries, chopped		

Sift all dry ingredients into a large bowl. Stir in nuts, cranberries and orange rind. Combine oil, eggs and buttermilk. Stir into first mixture, blending well. Pour into a well greased and floured 10 inch tube or bundt pan. Bake at 350° for 1 hour or until done. Cool in the pan for 30 minutes; remove to a wire rack. Combine orange juice and sugar. Stir until the sugar is dissolved and use as a basting sauce. When well basted, wrap in foil and refrigerate for 24 hours before serving. Serves 16 to 20.

Florence Batey
Lone Star Legacy

14 Karat Cake

2	cups flour	1	cup white sugar
2	teaspoons baking powder	2	cups grated carrots
1½	teaspoons baking soda	1	can (8 ounces) crushed
1½	teaspoons salt		pineapple, drained
2	teaspoons cinnamon	1½	cups chopped nuts
1	cup brown sugar	1	can (3½ ounces) coconut,
4	eggs		optional
1½	cups oil		

Orange Cream Cheese Frosting:

½	cup butter	1	teaspoon orange juice,
8	ounces cream cheese		optional
1	teaspoon vanilla	1	teaspoon orange rind,
1	pound powdered sugar		optional

Combine flour, baking powder, baking soda and salt. Add remaining ingredients, including coconut, if desired. Grease and flour three 9 inch pans. Bake at 350° for 35 to 40 minutes. Cool completely before frosting. To make frosting, cream butter, cream cheese, vanilla and powdered sugar together and spread on cake.

Variation: Spread buttermilk glaze over hot cakes while still in pans. When cool add Orange Frosting.

Mrs. John Carrell (Jane)
Lone Star Legacy

Buttermilk Glaze

1	cup sugar	½	cup butter
½	teaspoon baking soda	1	tablespoon light corn syrup
½	cup buttermilk	1	teaspoon vanilla

Combine sugar, baking soda, buttermilk, butter and corn syrup in heavy saucepan. Bring to a boil; cook 4 minutes, stirring often. Remove from heat and add vanilla. Spread glaze over layers immediately after removing them from oven. Cool, remove from pans, and frost with cream cheese frosting on top of glaze.

Mrs. Jim Rado (Vicki)
Lone Star Legacy

Vi's Super Carrot Cake

2	cups all-purpose flour	2	cups sugar
2	teaspoons baking soda	1½	cups vegetable oil
1	tablespoon cinnamon	3	cups grated carrots
1	teaspoon salt	1	cup yellow raisins
4	eggs, beaten		(optional)

Icing:

½	cup margarine, softened	1	(16 ounce) package
1	(8 ounce) package cream		powdered sugar
	cheese, softened	½	cup chopped pecans,
2	teaspoons vanilla		toasted (optional)

Sift flour, baking soda, cinnamon and salt. In large mixing bowl, combine eggs, sugar, oil and carrots. Mix well. Gradually add dry ingredients to wet ingredients and mix well. (Add raisins if desired.) Pour batter into 3 greased and floured 8-inch round baking pans. Bake at 350° for approximately 20 to 25 minutes or until wooden pick inserted in middle of cake comes out clean. Let cake cool and remove from pans. Using electric mixer, cream margarine and cream cheese. Add vanilla. Mix well. Gradually add powdered sugar, mixing well after each addition. Place icing between cake layers and on top and sides of cake. Sprinkle toasted pecans on sides of cake if desired. Serves 16.

Ginny Ashley
Changing Thymes

Per serving

Calories 575 Protein 4.54 g Carbohydrates 68.2 g Fat 32 g Cholesterol 68.6 mg
Sodium 369 mg

White Texas Sheetcake

2 cups sugar	1 teaspoon vanilla
2 eggs	1 (20 ounce) can crushed
2 cups all-purpose flour	pineapple, undrained
2 teaspoons baking soda	1 cup chopped walnuts

Frosting:

1 (8 ounce) package cream cheese, softened	1 teaspoon vanilla
½ cup margarine, softened	1½ cups powdered sugar

Cream sugar and eggs together until smooth. Combine flour and baking soda. Add dry ingredients to egg mixture, mixing well. Stir in vanilla, pineapple and walnuts. Spread batter on greased and floured 18 × 12 × 1-inch jelly roll pan. Bake at 350° for 25 to 30 minutes. Let cake cool. Prepare frosting by blending cream cheese, margarine, vanilla, and powdered sugar, beating until smooth. Spread frosting on cooled cake. Serve 16.

Mary Lauderman Tavcar
Changing Thymes

Per serving_____

Calories 371 Protein 4.75 g Carbohydrates 53.8 g Fat 16g Cholesterol 42.1 mg Sodium 221 mg

Pumpkin Cake

1	(16 ounce) can pumpkin	1½	teaspoons baking soda
3	eggs	1¼	teaspoons salt
¾	cup vegetable oil	1	teaspoon nutmeg
½	cup water	1	teaspoon cinnamon
2½	cups all-purpose flour	1	cup yellow raisins
2½	cups sugar		

Frosting:

½	(8 ounce) package cream cheese, softened	1	teaspoon vanilla
3	tablespoons butter or margarine, softened	½	(16 ounce) package powdered sugar

Combine pumpkin, eggs, oil and water, beating until smooth. Combine flour, sugar, baking soda, salt, nutmeg and cinnamon. Add dry ingredients to pumpkin mixture, mixing until smooth. Stir in raisins. Pour batter into greased and floured bundt pan. Bake at 350° for 1¼ hours. Cool cake in pan for approximately 20 minutes, then invert on wire rack to cool completely. Prepare frosting by blending cream cheese, butter or margarine, vanilla and powdered sugar, beating until smooth. Spread frosting on cooled cake. Serves 16.

Ginny Ashley
Changing Thymes

Per serving

Calories 426 Protein 4.42 g Carbohydrates 68.1 g Fat 16 g Cholesterol 53.4 mg Sodium 302 mg

Annie's Pumpkin Pie Cake

1	(16 ounce) can pumpkin	1	(18½ ounce) package
4	eggs, beaten		yellow cake mix
1	(12 ounce) can	1	cup margarine, melted
	evaporated milk	¾	cup chopped pecans
1¾	cups sugar		Whipped cream (optional)
1	tablespoon pumpkin		
	pie spice		

Combine pumpkin, eggs, milk, sugar and pie spice, blending well. Pour batter into ungreased 13 × 9 × 2-inch baking pan. Sprinkle cake mix evenly on batter. Drizzle margarine over cake mix and sprinkle with pecans. Bake at 350° for 1¼ hours. Place pan on wire rack to cool. Cut into squares and serve with whipped cream. Serves 24.

Gwen Walden Irwin
Changing Thymes

Per serving_____

Calories 281 Protein 3.55 g Carbohydrates 35.3 g Fat 14.5 g Cholesterol 39.9 mg Sodium 258 mg

Piña Colada Cake

1	(18½ ounce) package	1	(20 ounce) can crushed
	white cake mix (without		pineapple
	pudding)	1	(8 ounce) carton frozen
1	(16 ounce) can cream		whipped topping
	of coconut	¼	cup flaked coconut

Prepare cake according to package directions. Pour batter into greased and floured 13 × 9 × 2-inch baking pan. Bake as directed. Pour cream of coconut over warm cake. Spoon pineapple on cake. Spread whipped topping on cooled cake and sprinkle with coconut. Refrigerate. Serves 24.

Donna Earle Crain
Changing Thymes

Per serving_____

Calories 150 Protein 1.63 Carbohydrates 19.8 g Fat 7.5 g Cholesterol 0 Sodium 119 mg

Almond Amaretto Cake

½ cup sliced almonds
1 tablespoon butter
1 (18½ ounce) package yellow cake mix

4 eggs
½ cup amaretto liqueur
½ cup water
½ cup vegetable oil

Glaze:
½ cup sugar
¼ cup margarine

2 tablespoons amaretto liqueur
¼ cup water

Lightly brown almonds in butter in small saucepan. Pour almonds and butter into greased and floured 10-inch bundt pan. Combine cake mix, eggs, amaretto, water and oil, blending well. Pour batter over almonds. Bake at 325° for 45 minutes. Place pan on wire rack to cool while preparing glaze. Prepare glaze by combining sugar, margarine, amaretto and water in saucepan. Cook over medium heat, stirring until sugar is dissolved. Invert cake on serving plate. Pour glaze over cake. Serves 16.

Barbara Stromberg Boyd
Changing Thymes

Per serving_____

Calories 318 Protein 3.62 g Carbohydrates 35.6 g Fat 17 g Cholesterol 55.6 mg Sodium 270 mg

Simply Scrumptious Sherry Cake

1 package (18½ ounces) yellow cake mix
1 package (3 ounces) instant vanilla pudding
4 eggs

1 cup oil
1 cup sherry
1 teaspoon nutmeg
Powdered sugar for garnish

Combine all ingredients except powdered sugar and mix well. Pour into a greased bundt pan or an angel food cake pan. Bake at 350° for 45 minutes. Cool 20 to 30 minutes. After removing from pan, sprinkle with powdered sugar. Let stand 15 minutes before slicing or serving. Serves 16.

This moist and rich cake seems like it would take much more effort to make than it does. It is a nice dessert for brunches or buffets.

Mrs. Jette Campbell (Sally)
Lone Star Legacy II

Banana Applesauce Cake

2½ cups all-purpose flour	½ cup water
2 cups sugar	½ cup vegetable shortening
½ teaspoon baking powder	1 cup canned applesauce
½ teaspoon baking soda	1 cup mashed bananas
¾ teaspoon salt	2 eggs
1 teaspoon cinnamon	½ cup chopped nuts
½ teaspoon ground cloves	¾ cup raisins
½ teaspoon ground allspice	

Combine flour, sugar, baking powder, baking soda, salt, cinnamon, cloves and allspice in large mixing bowl. Add water, shortening, applesauce and bananas to dry ingredients. Using electric mixer, beat until creamy. Add eggs and beat at medium speed for 2 minutes. Stir nut and raisins into batter. Pour batter into 13 × 9 × 2-inch baking pan lined on bottom with wax paper. Bake at 350° for 45 minutes. Invert on wire rack, remove wax paper and turn, right side up, while still warm. Sift powdered sugar on cake just before serving. Serves 24.

Ann Bommarito Armstrong
Changing Thymes

Per serving

Calories 196 Protein 2.29 g Carbohydrates 33.3 g Fat 6.5 g Cholesterol 17.7 mg Sodium 41 mg

Poppy Seed Cake

1½ cups sugar	1 teaspoon baking soda
1 cup margarine	1 cup sour cream
4 eggs, separated	2 cups sifted flour
⅓ cup poppy seeds	

Cream sugar and margarine. Beat egg yolks and add to creamed mixture. Add poppy seeds. Dissolve soda in sour cream and add the sour cream alternately with flour to the mixture. Beat egg whites until stiff and fold in. Pour into a lightly greased tube pan and bake at 350° for 1 hour. Serves 16.

This makes a good cake for morning coffee.

Mrs. Greg Gordon (Kathy)
Lone Star Legacy II

Carmon's LBJ Cake

1	cup flour	2	small packages instant pudding mix, vanilla or chocolate or 1 of each
1	stick margarine, melted		
1	cup chopped pecans		
8	ounces cream cheese, softened	3	cups milk
		1	carton (12 ounces) whipped topping
1	cup powdered sugar		
		1	cup toasted coconut

Mix flour and melted margarine. Add pecans and pat mixture in bottom of 9 × 13 inch pan. Bake at 350° for 20 minutes. Cool. Mix cream cheese and powdered sugar; spread over flour mixture. Mix pudding and milk and when thick fold in one cup topping. Spread on top of cheese mixture. Top with remaining whipped topping and sprinkle with toasted coconut. Refrigerate 4 hours. Serves 12.

Mrs. Lee Dickerson (Carol)
Lone Star Legacy

Surprise Cupcakes

1	package (18½ ounces) chocolate cake mix	1	egg
		⅛	teaspoon salt
8	ounces cream cheese, softened	1	package (6 ounces) semisweet chocolate chips
⅓	cup sugar		

Prepare cake mix according to directions on package. Place paper baking cups in muffin pans and fill ⅔ full with cake mix. Cream the cheese with sugar and beat in egg and salt. Stir in chocolate pieces, then drop one rounded teaspoon of mixture into each cupcake. Bake at 350° for 25 to 30 minutes. Refrigerate until served. Yields 18 cupcakes.

Mrs. Ed Fomby (Beaty)
Lone Star Legacy II

Banana Split Pie

8	ounces cream cheese, softened	1	can (8 ounces) crushed pineapple, drained
1	cup powdered sugar	1	carton (8 ounces) whipped topping
5	tablespoons milk		
1	graham cracker crust, 9 inch	1	bottle (6 ounces) maraschino cherries, drained
2	bananas, sliced		

Mix cream cheese, powdered sugar and milk together and put into graham cracker crust. Slice the bananas and place on top of mixture. Top with crushed pineapple, followed by the whipped topping. Add the cherries for decoration. Refrigerate for several hours or overnight before serving. Serves 6.

Claire Shavers Hayden
Lone Star Legacy II

Amaretto Pie

1	cup whipping cream, whipped	1	tablespoon Amaretto
1	can sweetened condensed milk	2	tablespoons Cream de Cacao
1	tablespoon Gran Marnier	1	graham cracker crust, 9 inch

Mix filling ingredients and pour into pie crust. Freeze 4 hours. Serves 10.

For a different taste use other liqueur combinations and a chocolate crumb crust.

Mrs. Steve Scheffe (Betsy)
Lone Star Legacy

Southern Pecan Pie

½ cup dark corn syrup	1 teaspoon vanilla
1 cup sugar	½ cup butter, melted
1 teaspoon flour	1¼ cups pecan halves
2 eggs	1 unbaked 9 inch pie crust
2 teaspoons milk	

Combine all filling ingredients and pour into crust. Bake at 350° for one hour. Serves 6 to 8.

Mrs. Charles Cantwell (Winn)
Lone Star Legacy

Brownie Pecan Pie

⅔ cup sugar	3 eggs, slightly beaten
⅛ teaspoon salt	1 teaspoon vanilla
1 cup light corn syrup	1 cup coarsely chopped pecans
1 package (4 ounces) German sweet chocolate, broken in pieces	1 unbaked 9 inch pie shell
3 tablespoons margarine	Whipped cream to garnish

Combine sugar, salt and corn syrup in a saucepan. Bring to a boil over medium heat, stirring until sugar dissolves. Boil 2 minutes. Remove from heat. Add chocolate and butter and stir until melted. Cool. Gradually pour chocolate mixture over the eggs, mixing well. Add vanilla and pecans. Pour into pie crust and bake at 350° for 50 minutes. Cool. Serve topped with whipped cream. Serves 6 to 8.

Mrs. Joe Bowles (Mary)
Lone Star Legacy

Chocolate Mousse Pie

1	(8 ounce) package bittersweet chocolate, chopped
¼	cup rum
¼	cup plus 2 tablespoons unsalted butter, softened
1	envelope unflavored gelatin

¼	cup cold water
4	egg whites
½	cup sugar
1	cup whipping cream, whipped

Crust:

2	cups graham cracker crumbs
½	cup unsalted butter, melted

2	tablespoons sugar

Prepare crust by mixing graham cracker crumbs, butter and sugar. Press crumbs in bottom and along sides of deep 9-inch pie plate. Bake at 350° for 8 minutes. Set aside. Combine chocolate and rum in top of double boiler over boiling water. Stir until melted and smooth. Remove from heat and add butter, whisking to blend. Dissolve gelatin in cold water in small saucepan. Stir over low heat until clear. Blend into chocolate mixture. Set aside to cool. Beat egg whites to soft peaks. Add sugar and beat until stiff. Drizzle chocolate mixture over egg whites, folding to incorporate evenly. Fold in whipped cream, blending well. Spoon chocolate filling in cooled crust. Chill for several hours or overnight. Serves 10.

For an elegant dessert without the crust, mousse may be piped into individual dessert dishes before chilling.

Vicki Ashley Atkins
Changing Thymes

Per serving

Calories 504 Protein 5.99 g Carbohydrates 42.3 g Fat 36.5 g Cholesterol 76.1 mg Sodium 179 mg

Old Fashioned Chocolate Pie

¾ cup sugar
2 heaping tablespoons flour
3 eggs, separated
1 cup milk
3 tablespoons cocoa or
1 square unsweetened
chocolate

⅛ teaspoon vanilla
1 tablespoon butter
1 baked 8 inch pie shell

Mix sugar, flour, egg yolks, milk, and chocolate in top of double boiler. Cook until thick. Using electric mixer, beat in vanilla and butter. Pour into baked crust. Top with meringue made by beating egg whites with an additional 6 tablespoons of sugar. Brown in 325° oven. Serves 8.

Mrs. Jim Smith (Jare)
Lone Star Legacy

Chocolate Chess Pie

3 eggs, whipped lightly
1¾ cups sugar
1 tablespoon flour
1 tablespoon corn meal
¼ cup cocoa

1 stick margarine, melted
1 teaspoon vanilla
½ cup milk
1 unbaked 9 inch pie crust,
optional

Combine all filling ingredients and pour into pie shell. Bake at 350° for 45 minutes. Serves 8.

This filling is equally as good baked without the pie shell.

Mrs. Jim Smith (Jare)
Lone Star Legacy

Coconut Chess Pie

3 eggs, beaten
1½ cups sugar
½ cup butter, melted
4 teaspoons lemon juice

1 teaspoon vanilla
1 can (3½ ounces) flaked
coconut
1 unbaked 9 inch pie shell

Combine ingredients in order given and pour into pie shell. Bake at 350° for 40 minutes or until set. Serves 6 to 8.

Mrs. Jerry Dow (Annette)
Lone Star Legacy

Mom's Peanut Butter Cookies

1¼	cups smooth peanut butter	2	teaspoons vanilla extract
1	cup sugar	2½	cups flour
1	cup brown sugar	1½	teaspoons baking soda
1	cup shortening	1	teaspoon baking powder
2	eggs		

Blend until smooth the peanut butter, sugars, shortening, eggs and vanilla. Measure, then sift together, the remaining ingredients. Add to sugar mixture and blend well. Make into small balls, using about a teaspoon of dough for each. Place on an ungreased baking sheet. Flatten each ball slightly using a fork dipped in sugar, creating a crisscross pattern. Bake at 375° for 9 to 10 minutes. Yields 50.

Mrs. Sid Mann (Kathi)
Lone Star Legacy II

Gingerbread Men Cookies

Dough:

½	cup shortening	3	cups flour
½	cup sugar	¼	teaspoon salt
½	cup molasses	½	teaspoon baking soda
½	tablespoon vinegar	½	teaspoon cinnamon
1	egg, beaten	½	teaspoon ginger

Place shortening, sugar, molasses and vinegar in a saucepan and bring to a boil. Remove from heat and cool. Stir in egg. Sift together dry ingredients and add to molasses mixture. Mix well and chill dough for 30 to 45 minutes. Roll the dough out to ¼ to ½ inch thickness and cut with a gingerbread man cookie cutter. Bake at 375° for 12 to 15 minutes on a greased cookie sheet.

Decorator Icing:

1	box (16 ounces) powdered sugar	¼	cup almost boiling water
½	cup shortening	1	teaspoon vanilla extract
		⅛	teaspoon salt

Cut shortening into powdered sugar, then add very hot water. Mix well; add vanilla and salt. Drizzle over cookies. Yields 30 cookies.

These cookies were sold in the gift shop at Christmas at Caswell House in 1984.

Mrs. Jim Rado (Vicki)
Lone Star Legacy II

Magic Window Cookies

¾ cup butter
1 cup sugar
2 eggs
½ teaspoon lemon extracts

2½ cups flour
1 teaspoon baking powder
½ teaspoon salt
6 packages of Lifesavers

Mix together butter, sugar, eggs, and lemon extract. Blend in flour, baking powder, and salt. Cover and chill at least one hour. Roll dough ⅛ inch thick on a lightly floured board. Cut into desired shapes. Cut a small hole in center of each cookie with a sharp knife. Place cookies on foil covered baking sheet. Place a Lifesaver in the center of each cookie. Bake at 375° for 7 to 9 minutes until lightly browned or until candy is melted. Cool on baking sheet. Store in layers between waxed paper. These freeze nicely. Yields 6 dozen.

Marian Hidell
Lone Star Legacy

Snickerdoodles

1 cup shortening
1½ cups sugar
2 eggs
2¾ cups flour
1 teaspoon baking soda

½ teaspoon salt
¼ teaspoon cream of tartar
2 tablespoons sugar
2 teaspoons cinnamon

Cream shortening with sugar. Add eggs and beat well. Meanwhile, sift together the dry ingredients, except sugar and cinnamon. Stir them into the creamed mixture. Chill the dough for an hour. After chilling, roll the dough into small balls. Roll these balls in sugar-cinnamon mixture. Place about two inches apart on an ungreased cookie sheet and bake at 400° for 8 to 10 minutes. Yields 5 dozen.

This recipe has been passed through several generations in my family—it's always one of the favorites.

Mrs. Ken Moyer (Bonnie)
Lone Star Legacy

Sugar Cookies

1	cup shortening	2¾	cups flour
1	cup sugar	¾	teaspoon salt
2	eggs	½	teaspoon baking powder
1	teaspoon vanilla	½	teaspoon baking soda

Cream shortening and sugar. Beat in eggs and vanilla. Gradually blend in dry ingredients. Chill 3 hours. Roll ⅛ to ¼" thickness. Cut out with cookie cutters. Bake at 375° for 8 to 10 minutes. Yields 2½ dozen.

I use this recipe at Christmas and ice the cookies with butter and powdered sugar icing—always popular. To make small round cookies I use the spout on a tupperware lid as a cutter.

Mrs. John Perkins (Sandy)
Lone Star Legacy

Texas Cow Patties

2	cups margarine, softened	4	cups all-purpose flour
2	cups sugar	2	teaspoons baking powder
2	cups firmly-packed brown sugar	2	teaspoons baking soda
4	eggs	1	(6 ounce) package semisweet chocolate morsels
2	teaspoons vanilla		
2	cups quick-cooking oats	2	cups chopped broken pecans
2	cups corn flakes		

Cream margarine, sugar and brown sugar together until light and fluffy. Add eggs, 1 at a time, beating well after each addition. Stir in vanilla. Add oats and corn flakes to creamed mixture, mixing thoroughly. Sift flour, baking powder and baking soda together. Gradually add to creamed mixture, beating slowly to mix. Stir in chocolate morsels and pecans. Drop by rounded tablespoons onto cookie sheets. Bake on top rack of oven at 325° for 17 minutes. Cool on wire rack. Makes 2 dozen.

Wendy Coffin
Changing Thymes

Per cookie_____

Calories 470 Protein 5.68 g Carbohydrates 57.4 g Fat 25.5 g Cholesterol 35.3 mg Sodium 286 mg

Texas Trail Busters

¾	cup butter, softened	2	teaspoon salt
1	cup vegetable shortening	3	cups regular oats
2	cups sugar	2	cups coconut
2	cups firmly-packed dark brown sugar	2	cups raisins
4	eggs	1	(6 ounce) package semisweet chocolate morsels
2	teaspoons vanilla		
3	cups all-purpose flour	1	cup chopped nuts
2	teaspoons baking soda		

Cream butter, shortening, sugar and brown sugar together until light and fluffy. Add eggs, 1 at a time, beating well after each addition. Stir in vanilla. Combine flour, baking soda and salt. Add dry ingredients to creamed mixture, mixing thoroughly. Add oats, coconut, raisins, chocolate morsels and nuts, kneading to blend. Drop dough by heaping teaspoonfuls 2 inches apart onto greased cookie sheet. Bake at 350° for 8 minutes or until cookies are golden brown. Cool on wire rack. Makes 7 dozen.

For best results, shape dough into rolls, wrap in wax paper and chill for several hours. Cut in slices and bake as directed.

Carol Willis
Changing Thymes

Per cookie_____

Calories 148 Protein 1.7 g Carbohydrates 20.3 g Fat 7.5 g Cholesterol 14.5 mg Sodium 97.1 mg

LBJ'S Favorite Macaroons

2 egg whites	1 cup shredded coconut
Pinch of salt	½ teaspoon vanilla extract
½ cup sugar	½ teaspoon almond extract

Using electric mixer, beat egg whites well. Add salt and beat until peaks form. Gradually add sugar, beating until glossy. Stir coconut, vanilla and almond extract into egg whites. Drop dough by mounded tablespoonfuls 2 inches apart onto lightly greased cookie sheets. Bake at 325° for 20 minutes. Cool on cookie sheets for 5 to 6 minutes, then place on wire rack to cool completely. Makes 3 dozen.

Vera Alexander Dufour
Changing Thymes

Per cookie_____

Calories 25 Protein .269 g Carbohydrates 4.03 g Fat 1 g Cholesterol 0 Sodium 40.3 mg

Melissa's Coconut Crispies

¾ cup butter or margarine, softened	2 cups all-purpose flour
1 cup sugar	¾ teaspoon baking powder
1 egg	¼ teaspoon salt
1 teaspoon vanilla	1½ cups shredded coconut

Using electric mixer, beat butter, sugar, egg and vanilla together until fluffy. Combine flour, baking powder and salt. Add dry ingredients to creamed mixture and beat at low speed just until moistened. Stir in coconut, mixing by hand. Drop tablespoonfuls of dough onto ungreased cookie sheet, pressing each to ¼-inch thickness. Use back of fork tines, dipped in flour, to press ridges in each cookie. Bake at 375° for 10 to 12 minutes or until edges are golden. Cool on wire rack. Makes 3 dozen.

Jeanne Cassidy
Changing Thymes

Per cookie _____

Calories 103 Protein 1.04 g Carbohydrates 12.8 g Fat 5.5 g Cholesterol 5.89 mg Sodium 71.6 mg

Butterscotch Oatmeal Thins

1	cup uncooked regular oats	3	tablespoons all-purpose
1	cup sugar		flour
½	cup butter, melted	¼	teaspoon salt
1	egg	¼	teaspoon baking powder
½	teaspoon vanilla		

Combine ingredients. Drop by half teaspoon on cookie sheet covered with parchment paper. Space 3 inches apart. Bake 5 to 10 minutes at 350°. Cool and peel off paper. Makes 4 dozen.

Kathy Marsh
Changing Thymes

Per cookie _____

Calories 43 Protein .472 g Carbohydrates 5.69 g Fat 2 g Cholesterol 9.59 mg Sodium 32.1 mg

Love Bites

1	(12 ounce) package semisweet chocolate morsels	1	(8½ ounce) package chocolate wafers, crushed
1	(14 ounce) can sweetened condensed milk	1	cup chopped nuts, divided

Melt chocolate in top of double boiler over very hot (not boiling) water or in microwave, stirring until smooth. Add condensed milk, wafer crumbs and ½ cup chopped nuts to chocolate. Stir to blend well. Press mixture into foil-lined 8 × 8 × 2-inch baking pan. Press remaining nuts into chocolate layer. Let stand at room temperature until firm. Cut into 2-inch squares. Makes 16 squares.

Nanci Norin Jordt
Changing Thymes

Per square _____

Calories 296 Protein 4.43 g Carbohydrates 39.2 g Fat 15.5 g Cholesterol 8.65 mg Sodium 121 mg

Fudge Cookies to Die For

6	tablespoons butter	1	(14 ounce) can sweetened
1	(12 ounce) package		condensed milk
	semisweet chocolate	1	cup all-purpose flour
	morsels	2	cups chopped pecans

Combine butter, chocolate and milk in heavy saucepan. Cook over low heat, stirring often, until chocolate is melted and mixture is smooth. Stir flour and pecans into chocolate mixture. Drop dough by teaspoonfuls onto lightly greased cookie sheet. Bake at 300° for about 10 minutes or until light glaze forms on cookies. Makes 3 dozen.

Cookies will not appear done but do not overbake. Cool on wire rack.

Donna Earle Crain
Changing Thymes

Per cookie_____

Calories 154 Protein 2.16 g Carbohydrates 15.8 g Fat 10 g Cholesterol 8.89 mg Sodium 34.7 mg

Fat Ladies

1	(16 ounce) package	32	caramels
	refrigerated chocolate	¼	cup half and half
	chip cookie dough	1	cup chopped pecans
1	(6 ounce) package		
	semisweet chocolate		
	morsels		

Spread cookie dough evenly into the bottom of 13 × 9 × 2-inch baking pan. Bake for 15 to 20 minutes at 350°. Sprinkle with chocolate chips while hot. They will melt and form a layer of chocolate. Melt together the caramels and half and half. Pour over the chocolate layer. Sprinkle with chopped pecans. Cool and cut into small bars. Makes 2 dozen.

Donna Earle Crain
Changing Thymes

Per bar_____

Calories 113 Protein 1.27 Carbohydrates 14 g Fat 6.5 g Cholesterol 1.8 mg Sodium 29 mg

Applesauce Bars

1½ cups sugar	2 tablespoons cocoa
½ cup margarine	2 cups applesauce
2 eggs, beaten	2 tablespoons sugar
2 cups flour	½ cup chopped nuts
1½ teaspoons baking soda	1 package (6 ounces)
½ teaspoon salt	semisweet chocolate
½ teaspoon cinnamon	chips

Cream 1½ cups sugar and margarine; add eggs beating well. Stir in flour, soda, salt, cinnamon, and cocoa. Add applesauce. Put in greased and floured 9 × 13 inch pan. Combine remaining sugar, nuts and chocolate chips; sprinkle over batter. Bake at 350° for 25 to 30 minutes. Cut into squares and serve. Yields 24 bars.

Mrs. Tim Bauerkemper (Pam)
Lone Star Legacy

Praline Bars

12 unbroken graham crackers, 4 squares to each	1 cup packed brown sugar
2 sticks unsalted butter	1 cup chopped pecans

Place graham crackers on a jelly roll pan with sides. Melt butter in saucepan; add sugar and pecans. Boil slowly for 2 minutes. Pour over graham crackers. Bake at 300° for 15 minutes. Cool 10 minutes, then cut into bars. Yields 3 dozen.

Very simple, good recipe for children to make, taste like a Heath bar.

Mrs. Don Harris (Nancy)
Lone Star Legacy

Chewy Brownies

2	squares (1 ounce each) unsweetened chocolate	1	cup unsifted flour
1/3	cup butter	1/4	teaspoon baking powder
1	cup sugar	1/4	teaspoon salt
2	eggs	1/2	teaspoon vanilla extract
		1/2	cup chopped pecans

Place chocolate squares in medium glass bowl. Microwave on MEDIUM for 1 minute. Add butter and microwave for 1 minute more, or until melted. Stir in sugar and beat in eggs. Stir in remaining ingredients. Spread batter into a 8 × 8 glass baking dish and microwave on LOW for 7 minutes. Then increase baking speed to HIGH for 3 to 4 minutes, or until puffed and dry on top. Cool until set; cut into bars. Yields 16 square brownies.

Mrs. Ken Moyer (Bonnie)
Lone Star Legacy II

Congo Bars

3	cups brown sugar	1/2	teaspoon salt
2/3	cup shortening	1	small package chocolate chips
3	eggs		
1	teaspoon vanilla	1/2	small package butter-scotch chips (optional)
2¾	cups flour		
1½	teaspoons baking powder	¾ to 1	cup chopped nuts

Cream sugar and shortening. Add eggs and vanilla. Add dry ingredients and mix. Stir in chips and nuts. Press in greased 9 × 13 inch pan. Bake at 350° for 30 to 40 minutes. Cut into bars when cool.

Can be frozen. Good when partially frozen.

Marian Carlson Hidell
Lone Star Legacy

Chocolate Cloud

3	egg whites	1	cup Ritz cracker crumbs
1	teaspoon vanilla	½	cup chopped pecans
1	teaspoon baking powder	1	cup whipping cream
¾	cup sugar	2	tablespoons sugar
1	package (4 ounces) German sweet chocolate, grated	1	teaspoon vanilla

Beat egg whites and vanilla to soft peaks. Combine baking powder and sugar and gradually add to whites, beating until stiff peaks form. Reserve 2 tablespoons chocolate and add remaining chocolate with crackers and pecans to egg white mixture. Spread in a 9 inch pie plate. Bake at 350° for 25 minutes. Cool thoroughly. Whip cream with sugar and vanilla and spread on top of pie. Garnish with reserved chocolate. Refrigerate at least 8 hours. Serves 8.

Mrs. Dan Ross (Lamonte)
Lone Star Legacy

Chewy Peanut Butter Bars

⅓	cup shortening	1	cup flour
½	cup peanut butter	¼	teaspoon salt
¼	cup brown sugar	1	teaspoon baking powder
1	cup sugar	1	can (3½ ounces) flaked coconut
1	teaspoon vanilla extract		
2	eggs		

Cream shortening, peanut butter and sugars together. Add vanilla and eggs. Mix in flour, salt and baking powder. Stir in coconut. Spread evenly in a greased 9 × 12 inch pan. Bake at 350° for 25 minutes. Cool and cut into squares. Yields 24.

Mrs. Roger Borgelt (Cindy)
Lone Star Legacy II

301

Cream Cheese Brownies

1	package (4 ounces) sweet baking chocolate	1½	teaspoons vanilla extract, divided
5	tablespoons butter, divided	½	cup unsifted flour
3	ounces cream cheese, softened	½	teaspoon baking powder
		¼	teaspoon salt
1	cup sugar	½	cup coarsely chopped pecans
3	eggs, divided		
1	tablespoon flour	¼	teaspoon almond extract

Melt chocolate and 3 tablespoons butter over very low heat, stirring constantly. Cool. Cream remaining butter with cream cheese until softened. Gradually add sugar, beating until light and fluffy. Blend in 1 egg, 1 tablespoon flour and ½ teaspoon vanilla. Set aside. Beat remaining eggs until thick and light in color. Gradually add remaining ½ cup flour, baking powder and salt. Blend in cooled chocolate mixture, pecans, almond extract and remaining 1 teaspoon vanilla. Measure 1 cup chocolate batter and set aside. Spread remaining chocolate batter into a greased 9 inch square pan. Top with cheese mixture. Drop measured chocolate batter by tablespoon onto cheese mixture, and swirl with spatula to marble. Bake at 350° for 35 minutes. Cool before cutting into squares. Cover and store in refrigerator. Yields 16 brownies.

Mrs. Ron Bruney (Carol)
Lone Star Legacy II

Kiwi Cheese Cake

3 to 4 kiwi, peeled, puréed
and strained
16 ounces cream cheese,
cubed at room
temperature
1 pound Ricotta cheese
2 cups sour cream
5 eggs
2 cups sugar
½ cup flour

½ cup butter
2 tablespoons fresh lime
juice
1 teaspoon vanilla extract
Pinch salt
3 kiwi, peeled and sliced
½ cup apricot preserves
1 tablespoon fresh lemon
juice

Butter bottom and sides of a 10 inch springform pan. Cook puréed kiwi in a small saucepan over medium heat until reduced to ¼ cup. In a mixing bowl combine kiwi, cheeses, sour cream, eggs, sugar, flour, butter, lime juice, vanilla extract and salt. Blending well at low speed, increase speed to medium and beat 20 minutes. Pour batter into prepared pan. Set pan on a baking sheet in the middle of the oven. Bake at 250° for 2¼ hours. Turn off heat and let cake remain in oven with door closed 1 hour longer. Transfer cake to rack and let cool in pan. Arrange sliced kiwi in overlapping pattern around outer edge of cake. Melt apricot preserves in a small saucepan over low heat. Press through sieve set over a small bowl. Stir in lemon juice. Brush apricot mixture over kiwi slices and top of cake. Cover and refrigerate overnight. To serve, bring cheese cake to room temperature. Remove springform pan and cut. Serves 10 to 12.

Mrs. Marcus Bone (Beverly)
Lone Star Legacy II

Butterscotch Cheesecake Bars

1	package (12 ounces) butterscotch chips	8	ounces cream cheese, softened
1/3	cup margarine, melted	1	can (14 ounces) sweetened condensed milk
2	cups graham cracker crumbs	1	teaspoon vanilla extract
1	cup chopped pecans	1	egg

In a medium saucepan melt butterscotch chips and margarine over medium heat. Remove from heat and stir in crumbs and pecans. Press half the mixture firmly into bottom of a greased 9 × 13 inch baking pan. Beat cream cheese until fluffy. Add condensed milk, vanilla and egg and mix well. Pour on top of crumbs, and top with remaining crumb mixture. Bake at 325° for 25 to 30 minutes. Cool to room temperature, then chill before cutting into bars. Refrigerate leftovers. Yields 48 bars.

Mrs. Tommy Gardner (Peggy)
Lone Star Legacy II

Flaming Bourbon Apples

1	large tart apple, cored, peeled and cut into 1/8 inch slices	2	tablespoons butter
		2	tablespoons brown sugar
1	tablespoon fresh lemon Juice	2	tablespoons warmed bourbon
			Topping of your choice

Combine apple slices and lemon juice in a bowl and toss gently. Melt butter in a medium skillet; and add apples and cook, turning frequently, until crisp-tender, about 10 minutes. Stir in brown sugar. Add bourbon and flame, shaking skillet gently until flame subsides. Serve warm with desired topping. Serves 2.

This is a versatile dessert and is delicious served with a dollop of sour cream, yogurt or vanilla ice cream.

Mrs. Cecil Smith (Diana)
Lone Star Legacy II

Bread Pudding with Rum Sauce

Pudding:

3 tablespoons butter	3 eggs
1 loaf (1 pound) French bread	2 tablespoons vanilla extract
1 quart milk	1 cup raisins
2 cups sugar	

Preheat oven to 350°. Melt butter in a 4 quart baking dish over low heat. Cool. Tear bread into large pieces and place in a very large bowl. Pour milk over. Let stand several minutes, then lightly stir bread until soaked through. Beat sugar, eggs and vanilla in a medium bowl to blend. Add to bread mixture. Stir in raisins. Pour into prepared dish. Bake at 350° for about 2 hours or until firm. Let cool.

Rum Sauce:

1 egg, room temperature	½ cup butter, melted and hot
1 cup sugar	2 to 4 tablespoons rum

Beat egg in a small bowl until thick and lemon colored. Gradually, add sugar, beating constantly until thick, 2 to 3 minutes. Add hot, melted butter and stir until smooth. Blend in rum. If sauce is too thick, thin with water to desired consistency. Pour sauce over pudding. Serves 6.

Mrs. Marcus Bone (Beverly)
Lone Star Legacy II

Pan Chocolate Eclairs

Cake:

1   package (16 ounces)
    graham crackers, divided
2   packages (3 ounces each)
    instant vanilla pudding

3⅓ cups milk
1   carton (8 ounces) whipped
    topping

Butter the bottom of a 9 × 13 inch cake pan and line with graham crackers, trying to fit right to the edges. Mix the pudding with milk and beat at medium speed for 2 minutes. Fold in whipped topping and pour half the pudding mixture over the crackers. Place a second layer of whole graham crackers over the pudding and pour the remaining pudding on top. Place a third and final layer of graham crackers on top and cover with plastic wrap. Refrigerate for 2 hours.

Frosting:

¼   cup cocoa or 1 square
    (1 ounce) unsweetened
    chocolate, melted
2   teaspoons white corn
    syrup

2   teaspoons vanilla extract
2   tablespoons margarine,
    softened
1½ cups powdered sugar
3   tablespoons milk

Beat all frosting ingredients together until smooth and spread over cooled cake. Cover and refrigerate for 24 hours. Serves 16.

Mrs. Chris Reed
Lone Star Legacy II

Fruit Party Pizza

1 package (16 ounces) sugar
   cookie dough
8 ounces cream cheese,
   softened
½ cup powdered sugar

Fresh fruits to cover
1 cup apricot or peach
   preserves
6 tablespoons water

Press cookie dough into a 15 inch pizza pan and bake at 350° for 10 minutes. Cool. Sweeten cream cheese with powdered sugar and spread over baked cookie dough. Place fruits on crust. Use bananas, strawberries, pineapple, grapes, mandarin oranges, or any fruit to make a colorful assortment. Thin preserves with water and cook until a glaze forms. Drizzle glaze over fruit. Serves 8 to 10.

This is a beautiful dessert and is really good for a brunch or luncheon.

Mrs. Linden Welsch (Phyllis)
Lone Star Legacy

Coconut Amaretto Fluff

1 (8 ounce) package cream
   cheese, softened
¼ cup plus 2 tablespoons
   amaretto liqueur
1 (8 ounce) carton frozen
   whipped topping, thawed

½ pound crisp macaroon
   cookies, crumbled
   (approximately 16)

Beat cream cheese until smooth. Add amaretto and beat well. Fold whipped topping and cookie crumbs into cream cheese mixture. Makes approximately 2½ cups.

Serve with assorted fruit or pieces of angel food cake.

Kathy Marsh
Changing Thymes

Per tablespoon

Calories 72 Protein .847 g Carbohydrates 6.3 g Fat 4.5 g Cholesterol 11.2 mg Sodium 38.2mg

Hill Country Peach Cobbler

2 to 3 cups sliced peaches	1 cup all-purpose flour
1¾ cups sugar, divided	1 teaspoon baking powder
3 tablespoons butter or margarine, softened	½ teaspoon salt, divided
	1 tablespoon cornstarch
½ cup milk	1 cup boiling water

Place peaches in 9 × 9 × 2-inch baking pan. Combine ¾ cup sugar and butter, beating until smooth. Add milk, flour, baking powder and ¼ teaspoon salt to creamed mixture and mix until smooth. Pour batter over peaches. Combine 1 cup sugar, ¼ teaspoon salt and cornstarch. Sprinkle over batter. Pour boiling water over batter. Bake at 375° for 1 hour. Serves 9.

Rhonda Copeland Gracely
Changing Thymes

Per serving_____

Calories 267 Protein 2.26 g Carbohydrates 56.3 g Fat 4.5 g Cholesterol 1.84 mg Sodium 172 mg

Flan

1 cup sugar, divided	3¼ cups milk
5 eggs	¼ cup rum
1 teaspoon vanilla extract	

Cook ½ cup sugar slowly in heavy skillet until melted, using a wooden spoon to stir. Beat eggs, sugar and vanilla. Add milk and rum. Pour into a buttered 5 cup ring mold on top of melted sugar. Place in a shallow pan filled with 1 inch of water. Bake at 325° for 1 to 1½ hours. Chill at least 1 hour before unmolding. Serves 4 to 6.

For a coffee flavored flan use 4 to 6 teaspoons instant coffee dissolved in ⅛ cup hot water.

Mrs. Jim Rado (Vicki)
Lone Star Legacy II

308

Chocolate Dipped Fruit

1	(12 ounce) package semisweet chocolate morsels
¼	cup vegetable shortening

Washed and dried fresh strawberries or mandarin orange slices, drained or pineapple chunks, drained, or maraschino cherries

Over hot (not boiling) water, combine chocolate morsels and shortening. Stir until morsels melt and mixture is smooth. Remove from heat, but keep chocolate over hot water. If chocolate begins to set, return to heat and add one to two teaspoons shortening. Dip pieces of desired fruit into chocolate mixture, shaking off excess chocolate. Place on foil-lined cookie sheets. Chill in refrigerator for 10 to 15 minutes until chocolate is set. Gently loosen fruit from foil. Serves 18.

Ada Smyth
Changing Thymes

Per serving_____

Calories 123 Protein .94 g Carbohydrates 13.7g Fat 8.5 g Cholesterol 0 Sodium 2.32 mg

Crepes

4	eggs	2	tablespoons sugar
2	cups milk	½	teaspoon salt
1½	cups sifted flour		

Place all ingredients in a blender container, cover and blend on high until smooth. Chill 1 hour. Lightly butter a 6 to 8 inch crepe pan and set over medium heat. For each crepe, pour 2 tablespoons batter onto pan. Bake until golden brown on both sides, turning once. Cool. Serves 12.

The Cookbook Committee
Lone Star Legacy II

Sopaipillas

4	cups flour	3	tablespoons shortening
1	tablespoon baking powder	1¼ to 1½ cups cold water
1	teaspoon salt	Oil

Combine dry ingredients. Cut in shortening, and add water gradually to make a soft dough. Roll out as for pie crust and cut into 3 inch squares. Heat oil in a deep fryer, and fry sopaipillas until golden brown. Drain on paper towels and serve immediately with butter and honey. Yields 4 to 5 dozen.

Brandi and Cynthia Bradford
Lone Star Legacy II

Cognac Ice Cream

8	cups milk	4	tablespoons vanilla extract
4	cups sugar, divided	16	egg yolks
1	cup cognac	4	cups whipping cream

Combine milk, 2 cups sugar, cognac and vanilla in a large saucepan. Bring to a simmer over medium heat. Remove from heat and cool 10 minutes. Combine remaining 2 cups sugar with egg yolks in a large mixing bowl and beat at medium speed until mixture is thick and falls from beaters in ribbons. With mixer running, add warm milk to yolk mixture in a slow, steady stream, blending well. Return to saucepan. Cook over medium low heat until thickened. *Do not boil.* Cool at room temperature. Blend in cream and transfer to a chilled freezer canister and freeze according to manufacturer's directions. Yields 1 gallon.

Mrs. Jim Rado (Vicki)
Lone Star Legacy II

Grapefruit Sorbet

8	large Texas Ruby Red grapefruit	2	cups sugar
		32	ounces water

Remove all peel and section the grapefruit. Place the sections in a ceramic or stainless steel pan. Mix sugar and water and simmer on low heat until all sugar is dissolved. Cool. Pour the light syrup over grapefruit sections and freeze. Before serving, place sorbet in food processor with steel blade; blend quickly. Scoop mixture into balls for serving and return to the freezer to firm and hold shape until serving. Yields 2 quarts, 16 (4 ounce) scoops.

Mrs. Mark White (Linda Gayle)
Lone Star Legacy II

Creamy Pralines

2½	cups sugar	¼	cup butter
1	cup buttermilk	1	teaspoon vanilla extract
1	teaspoon baking soda	3	cups pecan halves
¼	teaspoon salt		

In a large, heavy saucepan combine sugar, buttermilk, soda and salt, stirring frequently, until sugar is dissolved. Continue, cooking over low heat to soft ball stage or 234°. Remove from heat and add butter and vanilla. Cool about 5 minutes. Beat until smooth and slightly thickened. Stir in pecans. Immediately drop from a tablespoon onto waxed paper. Yields 18 large pralines.

Do not attempt to make these pralines when it is humid.

Mrs. Jim Stasswender (Linda)
Lone Star Legacy II

Microwave Fudge Delight

1	box (16 ounces) powdered sugar	½	cup butter, softened
½	cup cocoa	1	tablespoon vanilla extract
¼	cup plus 3 tablespoons milk	½	cup chopped pecans or crunchy peanut butter

Blend sugar and cocoa in a 2 quart mixing bowl. Add milk and butter. *Do not stir.* Microwave on HIGH for 2 minutes. Remove bowl from microwave and mix well with hand mixer for 1 to 2 minutes. Add vanilla and pecans or peanut butter. Pour into a greased 8 inch square dish. Place in refrigerator for at least 1 hour. Yields 64 one inch squares.

Mrs. Jerry Holder (Pat)
Lone Star Legacy II

Date Balls

2	cups chopped dates	1	teaspoon vanilla
1	stick margarine	2	cups Rice Krispies
2	egg yolks	1	cup chopped pecans
2/3	cup sugar		Powdered sugar

Cook dates, margarine, egg yolks, sugar and vanilla in heavy skillet, stirring until mixture boils. Simmer 2 to 3 minutes. Add Rice Krispies and nuts. Shape into bite size balls and roll in powdered sugar. Keep hands buttered when handling hot dates. Yields 5 dozen.

For a special effect, these can be formed into strawberry shapes, rolled in red sugar, and topped with leaves, using green decorator icing.

Mrs. Robert West (Linda)
Lone Star Legacy

White Chocolate Surprises

2	pounds white chocolate	2	cups small pretzel sticks,
2	cups Spanish peanuts		broken

Melt chocolate in a double boner; stir in peanuts and pretzels. Drop by spoonfuls on wax paper. Work fast, as mixture hardens quickly. Yields 5 dozen.

This is especially nice to give for a Christmas gift.

Mrs. David Armour (Betsy)
Lone Star Legacy

Apples in Amaretto

8	apples, peeled and very thinly sliced	1½ cups Amaretto liqueur

Marinate apples in Amaretto overnight. About one hour before serving, place apples on a serving tray. Put in freezer. Remove just prior to serving. Use party toothpicks for serving. Serves 20.

Marian Hidell
Lone Star Legacy

BEST OF

Lone Star ★ Legacy

SERENDIPITY

Manifold Cooking

Cooking while driving, or manifold cooking, had its beginning with resourceful G.I.'s faced with the dreary prospect of cold beans. G.I.'s found they could heat their beans on the manifolds of their jeeps! This grew into the idea of wrapping packages of food in foil to place on the manifold of cars to cook while driving. Whatever you are cooking must be securely wrapped in several layers of extra heavy duty foil using the drugstore wrap and reversing the seam side with each wrapping. Try to wrap the packages to more or less conform to the shape of the manifold. The foil packages should be 'tied' onto the manifold with coated wire to prevent the wire from cutting the foil. Of course, no steam escapes during the cooking, so the food is literally cooked in its own juices. Meat does not brown; however, the meat may be quickly browned before packaging it. This also improves the flavor — just as it does when cooking in your kitchen. As with camp cooking, the exact cooking times are variable. As a general guideline, you can figure that 100 miles of manifold cooking, based on an average speed of 50 to 55 miles per hour, is equal to an hour in your home oven at 300° to 325°. In most cases, you should turn the package about halfway through the cooking period, but be careful not to puncture the foil! There are unlimited possibilities to manifold cooking — use your imagination! So, fill up the tank and let's go cooking! And may you never lose your pot roast.

Featured in Texas Monthly Magazine.

Mrs. Jim Albrecht (Donne)
Lone Star Legacy II

Basting Sauce for Barbecued Chicken

2	cups margarine	3	tablespoons paprika
1	cup lemon juice	1	tablespoon garlic powder
1	cup water	1	tablespoon curry
5	tablespoons salt	3	tablespoons black pepper

Melt margarine in a 2 quart saucepan. Add remaining ingredients; stir to mix well. Place halved chickens on grill. Turn frequently. Baste chickens liberally with a basting brush each time they are turned. Cook until leg bone is loose. Yields basting sauce for 4 chickens.

This sauce is not edible; however, it makes a fantastic barbecued chicken. The use of barbecue sauce when chicken is served is generally unnecessary.

Dr. Gerald A. Beathard
Lone Star Legacy II

Baked Potato Chips

3½ pounds red or white boiling potatoes	6	tablespoons butter, melted
		Salt and pepper

Position oven racks in upper and lower third of oven and preheat to 500°. Cut potatoes crosswise into ⅛ inch thick slices. Lightly grease 2 baking sheets. Arrange potato slices in a single layer on prepared sheets. Brush generously with butter. Bake 7 minutes; switch pan positions and continue baking until potatoes are crisp and browned about edges, about 7 to 9 minutes. Sprinkle with salt and pepper and serve immediately. Serves 6 to 8.

Mrs. Don Bradford (Melinda)
Lone Star Legacy II

Bread and Butter Pickles

16 cups (5 pounds) sliced cucumbers, about ¼ inch	5 cups sugar
	5 cups cider vinegar
6 cups (2½ pounds) thinly sliced boiling onions	1½ teaspoons celery seed
	1½ teaspoons mustard seed
½ cup salt	1½ teaspoons turmeric
Water	6 jars (1 pint) and lids
3 trays ice cubes	

In a large bowl mix well the cucumbers, onions and salt. Cover mixture with cold water and ice cubes. Let stand 3 hours. Drain, rinse well and drain again. Let set about 30 minutes more. In large pot mix sugar, vinegar and seasonings. Heat mixture to boiling, stirring well. Reduce heat and simmer 30 minutes or until syrup is formed. Prepare jars and lids and leave in hot water. Over high heat add cucumbers and onion to syrup. Heat until almost boiling. Ladle hot mixture into hot jars, leaving ¼ inch head space. Use a spatula and release air bubbles. Wipe jar and close. Place jars on a rack in canner full of boiling water and cover with 1 to 2 inches of water. Reduce heat after bringing to a gentle boil and boil for 15 minutes. Remove jars; cool on rubber racks for 12 hours. Test seal and store. Use within the next year. Yields 6 pints.

Mrs. David Hart (Sue)
Lone Star Legacy II

Holiday Coffee

1 pound ground coffee	4 to 6 tablespoons ground cinnamon
¾ to 1 ounce ground orange peel	

Combine all ingredients. Store in an airtight container until ready to use or to give as a gift. Yields 1 pound coffee.

Mrs. Denman Smith (Sandra)
Lone Star Legacy II

Caswell House Mulling Spices

1	pound cinnamon bark	½	ounce cinnamon oil
1	pound whole cloves	2	ounces orange oil
1	pound whole allspice	4	ounces lemon peel
1	pound orange peel	1	ounce whole coriander

Mix all ingredients together well to coat spices with oils. Store in airtight container 7 to 10 days to allow flavors and scents to mix. After 10 days remove and package in 2 ounce plastic bags. Tie with ribbon for Christmas gifts. Makes 34 (2 ounce) packages.

Austin Junior Forum
Lone Star Legacy II

Jalapeño Pepper Jelly

3	large green peppers, seeded and diced	5	pounds sugar
6 or 7	fresh jalapeño peppers, seeded and chopped	3	cups cider vinegar
⅓	cup water	3	pouches (3 ounces each) Certo
			Green food coloring

Process peppers in blender with water. Wear rubber gloves while handling jalapeños. In large saucepan, combine pepper mixture, sugar and vinegar; boil 4 minutes. Watch carefully because mixture boils over easily. Remove from heat and add Certo and food coloring. Stir well. Pour into sterilized jars and seal with paraffin. Yields 8 to 10 pints.

Mrs. Jim Schultz (Mary Kay)
Lone Star Legacy

Hot Spiced Cider

| ½ | gallon apple juice, cranapple juice or apple cider | 2 | ounces Mulling Spices |

Bring juice to simmer stage. Place spices in a tea ball or tie in a cheese cloth square. Add spices and cover; turn off heat and steep 15 to 30 minutes. Serves 8.

You can make another delicious drink for a cold winter night by substituting ½ gallon of Burgundy wine for the juice.

Austin Junior Forum
Lone Star Legacy II

Marinated Mushrooms

4	cups chopped mushrooms	2	tablespoons dry tarragon
4	cups chopped olives	2	cups vinegar
2	cups chopped carrots	½	cup olive oil
1	cup chopped onion	1	tablespoon salt
½	cup chopped pimiento		

Toss mushrooms, olives, carrots, onions and pimientos gently together and pack into jar. Bring remaining ingredients to a boil and pour over vegetables. Keep refrigerated up to 30 days.

These mushrooms just get better and better. Serve over any tossed salad or in the center of an aspic.

Mrs. Denman Smith (Sandra)
Lone Star Legacy

Jezebel Sauce

| 1 | jar (6 ounces) prepared mustard | 1 | jar (8 or 10 ounces) apple jelly |
| 1 | jar (6 ounces) prepared horseradish | 1 | jar (8 or 10 ounces) pineapple preserves |

Combine all ingredients. Serve as sauce with ham or pour over cream cheese and serve with crackers. Also good as an egg roll sauce.

Mrs. Jim Schultz (Mary Kay)
Lone Star Legacy

Cocktail Sauce

½ cup chili sauce
⅓ cup catsup
2 tablespoons horseradish
1½ teaspoons Worcestershire
sauce

¼ teaspoon salt
2 tablespoons lemon juice
Dash pepper
Tabasco to taste

Combine all ingredients and chill. Serve with seafood.

Mrs. Larry Nau (Rose)
Lone Star Legacy

Salsa Fresca

1 large tomato, seeded and
chopped
½ cup finely chopped onion
2 jalapeños, seeded and
chopped

¼ cup tomato sauce
1 teaspoon salt
2 teaspoons cilantro,
chopped

Mix all ingredients together and store in refrigerator for 30 minutes before serving to allow flavors to blend together. Yields about one pint.

This is an excellent side dish for any Mexican food or a good dip. Keeps for a couple of days in refrigerator but not much longer.

Mrs. Jim Rado (Vicki)
Lone Star Legacy

Blender Hollandaise Sauce

3 egg yolks
2 teaspoons lemon juice
¼ teaspoon salt

2 drops Tabasco
½ cup butter, melted

In blender, mix yolks, lemon juice, salt, and Tabasco. Slowly pour melted butter into blender while mixing on low speed. Refrigerate if not using immediately. Yields 1 cup.

To adapt Hollandaise sauce to a Bernaise sauce, add 1 tablespoon minced parsley, 1 tablespoon tarragon vinegar, and ½ teaspoon tarragon.

Mrs. Ken Moyer (Bonnie)
Lone Star Legacy

Hot Mustard Sauce

1	(16 ounce) jar apple jelly	1	(5 ounce) jar cream-style horseradish
1	(18 ounce) jar orange marmalade or pineapple preserves	1	(6 ounce) jar prepared mustard
			Salt and black pepper to taste

Combine all ingredients in blender container. Blend until smooth. Serve hot or cold with beef or ham. Makes 5½ cups.

Makes great gifts when bottled in small decorative jars.

Nanci Norin Jordt
Changing Thymes

Per tablespoon_____

Calories 33 Protein .179 g Carbohydrates 7.69 g Fat .5 g Cholesterol .696 mg Sodium 34 mg

Island Salsa

1	cup chopped pineapple	½	cup chopped purple onion
1	mango, peeled and chopped	¼	cup chopped cilantro
1	papaya, peeled and chopped	2	mild jalapeño peppers, seeds removed and chopped
1	medium-sized red bell pepper, chopped		Juice of 1 lime
2	kiwi, peeled and chopped		Ground white pepper to taste

Toss all ingredients together gently. May be prepared up to 3 hours in advance but no more. Makes approximately 5½ cups.

Wonderful with grilled meats or fish.

Vicki Ashley Atkins
Changing Thymes

Per ¼ cup serving_____

Calories 23 Protein .395 g Carbohydrates 5.86 g Fat .5 g Cholesterol 0 Sodium 1.51 mg

Index

Please send _____ copies of **Best of Lone Star Legacy Cookbooks**.

@ $19.95 (U.S.) each $_____

Plus postage and handling @ $6.00 each $_____

Texas residents add sales tax @ $1.45 each $_____

Check or Credit Card (Canada-credit card only) TOTAL $_____

Charge to my: ☐ Master Card or   ☐ Visa Card

Account # _____

Expiration Date _____

Signature _____

MAIL, CALL OR EMAIL:
Cookbook Resources, LLC
541 Doubletree Drive
Highland Village, Texas 75077
Toll-Free Orders: 866/229-2665
sheryn@cookbookresources.com

Name_____

Address _____

City _____ State _____ Zip _____

Phone (day) _____ (night) _____

— —

Please send _____ copies of **Best of Lone Star Legacy Cookbooks**.

@ $19.95 (U.S.) each $_____

Plus postage and handling @ $6.00 each $_____

Texas residents add sales tax @ $1.45 each $_____

Check or Credit Card (Canada-credit card only) TOTAL $_____

Charge to my: ☐ Master Card or   ☐ Visa Card

Account # _____

Expiration Date _____

Signature _____

MAIL, CALL OR EMAIL:
Cookbook Resources, LLC
541 Doubletree Drive
Highland Village, Texas 75077
Toll-Free Orders: 866/229-2665
sheryn@cookbookresources.com

Name_____

Address _____

City _____ State _____ Zip _____

Phone (day) _____ (night) _____

For copies of **Lone Star Legacy, Lone Star Legacy II and Changing Thymes,** please contact AUSTIN JUNIOR FORUM, P.O. BOX 26628, AUSTIN, TEXAS 78755 OR CALL 800-661-2537